THE VISION
OF DOROTHY KERIN

The Vision
of Dorothy Kerin

Morris Maddocks

Hodder & Stoughton
LONDON SYDNEY AUCKLAND TORONTO

British Library Cataloguing in Publication Data
Maddocks, Morris
  The vision of Dorothy Kerin.
  1. England. Kent. Christianity. Spiritual healing
  I. Title
  615.852092

ISBN 0-340-55992-6

Published by Hodder and Stoughton,
a division of Hodder and Stoughton Ltd,
Mill Road, Dunton Green, Sevenoaks, Kent TN13 2YA.
Editorial Office: 47 Bedford Square, London WC1B 3DP.

Typeset by Hewer Text Composition Services, Edinburgh.
Printed in Great Britain by Clays Ltd, St Ives plc.

CONTENTS

FOREWORD
BY BISHOP CUTHBERT BARDSLEY*

I must be one of the few bishops alive today who knew Dorothy Kerin, and can count her as a friend. It came about this way. For many years her episcopal adviser and confidant was Bishop Loyd, Bishop of Nasik and of St. Albans. Over a long period of time Dorothy Kerin turned to him for advice and counsel. It was therefore a great honour, when shortly after his death, she came to me one day and asked if I would carry on his work. This, in a very inferior way, I was privileged to do. She would write or wait until one of my periodic visits to Burrswood to confront me with a problem. Later there came a day when she said she felt the time had come to form a council. She was getting older and knew that her time in this world was limited. Her health was not good so she wanted to share her responsibilities; she asked me to be the first council chairman. This I was proud and happy to undertake. We met regularly to take counsel on the administration of the estate and to meet with officers on the staff such as the medical officer, the matron, the head cook, etc. We asked them to tell us about any problems or potential openings for further work and I think we were able to give much support to Dorothy in her latter years. There came a day when, in the fullness of time, she died, and it was then we realised how wise she had been in delegating responsibility to a council. Shortly afterwards we had the privilege of appointing her successor, a doctor from Guernsey whom she had met on one of her visits to that island. Dr. Edward Aubert was a first-rate choice

* Bishop Cuthbert Bardsley died in January 1991.

vii

for this important work, the work of Warden of Burrswood. He and his wife served humbly, devotedly and sacrificially. Indeed, one could almost say that he shortened his life by his determination to work long hours and be available to everybody on the staff who wanted to talk to him, to meet and to help any of the patients and visitors. Edward Aubert was, in every way, a worthy successor to Dorothy Kerin. He died in harness as he would have wished. In fact he died in the chapel during a Communion service.

To revert to Dorothy Kerin; she was, as I have said elsewhere, one of the few people who combined immense holiness with practical ability. She ran the community with remarkable efficiency, based entirely upon her life of prayer. She would get up very early in the morning to have an unhurried time of quiet devotion, and would allow nothing to prevent this. However late she went to bed, however tired she was, she always set aside time for this meeting with the Lord, when she opened her heart to Him and asked Him to help her to deal with the many problems which are inevitable in the running of a community. Dorothy Kerin was a holy woman. This holiness was reflected in her face. At times, it was a sad face because she knew what it was to suffer. She suffered from misunderstandings, from active hostility and jealousy, from overwork, and from a slowly ageing body. Suffering was, at times, very visible in her face; but equally present was joy and peace. Her laugh was natural and uninhibited. It was an unforgettable little laugh, which emerged from a naturally joyous personality. With this, and through this laughter and sorrow, she was able to get quickly alongside people. Those who came to see her did not have to spend a long time explaining their problems. Dorothy was very quick at discerning what their problems were. A few carefully chosen sentences, and the outpouring of genuine love enabled her visitors to find healing and peace. I have often myself seen people go into her room looking troubled and overwhelmed by the problems of life. Not very long afterwards, indeed often surprisingly quickly, they would emerge with a look of joy on their face, as one who had made the discovery of the love of

Jesus as the supreme answer to all their needs. Dorothy did not have to preach long sermons to these people in need. She was an acute listener and allowed them to talk, and then, led by the Spirit, she gave counsel and advice. I have emphasised this capacity for counselling, because to me, it was one of the most remarkable features of Dorothy's life. She was a superb counsellor; people went to her in large numbers. She also had, by virtue of her prayer life and holiness, a remarkable gift of healing. When she laid hands on the sick, they were conscious of the love of God, and in many cases were given a new power to respond to His healing touch. Not everybody who went to Dorothy Kerin was healed physically, but almost all were healed spiritually. Their faith in our Lord's faith in them was deepened and they were given the strength to face up to their problems and to overcome them. This gift of wisdom in counselling was, of course, especially marked in her dealings with the staff of the community. To run any community is never easy and her life was not easy, but everybody on the staff of the Burrswood community knew that, in Dorothy, they had a wise mature leader, a woman of God who sought guidance from Him every day, and who lived by grace.

Like many of the saints of old, she could make astonishingly courageous decisions, decisions which could turn upside down long cherished adherence to rules, decisions which could involve the use of a great deal of money, money which was not readily available. She went forward by faith, believing that God would provide if the decision which she had made had been the result of unhurried prayer. Sometimes her decisions astonished me and I was, at first, somewhat apprehensive, wondering whether what she had decided was wise and practical, but in many cases money came to hand in a remarkable way. She didn't wait to implement a decision until all the money was there. She acted in faith on many occasions and the money came.

This ability to discern what was right was manifest in all her dealings. In a remarkable way she knew when somebody was going to die. I can recall several occasions when she said to me,

"Of course, so and so hasn't long to live; we must help her to die peacefully". On other occasions, against all medical advice, she believed a person was going to be healed and restored to fullness of health, and again this happened in a remarkable way. This ability to look into the future has been the hallmark of many of the saints of old. It comes from total reliance upon God and from living very close to Him. Dorothy Kerin lived like Moses, as a friend of God. She knew Him, she loved Him, and she obeyed Him. This divine friendship helped her live in serenity, untroubled by the conflicts of the world. This doesn't mean that she did not know what the conflicts were. She was aware of evil and the power of the devil and, like many saints of old, she believed that life was a battle against the devil. Sometimes she would talk to me about this and she would know where, among the members of the community, the devil had got a hold. She had a nose for evil, she smelt it, was aware of it and fought it with prayer and faith.

I could continue at length, but I hope I have said enough, to make it clear how much I value the writing of this book by Bishop Maddocks. We need today, a reassessment of the vision of Dorothy Kerin. We need to rekindle in our lives something of her spirituality and powerful attack. We need more of her profound faith in the power of God and a far greater personal dependence on that power. Too many people today, including leaders, have lost heart and lost hope. They are fumbling in semi-darkness, rather than advancing with a light of personal faith and trust in God. They need a renewed conviction of the power of God to rule and to overrule, to reconcile and to heal. Dorothy Kerin is dead, but her spirit still lives on and is still greatly and mightily at work in that community of Burrswood which she founded, and which progresses in her name.

I hope that many people will read this book by Bishop Morris Maddocks, and will profit from it. I am proud to write this Foreword and commend this book to your careful and prayerful attention.

Cirencester
12th February 1990

x

PREFACE
BY BISHOP DONALD COGGAN

This is not just another biography of Dorothy Kerin, though it is fuller and more intimate than its predecessors. Here her life, her "spirituality" and her work are set against the background of the mystical tradition of the Church, and the parallels with other visionaries are of great interest. That is the framework of the book.

But it is by no means backward looking. Bishop Maddocks is concerned to depict not only what is now being done in the revival of the healing ministry of the Church, but also to look forward to its spreading and deepening in the years immediately ahead. To this, he and his wife are devoting their lives and energies. Why should this work not prove to be "for the healing of the nations"?

I can see this book being profitably used in study circles. I hope it will also be read by many individuals in Great Britain and further afield, and will prove to be a stimulus to prayer, thought and action in the fulfilling of the divine commission to go, to tell, to heal.

I add my warm commendation to that of Bishop Cuthbert Bardsley.

Winchester
St. Andrew's Day 1990

ACKNOWLEDGMENTS AND DEDICATION

I offer my gratitude to many people: to the Dorothy Kerin Trustees for their encouragement to write this book, and to the Trustees of the Acorn Christian Healing Trust for allowing me a sabbatical to complete it; to Dr. Gareth Tuckwell, Director of Burrswood, for his warm friendship and support, for reading the manuscript and for his contribution to Chapter 21; also to the Chaplain, the Reverend David Flagg.

I especially want to thank and acknowledge my debt to two bishops who have influenced my life and inspired my Christian pilgrimage: Bishop Cuthbert Bardsley and Bishop Donald Coggan.

Bishop Cuthbert Bardsley, whom I first met as an ordinand when doing military service in Berlin and who, after many intervening years, graciously invited me to succeed him as Bishop Visitor to Burrswood, has kindly written the Foreword.

Bishop Donald (now Lord) Coggan, who became my Archbishop in York and later consecrated me as one of his suffragan bishops, has done me the honour of writing the Preface. Throughout the time of our friendship, he and Lady Coggan have given Anne and me tremendous encouragement in our particular ministry, and even more importantly, have themselves promoted the healing ministry in the churches, not least when they were at Canterbury.

I am grateful to all the senior members of the Burrswood

community who worked with Dorothy: "Bocky" Caudwell, Marina Chavchavadze, the late Kathleen Davies (née Burke-Collis), Marisa Filmer, Maria Preston, and not least Gladys Modin and the late Kathleen Nest, who have given me much time, prayer and encouragement, and to Johanna Ernest, whose painstaking labours in collecting much valuable material and whose reassuring vision have been of inestimable help. I thank them, one and all.

I also thank all my Acorn colleagues for their prayers (and forbearance), not least Charles Longbottom for his ideas in the final chapter; and all the staff for their support during this time of writing.

I am grateful to my publishers, in particular to David Wavre who first mooted the idea, and to Carolyn Armitage for her patience and wisdom, and to Bryony Todman for seeing it through to publication; to Edward England, my agent, for his ready advice; and to June Hall who, having mastered a word processor, and though many miles away in York, has made the whole operation and its communication as easy as the five previous occasions when she has kindly typed my manuscripts.

Last, but not least, those who know me know that it is really "us" and that none of the work or writing would be possible without my wife, Anne. She survived eight gruelling weeks of constant writing and plied me with good meals and Mozart, prayer and laughter, love and Elgar, so that the work came to completion. I thank her from my heart. Together we dedicate this book to the Christian healing communities and organisations for whom the Acorn is a treasured symbol of growth and the coming of God's Kingdom.

Bishop Morris Maddocks

St. Mary's Cottage, Burrswood,
St. Luke'stide 1990

PROLOGUE

What is vision? Many have asked the question and the answers are as infinite and various as those who have attempted an answer. Here is one attempt, by someone who understood the mystics, which shows how many and varied are the ways in which a vision is perceived. Evelyn Underhill wrote in *The Spiritual Life*:

It was the voice of a child saying "take, read" which at last made St. Augustine cross the frontier on which he had been lingering and turned a brilliant and selfish young professor into one of the giants of the Christian Church; and a voice which seemed to him to come from the Crucifix, which literally made the young St. Francis, unsettled and unsatisfied, another man than he was before. It was while St. Ignatius sat by a stream and watched the running water, and while the strange old cobbler Jacob Boehme was looking at a pewter dish, that there was shown to each of them the mystery of the Nature of God. It was the sudden sight of a picture at a crucial moment of her life which revealed to St. Catherine of Genoa the beauty of Holiness, and by contrast her own horribleness; and made her for the rest of her life the friend and servant of the unseen Love. All these were various glimpses of one living Perfection; and woke up the love and desire for that living Perfection, latent in every human creature, which is the same thing as the love of God and the substance of the spiritual life. A spring is touched, a

1

Reality always there discloses itself in its awe inspiring majesty and intimate nearness, and becomes the ruling fact of existence; continually presenting its standards, and demanding a costly response.[1]

For Dorothy, the "spring was touched" supremely in her healing, but it will be seen how she was conscious that the "Reality was always there" and that she had many "glimpses of one living Perfection". She was someone to whom vision was a deep reality and who had a closer walk with God than most of us. Her vision was almost sight, her faith, knowledge.

Dorothy Kerin was born on 28th November, 1889 in Walworth, at that time one of the most densely populated areas of east London. Charlie Chaplin was born nearby in the same year. Not far away was the dreaded Newington workhouse and at the end of her own (Boyson) road, stood the asylum. She was born amongst suffering humanity.

Her father, William Augustus Kerin, who managed a ship-broking firm with his brother Charles, came from a family which hailed from the west of Ireland. Her paternal grandfather was, interestingly, an army doctor known and loved for his compassion. Her mother was called Emily Jenny (née Wilson) after Jenny Lind, the famous singer, who was a family friend. Music flowed in the veins of her maternal family; Jenny's mother was also a vocalist of note, while she herself was gifted with a glorious voice.

Tragedy was to hit this idyllic household. First Uncle Charles, the brains in the firm, died, and then William, who was no businessman, was forced to move the family to a smaller house in Epping and died soon afterwards, in 1902. Dorothy, who was particularly close to her father, was shattered and from that time, her health deteriorated and she became very ill. Her mother moved the family to a more convenient house, near to some friends in Herne Hill, and it was there, at 204 Milkwood Road, on 18th February, 1912, that Dorothy received her healing (Part I).

2

The remainder of her life falls conveniently into three periods of seventeen years. The first (1912–29) was spent in preparation for her life's work, chiefly in the home of Dr. Langford-James, a teacher and priest, who was gifted in music and mystical theology. He remedied the lack of formal education in his pupil, for Dorothy had only had five years schooling because of her illness. During this time she received the stigmata, the five wounds Christ was given on the cross. In Dorothy's case, these were open wounds on the hands, side and feet and were well attested (Chapter 7). As is usual, they were accompanied by acute pain and, although they eventually healed, for some time they remained indicators of spiritual distress. In the Roman Catholic Church the stigmata have never been a cause for canonisation, although the best-known examples were in fact saints – Francis of Assisi, Catherine of Siena and Teresa of Avila. The only English stigmatic seems to have been Julian of Norwich. To all of these Dorothy felt a particular affinity.

This period contained the acute trauma and aftermath of the 1914–18 war, a time of immense suffering in Europe whose "lights went out" and from which no family was immune. Dorothy had brothers at the front; her deep spirituality and profound compassion contributed to her out-of-body experiences at the time. It was a period of our history when the need for the Christian healing ministry had seldom been greater.

Countless lives had to be rebuilt, especially those who had suffered in the trenches and the families who had lost all their menfolk. It was a time of political turmoil, marked by vast unemployment and industrial unrest. It was such a period in which Dorothy was prepared and "called by Christ to heal" (Part II).

The second period (1929–46) was spent in Ealing, west London, where Dorothy gradually opened more and more nursing homes of Christian healing until she owned the whole road! Ten years of stable progress, during which she

3

became a household word in many places, were followed by another world war. Once again, because she was in London, Dorothy was near to the action and many of the war's "casualties" found their way to her door. This and the last period (1946–63), which covers her ministry in Kent, are described in Part III. In the latter Dorothy established Burrswood as the lasting focus of her future and on-going ministry, and also began an international ministry, travelling abroad during her last years. Internationally it was a period of rebuilding from the embers of yet another war. For Dorothy, building also became a major part of her life in more senses than one.

The climax of her building programme in the physical sense lay in the completion of the Church of Christ the Healer in 1960. The number of altar candles, the statues, the votive stands, the sacramental emphasis including Reservation, the vestments, the colour, the incense at the festivals, the dignity and the prayerfulness all speak of the Anglo-Catholic faith which was her inspiration and vehicle of devotion. She received her healing and was then educated by Dr. Langford-James at a time when the Anglo-Catholic expression of faith was at its zenith and for an Anglican mystic this would be a natural milieu. The expression of such a faith brought colour and life to an age that was for too many colourless and lifeless, especially in the industrial and poorer areas of the country. The movement produced some of the most caring and devoted priests in the Church of England, who were household names in their time. Dorothy resonated with this expression of the Christian faith and possibly saw it as the most likely vehicle for the healing of the churches as well as for the healing of individuals.

In Part IV, I try to relate her ministry to that of today and to perceive how her vision can bring some illumination to the life and ministry of the contemporary Church. The final decade of the second millennium has been designated by the mainline churches as a decade of evangelism. For such an exercise to bear fruit, the whole Christian body has to be grasped by the vision of a world won for Christ, a vision that is larger and more dynamic than our usual concerns, for it is the world Christ came to heal. Unless Christians see and are motivated by such a vision with true clarity and follow in obedience, the glorious gospel of Jesus Christ, our Saviour and Healer, will not be heard in His world.

This book is written with the conviction that Dorothy's vision and what she attempted under obedience to Christ the Healer has a word to say to the world as well as to today's Church as the purveyor of the Good News of Jesus Christ. It is not a biography, but includes a great deal of biographical material to support this conviction. My prayer is that her life and legacy will inspire and encourage Christians young and old to obey the vision God puts before them on their journey to wholeness, and will enable them to shine as lights of the world in their generation.

Note

1. (Mowbray, 1984).

Part I

Her Healing

1 HER "BEAUTIFUL DAY"

There can be little room for doubt that Dorothy Kerin was miraculously healed of a mortal sickness on Sunday, 18th February, 1912. There is the testimony of her doctors, of her mother and of her sister. There is her own testimony in three accounts, two written and one on tape, recorded in later life. There are the contemporary accounts written up in the national press. There is also the evidence of her subsequent life and ministry to thousands, in many of whom miracles of healing also took place; and there is the ongoing ministry in her foundation of Burrswood today.

The whole sequence of events began ten years earlier when she was twelve. The Jews have always seen that the age of twelve is a significant time for a child. It was certainly to be a milestone in the life of Dorothy, for in that year her father died. Dorothy was a child who was devoted to both her parents and the tie with her father seemed especially close. She would not leave his side during his final illness. She was always a person who felt things essentially through her body and she felt her father's death in every fibre of her being. It is not surprising that it began to break her health. The family doctor realised at once how delicate the child had become and told her mother she would need constant watching and care. Her mother nursed her devotedly for the next ten years.

After four years she caught diphtheria and was sent to an isolation hospital in Tooting. It was a severe illness and took a great toll of her health so that she had to convalesce

9

in a sanatorium for nine months. She was still unwell on her return home and was ordered to rest. Then a chill resulted from resting out of doors, pneumonia and pleurisy set in and she nearly died. This illness began long years of confinement to her bed. Later on a microscopic examination showed that she was suffering from a general tuberculosis.

Let her mother take up the story:

As the time went on her suffering became more intense. It was distressing to see her frame racked with pain and cough. We realised how helpless we were, for the doctor had said that nothing more could be done, and that it was just a question of time. During the last six months she grew rapidly worse, and so great was her exhaustion that on some days she was too weak to speak or lift a hand. In all this time she never made an impatient murmur, but often remarked that it was a privilege to suffer with Christ.

The end was apparently near in January 1912, when the doctor diagnosed tubercular peritonitis. For four weeks we kept her alive by means of starch and opium injections and other stimulants. She was not allowed to take any food by mouth, and during this time haemorrhage occurred frequently. Her suffering were so great that those who loved her could not wish her to linger on, and prayed that God in His love would soon call her.

On Sunday, February 4th, she asked for the Holy Communion to be brought her, and appeared to be conscious during the service, looking very happy and peaceful. We had noticed for some days that her sight seemed to be failing, and on the evening of this same day my younger daughter, Evelyn, was sitting by her bed, watching her, when Dorothy said, "I should like to hear 'Abide with me' sung; it is getting so dark." Within a few minutes the hymn was sung all the way through, and both children heard it. There was no one in the house singing. When it was over, Dorothy said, "Oh, Eve, how quickly God has answered my prayer."

10

After this she became quite blind and semiconscious and continued in this condition for two weeks. It was apparent to all who saw her that she was very near Heaven. Soon after she became blind we heard her joining in the Communion service. Her face at times was radiant with unearthly light.

About eight days before her healing we were watching by her bed when her face became lit up. Someone came in at that moment, but seeing her, drew back at once, exclaiming, "Oh, look quickly, what a lovely look there is on the child's face!" Dorothy was apparently talking to someone unseen to us, and was saying in a tiny, weak voice, "There were crowds and crowds of them; some had lilies and some had wings." In her delirium she was evidently talking of something she had seen. After this she constantly rambled about lilies and wings.

We procured for her a Madonna lily, and placed it near her face, and often heard her say, "This is His lily; Jesus sent it me; it is kissing me." We all realised that she was nearer Heaven than this world, and such a holy atmosphere was felt in the sick-room that it seemed almost sacrilege to enter.

In these last two weeks, all treatment had been stopped, the doctor having said that it was useless; and on Saturday the 17th, he told me that if there were any relations who would like to see her alive, I must send for them at once, as she could not live through the next day . . .

On Sunday several people came . . . and we distinctly heard Dorothy say, "Yes, I am listening." Her face was radiant with a beautiful smile . . . A beautiful light was all over her and in her face the Glory of the Father was reflected. As we looked, we saw her raised up in bed . . . Holding her head up as if in prayer, she said, "Mother, I am well; I am to get up now."[1]

The medical diagnosis had undoubtedly been correct. During this last fortnight, tubercular peritonitis had been followed

11

by delirium and she became both blind and deaf. The fatal diagnosis of tubercular meningitis was given to the family. The doctor was indeed right when he told them she had suffered enough to kill half a dozen people.[2] But out of her blindness and sufferings were to come new visions and hopes for many. For that fortnight of suffering and of unbearable grief for her mother and family was Dorothy's time of blessing and healing, her "beautiful day", God's time, as her own testimony describes:

My Beautiful Day

On Sunday morning, February 4, at nine o'clock, I received the Blessed Sacrament, and as the priest came towards my bed with the chalice, I saw wonderful golden lights radiating from it, which enveloped the priest. I had never seen this before, though all through my illness I had made my Communion every month. It was a beautiful experience, and the Divine Presence was indeed a reality. When the service was over, everything around me seemed to grow dim and misty, and I could see nothing clearly. In the evening I asked my little sister to sing "Abide with me," as all was then so dark. She did not know it well enough to sing, but as she sat by my bed with my hand in hers we heard it sung from beginning to end most beautifully. My sister heard it as distinctly as I did and said, "Oh, how wonderful." We are certain it must have been the Holy Angels who sang it, for there was no one singing either in the house or outside.

When the singing had ceased I seemed to drift into space. I was no longer conscious of my body, but my soul was overflowing with joy and love, and a transcendent feeling of supreme happiness, impossible to describe in ordinary language. I passed on and on, and as I went the way grew brighter and brighter, until I saw in front of me a wonderful altar formed by angels. There were six at the back, and in front one more beautiful than the rest holding a chalice, which he brought to me, and from which he gave me to drink. Then they disappeared, and as they went they seemed to be chanting words which I could not understand.

I passed on again, and soon I heard a great flocking sound, and saw coming from every direction white-robed figures, some of them were carrying lilies, while some had haloes. Their movements made lovely music, and they all looked as though they were coming and going with some definite purpose. No words of mine can exaggerate the exquisite beauty of the scene. As I looked I saw One coming towards me; I thought He was coming for me, and held out my hand towards Him, but He smiled and said, "No, Dorothy, you are not coming yet."

Again I passed on, and this time I seemed to go a much greater distance, until I could go no farther, when I heard a voice saying, "Dorothy," three times. I answered, "Yes, I am listening. Who is it?" Then a great light came all around me, and an Angel took my hands in his and said, "Dorothy, your sufferings are over. Get up and walk."

He passed his hands over my eyes and touched my ears, and then I opened my eyes and found myself sitting up in bed. My mother and a number of friends were standing round the bed, looking very frightened, and some clutching at each other. It seemed so strange to me, and I could not understand why they were all there. I asked for my dressing-gown, telling them that I was quite well, and that I must get up and walk; but they were all too astonished to answer me or to move.

The Angel again said to me, "Get up and walk." Then they brought the dressing-gown, and when I had put it on I got out of bed unassisted. Part of the light came to the right side of the bed, and I put my hand on it, and it led me out of the room and along a passage and then back into my room again. Though I had not walked for five years, I now walked quite steadily, and was not the least bit shaky; indeed I felt so well and strong that

I might never have been ill at all. Very soon I realised that I was hungry, and asked for food. They brought me milk in a feeding-cup, but I refused it, and finally I went down myself the two flights of stairs to the larder and brought back the materials for a real meal of meat and pudding. How I enjoyed that meal! It was the first solid food I had been able to digest for years, and I had not the slightest pain or discomfort after it.

Sixteen people were in the room, and all were mystified and amazed at what they saw. I was perfectly well, all pain had left me, my sight was restored, and I felt better and stronger than I can ever remember feeling before. It was half-past nine in the evening when I got up, and at twelve o'clock, midnight, I went back to bed, and slept until eight o'clock the following morning. When I got up, my mother and friends, who knew that I had been like a skeleton the day before, were amazed to see that my body was in a perfectly normal condition; all discoloration had entirely disappeared, and I was quite plump, my bones being covered with firm, healthy flesh – all this in the space of twelve hours.[3]

The two accounts together, the one by her mother and the other by Dorothy, make an interesting comparison. It is as though the one was seen through earthly and the other through heavenly eyes. But the mother's account, if factual, is yet a perceptive comment on Dorothy's own account of her healing, while Dorothy's enlightens and confirms what her mother heard and saw – Dorothy's joy in suffering with Christ, the angelic singing of the hymn, her radiant face, her closeness to the angels and heaven, her obedience in listening and her final raising up.

Dorothy's account from *The Living Touch*, written two years after her healing, is corroborated by her account in *Fulfilling*,[4] written nearly forty years later, and on the tape-recording made near the end of her earthly life, but with one major difference: in these accounts she telescoped her "beautiful day" from a fortnight into twenty-four hours, rather like the author of the fourth gospel, writing in later years, telescoped the Great Forty Days by recording Jesus's gift of the Spirit to his disciples as happening on the evening of Easter Day.

Joan Ashton makes the comment concerning the account in *The Living Touch* that "it may well have been composed while she was still overwhelmed by the experience and it was only later, when recollected in tranquillity and in conversation with people she could trust, that she was able to get the story in the right sequence. But it seems certain that her honesty in this matter is without question and that psychological fantasy played no part".[5] In any case, as in the example of the Gospels, the fact is that as regards the essential truth of the matter, they corroborate each other.

The doctor, who had generously and devotedly looked after Dorothy – when he called in specialists he himself paid their bills and seldom if ever sent in one of his own – told the press the next day that in his experience this case and its outcome was unique. In attending her he had found all the gravest symptoms of advanced tuberculosis, of diabetes and other complications. He had had no less than twelve nurses attending her during the course of her illness and the chart they kept of her temperature showed violent fluctuations. On the Saturday he had given up hope. Little wonder he could not believe it was the same girl he left dying the day before who ran to greet him. When he asked her to climb the stairs to test her, she ran up two flights. He told his questioners that all he could exclaim was "Great God, what is the meaning of it all?" What indeed! The incontrovertible fact is that Dorothy was miraculously healed from mortal sickness with an immediacy and thoroughness that defied human reason.

Dorothy's own witness was unequivocal:

The whole fortnight to me was as one beautiful day, passed in an indescribably lovely place, where everything, both to

15

see and to feel, was exquisite harmony; and it was at the
end of this, my beautiful day, that Jesus made manifest
His healing power in my diseased body, and raised me
up from my bed of sickness, every whit whole, strong in
every organ and limb.[6]

She obviously underwent the death–life cycle which many
have experienced as they approach the hinterland of the
dying process. In this "between" situation, dying people
have asked to be left alone because "all is so beautiful".
In all probability Dorothy went as far on this journey as
any have gone who eventually returned. As she relates,
she passed "on and on" and the way grew "brighter and
brighter". The experience she related seems to describe the
courts of heaven which on this earth we can only faintly
imagine. But she did experience them and this event alone
set her apart as a true visionary and gave her life an added
dimension.

Frank Drake, once chaplain at Burrswood and builder of
the chapel of Christ the Healer on Guernsey, in 1957, in
the course of a book about his son's death, put this other
dimension of Dorothy's life in its context:

She might with justice be described as a genius, in her
own field. But this word is never used of Dorothy because
it would imply a purely human quality of her own, an
implication which she would never allow. It should be
said rather that she is a direct channel of God's love to
a degree which amounts to genius. But to appreciate her
quality you must never make the mistake which many
have made who do not know her, of supposing that she is
by nature, in her own right as it were, a very joyful person,
a very mirthful one, or even a very tender or loving one.
She is these things of course; outstandingly so. But they
would cease if her Master left her. Her joy, her mirth,
her tenderness are the joy, the mirth and the tenderness
of One who pours His own gifts into her, and through

16

her, so that they may bless the folk whom He sends her. If He were to leave her – He will not, of course, because He promised not to – her joy would vanish at once, and I do not think that even joy would remain! Indeed I know it would.

How can these things be? To understand how this came about, you must realise that as a girl Dorothy was not merely ill for nine long years, but at the end had been for long months a skeleton, a shadow, a ghost, lying motionless for week after week, emaciated and exhausted. The long slowness of this near approach to death burned out of her personality almost all the usual desires, greed and fear, almost I believe all the normal self which lives in the flesh. Then for the last two weeks, while her unconscious, almost lifeless, body lay upon its bed, her spirit soared away into Heavenly places, moved with angels and archangels and all the company of Heaven, heard the singing of angelic choirs and spoke with the Master Himself. Purged and purified by her long illness, she then returned from Heaven, as I believe, bearing the actual touch of Our Lord Himself. Many, many times since then Our Lord has been beside her and she has heard His voice . . . When therefore Dorothy talks of matters relating to God and man, . . . she speaks firmly and with conviction. She knows. She has been there.[7]

Before we leave this remarkable day, 18th February, 1912, whose significance we shall see gradually worked out in the life and ministry of Dorothy, two comments are of interest. The first is that it happens to be the feast day of St. Bernadette of Lourdes.[8] If, as is sincerely to be hoped, Dorothy is one day given a day in the Anglican calendar, then probably it should be this date, the anniversary of her healing, which is always kept in her church of Christ the Healer at Burrswood. The other comment is from the pen of a journalist who was on the staff of the *Daily Chronicle*, later to become the *News Chronicle*, who interviewed her on the morning after her healing. In a letter to Dorothy not long before she died, he wrote:

> I well remember your telling me of your heavenly vision, and of the voice saying, "Dorothy, your sufferings are over. Get up and walk."
>
> When you told me of your wonderful experience, you were sitting by the fireside wrapped in two blankets. The only dresses of your own that your mother possessed were some you had worn before you were bedridden. That was several years before. Then you were a child, now you were a young woman. And in those days there were no such places as Marks and Spencers where you could have a ready-made dress. A dressmaker had to be sent for to take measurements, buy material and make it up. It took a week or a fortnight. So there you were wrapped up in blankets.
>
> I remember telling my parents you looked exactly like some pictures of the Virgin Mary. There was the same type of feature and your face bore such a lovely expression of divine beauty and peace. I remember it as well as if I had only seen you yesterday.[9]

It was, after all, the expression of one who had been in the presence of Christ and experienced His healing touch. It had not been only her "beautiful day", but a day of significance for the Church of God.

Notes

1. Dorothy Kerin, *The Living Touch*, first published in 1914, pp. 51–55.
2. I am indebted to Dr. Gareth Tuckwell, Director of Burrswood, for confirmation of the medical diagnosis.
3. Dorothy Kerin, *The Living Touch*, pp. 8–13.
4. Dorothy Kerin, *Fulfilling* (Hodder and Stoughton, 1952). This account and a transcription of her tape-recording are printed in

full in Appendix A and make an interesting comparison with the account printed in this chapter.

5. Joan Ashton, *Mother of Nations: Visions of Mary* (Lamp Press, Marshall Pickering, 1988) p. 47.
6. Dorothy Kerin, *The Living Touch*, p. 8.
7. Frank Drake in *Thy Son Liveth* (Hodder and Stoughton, 1959) pp. 53 ff.
8. See Johanna Ernest, *The Life of Dorothy Kerin* (Dorothy Kerin Trust, 1983) p. 64.
9. Quoted by Dorothy Musgrave Arnold in her *Dorothy Kerin: Called by Christ to Heal* (Hodder and Stoughton, 1965) p. 18.

2   HER MESSAGE

News travels fast and this was true even in 1912. The small terrace house in Herne Hill was soon besieged by the press, interested doctors, friends old and new, and the curious. The London *Evening News* reported the facts of the case on 20th February "without comment", except to say that it could offer no explanation for them. The *Daily Chronicle* published its account a day later, including an interview with the doctor, in which he stated: "Had I read of it I certainly should not have believed it. She is well, but how she got better I don't know." Dorothy herself gave countless interviews and was examined by other doctors.

One of them, Dr. Edwin Ash, who had a specialist practice in Portman Square, saw the stress being caused to the family and determined to bring some relief to the situation. He asked her mother if he could take Dorothy home and continue his examination in more peaceful surroundings. She stayed with him for six weeks, during which time he and some trusted colleagues were able to make a full examination. They found that the normal, healthy flesh had returned at once, quite new lungs had replaced the old ones wasted away with the disease and blood tests showed her to be in perfect health. In fact she had been made "every whit whole". But her stay in Dr. Ash's house was also important for another reason: the receiving of God's message, delivered in a vision by the Virgin Mary. It was the answer to her own doctor's question, "what does it all mean?" She described it in these words:

On Sunday, March 11th, I was wakened out of sleep by a voice saying, "Dorothy." I sat up, and saw at the foot of my bed a wonderful light, out of which came the face of a beautiful woman holding a lily. She came very near to me and said:

"Dorothy, you are quite well now. God has brought you back to use you for a great and privileged work. In your prayers and faith many sick shall you heal; comfort the sorrowing and give faith to the faithless. Many rebuffs will you have, but remember you are thrice blessed: His grace is sufficient for thee. He will never leave thee."

After making the sign of the Cross over me with her lily, the figure disappeared; and when I woke in the morning, the room was still full of the scent of the lily.

The answers to my prayers had come. All unworthy as I know myself to be, God has a work here for me, and I can only thank Him for His great love, and pray that He may purify and make worthy the very imperfect channel He has chosen.[1]

This was the purpose of her healing and this was to be the focus of her future ministry and of her message to the world – to heal the sick, comfort the sorrowing and give faith to the faithless. For this purpose the gifts of prayer and faith had obviously been given to Dorothy and in her healings she was indeed thrice blessed. The promise of rebuffs would for the time being be a mystery yet become a reality soon enough, but the promises to St. Paul (2 Cor. 12:9) and to the Apostles (Matt. 28:20) were repeated to Dorothy as an assurance of the divine presence and help at all times.

It was interesting that Dorothy in her role as the visionary did not name the Virgin Mary, preferring to describe her as "a beautiful woman holding a lily", but the sign of the cross made with the lily and the lingering scent, together with the manifest authority with which the message was delivered, leave us in little doubt that the beautiful woman was none other than the Virgin Mary. As Joan Ashton comments,

21

"The vision and prophecy enabled her to bear with patience the long years of preparation before her life's work began".[2] In fact the vision and the message were to be central to her life and work for the next fifty years. Herein lay the purpose of her healing. Here was the essence of her message. Here was the focus of her vision.

Her stay in Portman Square was a God-given space for quiet contemplation. It enabled her prayerfully to ponder on what had happened to her, physically, spiritually and emotionally. It was a time of adjustment to facing life again, but now with a very different purpose, for she had received a divine call. She knew she had to share this with the world, that she had to go and tell how much the Lord had done for her.[3] This was obviously at the forefront of her mind during this time of quiet, and eighteen weeks after her healing she was given an opportunity to do just this. The magazine section of the *London Budget* asked for a piece and gave it the whole of its front page on Sunday, June 30th, 1912. The Reverend J. L. Thompson, who had ministered to Dorothy during the five years of her illness until her healing, wrote in his monograph *London's Modern Miracle* that possibly the most remarkable factor connected with Dorothy's healing was this message she gave to the Church and to the world. It is so important in assessing her vision that it must be quoted in full:

> In my restoration to health, I have been entrusted with a message to the whole world, a promise of healing to the sick, comfort to the sorrowing and faith to the faithless. This message is for everybody as soon as they are ready to accept it and have the desire.
>
> How these things are going to be brought into practice has not been revealed to me yet. I only know that it will depend largely upon Prayer and Faith. I do know there is a beautiful truth for us as soon as we are ready for it.
>
> I am confident that as soon as people are brought to open their spiritual eyes, these great and beautiful

manifestations will be for them also. The vast multitude build up a barrier between the seen and the unseen – between spiritual beauty and themselves – by worldly lives and by foolishness, but as soon as this barrier is broken down there will be a great inrush of spiritual beauty and glory. I have seen it and I know.

People do not realise that the spiritual part is much the greater portion. It is the true inheritance of all, but we do not claim it. Sometimes when I see people who have not this beautiful outlook upon things that are external, I wonder how they can exist; it is puzzling to me.

I believe we are on the threshold of a great revelation from the Spirit that is Infinite. I feel that man is about to have a great awakening. What strengthens me in my belief? PRAYER. I am confident that Prayer is the tonic that will create an appetite for the things of the spirit. Through Prayer we shall receive the Great Benediction. Prayer is the desire of the soul for spiritual things. There is a form of Prayer without words, a voiceless prayer in the heart, that God and God only understands.

People ask me how the Divine Presence, or God, appears to me. God appears to me as an inexpressibly beautiful BEING – an Infinite Power impossible to describe. I know that with God all things are possible.

I am asked if I feel that there will come another revelation to me. I answer that in God's own time all will come right. In the kingdom of the unseen one cannot presume to make plans for oneself. People say to me, "What are you going to do with your life?" If you ask me what God is going to do with my life, I answer, "I do not know". It will come from God. One life lifted from the shadow of death and brought into the sunshine of happiness should be enough to convince the world. I am asked whether when the revelation, which I await in faith and trust, comes to me, pointing the way for ministration, I will announce it, and I say I will, of course. I know that it is by prayer, faith and obedience that it will come. *It will belong to the world.*

I know that it was not for me alone, but that there is a divine purpose in my being singled out to manifest the healing power of the spirit. God knows the way. I do not know. I know that whereas I was prostrate, now I am well. I am an instrument in God's hands. I know that He closed my human eyes and ears so that I might know spiritual realities. And the harmony and health and happiness that have come to me are so complete, that of the pain and suffering of those years I remember nothing.

People ask me if I attribute my recovery to any of the established systems of healing, such as healing by hypnotism, suggestion, the help of "friendly spirits", "faith healing", Christian Science, suggestive therapeutics etc. My restoration did not come through any of these or any other systems, nor did I pray for my recovery. I prayed that I might be happy in doing what God might will. I wondered sometimes why God ordained that I should suffer, but I was confident that it was for a purpose. I had no-one attempting to heal me by any means, except the regular physicians, but many people, knowing that the doctors had pronounced me incurable, and that I had been given up to die, think that my restoration was due in some way to some form of suggestion without my knowledge that that power was being invoked. There was no-one at my bedside to make suggestions, no-one attempting it – and had there been, how could an unconscious person have grasped them? No-one can claim my restoration but GOD. My healing came direct from Him alone. There was no intermediate agent or agency.

CHRIST is as much alive today as He was when upon earth, and is sending His message to those who will receive it. I feel no weight of care. Life is radiant when it is rightly lived, but there is swift retribution for those who are prodigal regarding the heritage which God gives. The Spirit of the Infinite lives in the truth, and the truth

24

should make us not only free but joyous. Religion should be like the song of the birds.

The glories of existence are all about us. The ineffable Power of Infinite Life is ours for the taking. There is nothing to hinder us except our own blindness. The Master in His day said they did not need to go to the mountain or to Jersualem to worship, for God was Spirit. It is possible for every door to open into Paradise. It is possible for every life to come into communion with the Infinite.

People say to me, "Come out into the world and live", but I say, "Come out from the world and live", and by that I do not mean come out and live your life away from your fellows. The old idea that people should go into the mountain or into the deserts and serve God by shunning society has been proved a fallacy. To be of help to your fellows; to share their joys and have them share yours; to smile with them; and if possible to banish their tears, are efforts worth while. What I mean by coming out from the world is to put aside the worldly things that pamper for a moment and perish – things that leave the soul empty and seared. It is not a renunciation, but the embracing of things that are supernal, things that are spiritual and do not die. The world has repeated for centuries, but without realising the full significance of the thought, that God is everywhere, and that the Kingdom of Heaven is within us. I believe that the world is ready today for a complete revelation of the literal and beautiful truth of these sayings that have largely come to be formal in their endless repetition.

The great truth is that POWER unlimited, sublime and free, is within reach of us all.

Yesterday, I was thinking much of my mission and message to the world, and wondered how I was going to bring it to execution. I prayed, "How is this to be done?", and I heard a voice say distinctly, "By prayer and faith".

Sometimes people in London come up to me in the

street and speak to me. The other day a man came to me in the street and said, "Excuse me, Miss, but may I touch you, perhaps the Spirit of the Master may pass through you into me".

You must break down the barrier before the inrush of glory can come in. The Spirit of God cannot come into the soul that is not receptive. Wealth could not buy my experience. It could not have effected my cure. It is the Spirit, the Spirit of Jesus, the Living God, that has given me this NEW LIFE.[4]

Dorothy Kerin
30th June, 1912

First of all she states the universality of her message. She believed that she had been given a sacred trust in her restoration to health: it was to take her message to the world. She believed that her being raised up "from the shadow of death and brought into the sunshine of happiness" should be a sufficiently convincing proof of the power of the Lord, a power that was available to all people, a power "unlimited, sublime and free". Certainly she was to be used as a channel of that power to many thousands and through this strong belief in its limitless quality, her vision of a world won for Christ the Healer was never diminished.

The content of the message was the sacred trust given to her by the Virgin Mary in that vision some weeks previously, "a promise of healing to the sick, comfort to the sorrowing and faith to the faithless". This will be discussed at greater length in other parts of the book, but it should be noted that her vision contained a three-fold thrust: not only the sick but also the sorrowing and the faithless were to be enfolded in her ministry. To all three she responded with obedience. They are also faithfully reflected in those who carry on the ministry today: caring and evangelism are also of vital importance to anyone "called by Christ to heal". Bereavement and lack of faith are diseases known by all at times. They too need the healing balm of Christ.

26

How was all this to be accomplished? The objectives had not yet been set, but the overall purpose was plain and could not be accomplished without the powerful trio of prayer, faith and obedience, all of which are cited in the text of the message as cornerstones for laying the foundations of the commission with which she had been entrusted. All of these will appear time and again. Prayer is "the tonic that will create an appetite for the things of the spirit". It prepares the atmosphere that is conducive to hearing the word of God and to seeing visions. It is a silent waiting upon the Lord. Only through prayer are great blessings received, because it breaks down the barriers between the seen and the unseen, between the temporal and the eternal. Dorothy herself had experienced this storming of the gates of Heaven and the consequent "inrush of spiritual beauty and glory". Her great desire was that all people should realise this was their true inheritance and claim it.

It was through prayer that she had received the gift of faith. She believed with all her heart that this was a key time in the history of God's dealings with his creation and that a great revelation was imminent, "that man is about to have a great awakening". This she awaited "in faith and trust". To prayer and faith was now added her very special gift of obedience. It was to be the hallmark of her life and ministry. This trio was to be the foundation of the disciplined life of her discipleship: the other side of the coin was the "harmony, health and happiness" for which she was so grateful throughout her life to Christ the Healer, to whom she dedicated her church at Burrswood in thanksgiving for her healing. The gift of this two-sided coin was her pearl of great price. It was this experience, whose price was above rubies, which she attributed solely to "the Spirit, the Spirit of Jesus, the Living God", for it was an experience of new and resurrection life. Her message was that she had seen and would now keep her spiritual eyes open and ready for further visions. Her prayer and the aim of her life's work was that all humankind would do the same.

Five years before she died, she was proclaiming her message in St Martin-in-the-Fields, and began with these words: "Today I stand here all unworthy and sinful as I am and dare to say to you in the presence of God and all the company of heaven that I have seen Jesus. I have heard His voice, I have felt His touch and I know that Jesus Christ is the same yesterday and today and forever."[5] By then she had become so totally identified with it that she had virtually become the message. The vision of Dorothy Kerin was in total focus.

Notes

1. Dorothy Kerin, *The Living Touch*, pp. 17–18.
2. Joan Ashton, *Mother of Nations: Visions of Mary*, p. 47 (Lamp Press, Marshall Pickering, 1988).
3. Cf. Mark 5:19.
4. A facsimile can be seen in *The Life of Dorothy Kerin* by Johanna Ernest (Dorothy Kerin Trust, 1983) p. 50. The author then quotes the important extracts. The full text can be seen in *Dorothy Kerin: Called by Christ to Heal* by Dorothy Musgrave Arnold (Hodder and Stoughton, 1965) pp. 14–17, as well as in Ruth Farr's *Will you go back?* (Dorothy Kerin Trust, 1970), pp. 10–14.
5. I was privileged to preach in the same church at the commemoration of the centenary of her birth and began my sermon with this quotation. (See Appendix B; see also Chapter 5 p. 51.)

3   THE TESTING OF HER OBEDIENCE

The vision of Mary and subsequent publication of the message was followed by a period of waiting which Dorothy obviously found hard. "One's soul had to be possessed in patience", was her comment. "It was so difficult to be still and wait when there were so many in spiritual darkness with whom one longed to share the joy of this new-found health and happiness."[1] She had a great burden for humanity, whom she saw as settling down in resignation to suffer its ills, both physical and spiritual, as though this was the divine intention. She viewed humankind as being in thrall, generation after generation, to the mistaken belief that God cannot and will not set them free in this life, but only in the next. Her vision of Christ in her healing and subsequently of His holy Mother led her to a different and more positive belief.

This period, notable for her exercise of obedience, was not, however, without incident. She herself recorded a miraculous deliverance from serious injury when boarding a bus which started off too soon. She felt her spine strike the curb and a creeping numbness, but suddenly she was enveloped in "a beautiful blue light" and heard a voice saying "God is love". She was lifted back on to the bus by unseen hands.[2]

In the autumn of the same year (1912), she was staying in Reigate where she had "several visions" of the Virgin Mary. She was at prayer one day in the local church, asking for guidance concerning the fulfilment of her commission, when she became conscious of a blue light towards the lady chapel, out of which appeared the figure of the Blessed Virgin. This time she was holding not a lily but a cross, in both her hands. She placed it on Dorothy's knees with the words, "Always by prayer and faith, but this must come first." The weight of the cross, though described by Dorothy as "visionary", was nevertheless "so heavy that I felt weighed down by it". She then looked up into the Virgin's face and saw her smile, a smile that she was always to remember. The smile "was so full of tenderness that as I gazed on it the weight of the cross became less and less, until it vanished in love".[3]

Dorothy was frequently to know the weight of the cross in her life and ministry, but possibly this vision was given to prepare her for the receiving of the stigmata, which in fact began to appear on one of our Lady's festivals. The serene smile of the Virgin, granted to her as a true visionary, would be a source of strength during her time of purgation and throughout her life. But this benediction was to be followed by an even greater one, the vision of the Lord Himself.

This time she was staying in Edmonton, at St. Aldhelm's Vicarage. The sound of exquisite music awakened her one Sunday night. Coloured light was again a feature of the vision, mauve, blue and pink merging together, and the song of the cherubim caught her up into the heavenlies. "Then a great blue (*sic*) mist cleared and revealed three transcendent forms: on the left hand I recognised the Angel who had been sent to heal me, on the right the Virgin Mary, and in the centre our Lord. He held His hands over me, and in the palm of each there shone a wonderful red jewel." Again it seems that Dorothy was being prepared to receive the stigmata for she experienced great rays of light coming from the sacred hands of Christ and permeating her whole being. The message was "Go and tell":

Go and tell my children what I have done, that they be not asleep when I come to judge the quick and the dead. Take no thought for to-morrow, for I will provide.[4]

At first she had been reluctant to record this vision which she regarded as the greatest of blessings since she was privileged to see the face of Christ. But in the end she felt it right to share the experience with others, "for it cannot fail to help some, who perhaps have been unable to do so before, to realise the ever-living presence of our Blessed Lord".[5] From now on her eyes seemed to shine with a certain intensity which is common to many visionaries. The spiritually perceptive could tell that they were eyes which had seen the Lord. But it was to signal the onset of spiritual warfare: the rebuffs would not long be delayed.

The following year she was on holiday at a friend's house in Paignton when she was mugged. She was flung to the ground and the chain which attached her purse to her third finger was bitten off by the assailant's teeth while he dashed her head on the pavement, leaving her unconscious. She came to in bed where she·lay in a critical condition for a month, being nursed night and day. Dr. George, who was obviously a man of faith, was in attendance and diagnosed a fracture at the base of the skull and a ruptured left ear drum. Ten days after the assault her temperature rose dramatically and the nurse called the doctor. On his arrival in the sick room all became conscious of an unseen presence and instinctively knelt down. Dorothy alone saw a great light, in the midst of which was our Lord himself. Laying His hand on her head He said,

> Fear not, for I am with thee. The time is not yet, but I will come again.

Then, in answer to her unspoken question as to whether in view of her healing it was right for her to have a doctor and nurses, he said further,

> Yes, I would not have thee exalted above other men, but as a daisy growing in the garden.[6]

The doctor, realising God had touched his patient in some way, took her temperature, which had fallen from 104 to 99 degrees.

This dilemma of how far to have recourse to medical help has exercised the minds of some Christians from the earliest times. No less a person than St. Basil the Great (329–79) treated the matter. He had had some medical training and founded and maintained what may have been the very first hospital – in the sense of a public institution devoted to the care of the sick – outside Caesarea. In *The Long Rules*, an important treatise on monastic life, he considered this question of "whether recourse to the medical art is in keeping with the practice of piety". He produced an answer that has stood the test of time and been the orthodox Christian view ever since. It also accords with the answer Dorothy received to her unspoken question. He stated that medical science has been given to mankind by God to be used when necessary, although not as the only decisive factor, and that "to reject entirely the benefits to be derived from this art is the sign of a petty nature".[7]

Dorothy was not, however, finally healed, for the pain in her head and ear continued, but now she had her Lord's promise that He would come again. The visionary was not to have preferential treatment, but was to be "as a daisy growing in the garden". Indeed a further complication was added almost at once for she contracted appendicitis. Everything was prepared for an operation, but the curate and parishioners kept a vigil of prayer in Paignton church and the trouble cleared up.

The pain in her head and haemorrhage in her left ear were now particularly troublesome and she became totally deaf. Dr. George wrote his prescription on a piece of paper for her to read: "It is an attack affecting your hearing. You must remember His promise. He *will* come again."

After he left, her friends came to sit with her. Almost at once Dorothy heard the angelic music again and was taken up into the midst of the angelic band where one asked her "Are you trusting Jesus?" to which she replied in the affirmative. Then our Lord Himself came and lifted her up with these words:

Many mighty works have I done, but they have not believed. Tell them the time is at hand when I shall come in Glory to gather mine elect, and the faithful will I carry as lambs in My bosom. Rest in My will, and I will lead thee.[8]

Dorothy related how she experienced so much in this vision but she did not feel able to reveal the detail to others. In fact this was her second healing. Dr. George pronounced her perfectly well, she walked two miles the same day and the night nurse could hardly believe that Dorothy's flesh had perfectly formed and her hair had grown again, all in a day; truly, another "beautiful day". For the next few days she was radiantly happy in her new-found health and spiritual blessings. She was all the more surprised when she learnt that the rebuffs were not yet over.

Once more it was the Virgin Mary who appeared to her. She came towards her in that same blue light, her face full of love and compassion, and said, "Dorothy, remember the message. The rebuffs are not yet over but fear not." Again the same fragrance of love remained. And again the rebuffs came in the form of sickness, this time a severe cold and a gastric ulcer. She was in great pain and despairing of holding on any longer, she cried out to the God of Love, asking for more patience and some sleep. Her prayer was answered at once and she awoke free from pain, and as on both previous occasions, there was no need for convalescence. Dr. George commented, "Is it possible? You are healed? He has touched you again."[9]

This was her third healing and the following day a special Eucharist of thanksgiving was celebrated in her room by the curate. All were conscious of the Lord's Presence on that morning, more powerful than in their previous experience. There was a feeling of completion and total wholeness about the third healing.

After this, Dorothy saw three more visions during the course of the next year which are recorded in *The Living*

Touch. With hindsight, it seems as if all the healings and visions were preparing her not only to fulfil her commission, which to her was always her priority, but also for the receiving of the stigmata, which we shall turn to in the next part of the book.

The first of these visions she called a "message", entrusted to her by "our blessed Lord" and which she asked should be "read with due reverence and, by the grace of God, be spiritually interpreted". Throughout her life, having been in the heavenly places and having heard the Lord's voice, she knew when it was He who called. Again she knew in this case that "the voice was unmistakably His," and, again, His caring was preceded by the same wonderful light. As the light became more beautiful she discerned three forms, "on either side a great Angel, and in the centre our Lord Himself". As in a previous vision, the Lord held His hands over her again and she was able to see the red jewels in each palm. This time she was given a definite message:

> Dorothy, I would have thee go and tell My children what I have wrought in thee. Many there are who will not believe, but I say, bitter is the cup of tribulation which they shall drink. Speak of these things in the secret places, and if they listen not, tell them not again. My Bride do I call, she will hear My voice, and will not slumber, for lo! the time is at hand when I shall come in Glory to gather Mine elect, and the faithful will I carry as lambs in My bosom. My love for them is mighty and embraces all things. Rest in My Love and fear not, for have I not said, "I will never leave thee"?[10]

This message was given to her on St Martin's Day, 11th November, 1913, a day that was to have great significance five years later, before which the whole world and life was to change. It was the third message of the twelve months since the previous November. In all three there had been a command to "go and tell". In the first and third the command was to witness to what the Lord had done in her and for her. The second, in which the command is just "tell", was to warn them that the *Parousia*, the coming of Christ in glory, was at hand. The Parousia was in fact mentioned in all three, giving a note of urgency to the visions. Another feature common to all three was the personal word of comfort given to the visionary at the close of each vision. It is interesting to see them in juxtaposition:

Take no thought for to-morrow, for I will provide.

Rest in My will, and I will lead thee.

Rest in My love and fear not, for have I not said "I will never leave thee"?

It can readily be seen that the messages are somewhat similar, but this is no reason to doubt their authenticity.[11] We must now turn to the other two visions of Dorothy.

The first came to her in the church of St. Mary, Brookfield, Highgate on 8th April, 1914. She had been awakened out of sleep by a voice which seemed to come from the church. As she entered the porch she was aware of that same beautiful atmosphere. Three sick people for whom she had been asked to pray came before her mind and she knew she had to take them to the altar of God that morning. At the consecration she saw a light in the shape of a dove, and golden rays passed from it through the priest's hands into the chalice. She saw now only "this glorious chalice" from which a mauve and blue mist arose, materialising into a great cross, on which was the form of Christ and again his hands glowed with the red jewels. She held the three sick people before him and heard the Crucified say, "It is finished". The vision then slowly disappeared. The three sufferers were completely healed from that time.[12]

It seems that this vision had a lasting influence on her ministry. It may well have given her a method of praying for the sick, which seems highly probable when "A Little Way of Prayer" is examined.[13] It also shows that all through this

period she was answering requests to pray for and minister
to the sick.

The other vision, and the last to be recorded in *The Living
Touch*, took place in Dublin, where she was staying with
friends, on 6th July, 1914. It was an unusual vision to say
the least, but it shows what manner of person she was and
is important for the influence it must have exerted on her
life and her attitudes. It seems right therefore to quote it in
full, particularly since it brings to an end her own accounts
of her healings and visions in *The Living Touch*:

I had retired to my room and had fallen into a deep sleep,
when an Angel appeared to me and took my hand in
his saying "Come quickly, the Lord has much to show
thee."

He took me a long, long way, so that I grew very tired,
and at last we came to a large and handsome building. I
tapped on the door, which was opened, and inside I saw
a great number of people, elaborately dressed, and, as it
seemed, rich and worldly. They were rejoicing, or rather
revelling and shouting, "We are the Bride of Christ!
Come in."

I was about to enter when a voice said, "Enter not, follow me," and as I drew back my foot, the door closed.

The Angel then appeared by my side again, and we
journeyed on, till, in the road, we came upon a great
company of monks, nuns, and other people, who were
doing violence to their bodies, distorting themselves, and
looking very wretched and weary. One very old man came
out from among them and asked me where I was going. I
replied that I was on my way to Heaven and that Jesus
had called me. He looked at me sadly and said, "You
will never get there. We have been trying through the
ages, and this is as far as we have got." He wanted me
to join them, when the voice again said, "Follow me."

On we went once more, and as we went we were
overtaken by a vast procession of gorgeous chariots, which

36

were galloping along and making a great noise. They stopped as they came up, and a woman leant out of one of them and asked me where I was going. I replied as before, that I was on my way to Heaven. She laughed at me and said, "You can never get there on foot. We have been trying through all the ages, and this is as far as we have got. You had better join us." Again the voice said, "Follow me."

My Angel led me forward, and though we were on foot we seemed soon to leave the chariots far behind. The way now became more difficult, and we passed many who had died under their burdens, some carrying their gold, others their treasures. At last we came to a magnificent cathedral, and being told to knock on the door, I did so, and it was immediately opened. The interior was filled with priests and acolytes chanting and burning incense. One asked me what I wanted there, and I said, "I have brought a message from Jesus, that He is soon coming." They all shouted, "Put her out, put her out!" And I was seized by the arms and turned out into the road so roughly that I cried out with the pain.

My Angel returned and led me on until we came to another large building, which I entered. Here, amid a great assembly of people, was gathered together wealth of every description, all the riches and treasures the world can provide. Every one was shouting, "We have the Christ! Come in to us." I was bewildered at what I saw, and again the voice said, "Follow me."

Again we continued our journey, and at last we reached a great gulf, on the brink of which were a multitude of men and women. They were trying to cross over to the other side, but could not, because they were encumbered with all kinds of burdens; some were hugging idols, some gold, some pictures, some children, some even crucifixes, which they could not leave behind. A great voice was crying continually, "No, no, nothing that defiles!" I wondered

37

how I was to get across the gulf, and, kneeling down, I prayed to God to take me safely over.

On opening my eyes I found that I was on the other side; everything had changed, and I looked upon an entirely different scene. Coming from every direction were crowds of people with upturned faces, all being drawn by the same object. They had nothing in their hands, and as we came nearer I saw in the firmament what it was that was attracting them. It was a great Heart, from which flowed a broad red stream. Under this the people passed, and as they did so they were changed into glorious beings, and their voices rose in one loud anthem of praise. I asked the Angel what was happening, and he replied, "They are even now being healed."

We went forward again, and before us we beheld a great gate magnificent in texture and beautiful beyond description. Issuing from the gate we heard music of indescribable loveliness, and I asked what it was. The Angel said, "The whole of Heaven rejoices, for the King is bringing home His Bride and they are preparing the banqueting hall."

My Angel guide then left me, and I heard the voice of our Lord. He told me many things, and finally spoke these words:

"I have shown thee these things that thou shouldst enter not into their temptations. The rebuffs are not yet over. There are those who will curse thee, bearing My witness. But fear not, for I have blessed thee and loved thee with an everlasting love."

Then I was sent back, and found myself lying on my bed.[14]

It is tempting to seek an interpretation to this vision. Some of it was later to be proved too near the truth for comfort. But it may not be right to interpret it allegorically. Dorothy herself indicated the more helpful way by interpreting it as a parable, a story that conveys one essential message. In

38

introducing her account of it she declared that it forcibly brought home to her "the fact that only Love counts; that Love is the Key that will unlock the gate of Heaven, through which we shall enter into the Kingdom of God."[15] All the graphic episodes of the vision pointed her to this one fact, that Love is supreme, the only Reality. It was to be central to her vision throughout her life, which was an embodiment of that love. After all, she had come face to face with its author and experienced the caress of His healing touch.

Notes

1. Dorothy Kerin, *The Living Touch*, p. 19.
2. Ibid. p. 21. Her descriptions were always precise about facts and it is interesting that the *blue* light was observed in this instance and the following vision. Blue is the colour associated with healing.
3. Ibid. p. 24.
4. Ibid. pp. 25 ff.
5. Ibid. p. 24.
6. Ibid. p. 29.
7. Quoted by Morton T. Kelsey in *Healing and Christianity* (SCM Press, 1973). See my *A Healing House of Prayer* (Hodder and Stoughton, 1987) pp. 72–74.
8. *The Living Touch*, p. 31.
9. Ibid. pp. 33–5.
10. Ibid. pp. 36 ff.
11. See the Medjugorje literature published by the Association of the Friends of Medjugorje in Milan, 1986 (not for sale).
12. Dorothy Kerin, *The Living Touch*, pp. 38–40.
13. See Chapter 19, pp. 207f.
14. Dorothy Kerin, *The Living Touch*, pp. 40–46.
15. Ibid., p. 40.

Part II

Her Spirituality

4   FIRST STEPS

From her earliest years it was obvious to her mother that
Dorothy was no ordinary child. "Even as a tiny child,"
she wrote later of Dorothy, "she had an immense love
of all that pertains to the spiritual, caring little for the
amusements which children are wont to indulge in, and
preferring pictures of angels and religious subjects to the
crudely humorous picture-books which most children love".[1]
She was an extremely sensitive child and could not bear
harshness in any form. This gift of heightened sensitivity
meant that any deficiency in schooling went unnoticed. Her
sister recalled that their mother used to declare that Dorothy
"could hear things almost before they were spoken" and
"always seemed to know what was going on in the house
without being told".[2] She was also clever in a practical way
and once she had seen something done, whether in sewing,
knitting, cooking, gardening or flower arranging, she could
do it as well or better than her teacher. From an early
age her powers of listening and apprehension were highly
developed.

Dorothy was born in Walworth, London, on 28th November, 1889. Boyson Road, in which the Kerins lived at number
6, was a street of terraced houses, each with a basement
kitchen and two floors above ground and an attic. Nearby
were the workhouse and asylum. Dorothy had a window
into suffering humanity even during her childhood.

Her father was an artist and caricaturist, reluctantly having
to turn his hand to the family business he inherited. Of

43

an old Irish family, he traced his descent from William of Wykeham (1324–1404), the founder of Winchester College and New College, Oxford.[3] Her mother came from a musical family. Dorothy's great-grandmother was an Italian prima donna. Her grandmother had a fine voice and married her music master at 20 years of age, by whom she had nine children, Dorothy's mother being the youngest. Dorothy grew up listening to the beautiful sound of her mother's fine coloratura voice echoing around the house. Music was to be an important factor in her spiritual awareness and gave her a listening ear.

When her father's business failed they moved to Epping and Dorothy spent five years at a dame school, the only schooling she received. She was very popular with all the children and always had a crowd around her. Possibly she was a great listener to them all. There seemed to be a "charisma" about her from early days and she was always possessed of an irrepressible sense of fun.

Dorothy herself occasionally said in later life how from her earliest years she was open to the spiritual life. She told the following story only two years before her death, but it is one of the great formative experiences she was given, even in those early days:

I would like to tell you a story, if I may. It is a story full of spiritual significance to me, and I want to share it with you, because there was a wonderful indication this morning that it was in God's pattern that I should do so. How many of you have wondered why you see such evidences of acorns and oak leaves at Burrswood? You see them in every conceivable place; you'll find them on the foundation stone; you'll find them in the decoration of the ceiling of this church, and everywhere they hang. It is because to me they have this special significance. One day, when I was a child, our Lord Jesus came to me, and in His hand He held a little brown object, and He said, *Tend this with obedience,*

44

and I will water it with the dew of my love, and one day you shall behold a mighty oak. That little brown object was an acorn, and those acorns have pursued me through my life. They come in the most unexpected way from various sources. And today that little acorn is represented in a mighty oak in this Church of Christ the Healer. Now, as this Church extends its branches, and drops its acorns, I pray that there will be many who will gather up these acorns, and tend them with obedience, and that our Lord will water them with the dew of His love, and that they may be planted in His Kingdom.[4]

The word that stands out from this vision is obedience and it was this key concept she was soon to learn, like her Master, through suffering. Thereafter she would make it the cornerstone of her spiritual life.

Before we leave the first twelve years, however, it should be emphasised that her childhood was essentially happy. Her mother had a very sweet nature and gave to her children a love of music and of beautiful things and of all that was good. The family was in tune with creation and the joy of life. Dorothy had a very special devotion to her father and there was a genuine bond of love between the two. All this made a fruitful soil for her faith. In later years she used to deny that she was a special child and she would often use the word ordinary about herself. But the kind of vision related above, and her resonance with the angels and things heavenly, must have shown her family and intimate friends that this was no ordinary child. Her mother realised that this child was special and so did her sister Evelyn. It was to become increasingly clear to them during the next twelve years.

This vision in her childhood is of profound significance. Firstly it links her with the long line of saints and mystics who saw visions and spoke with their Lord "face to face". It especially reminds us of the very similar vision

45

of Dame Julian of Norwich concerning the hazelnut, which was "all that is made" and showed her of God's infinite love. Secondly, Dorothy had a certainty about the event and related it perfectly naturally, which seems to indicate that even in her childhood she knew her Lord intimately and the occasions when He spoke to her were very real. Thirdly, this event gave her a vision for her life. Whatever her Lord called her to do, whatever task He assigned to her, would demand her obedience. Once that obedience was given, the Lord would give the increase: the acorns of work and ministry would become mighty oaks. In later life she would see her Lord being true to His promise as the acorns she planted with her obedience were indeed watered with the dew of His love and have become – and are still becoming – mighty oaks.

After Dorothy's healing, her mother made the comment that the terrible sufferings she had to watch her daughter undergo "proved that she possessed the great patience of which her childhood had given promise".[5] She went on to say:

> During this time all who saw her were deeply impressed by her patient cheerfulness, and would often remark that it was almost supernatural. She lived very near to the Master, and all who entered her room felt an unseen Presence. Many were the heartaches and burdens that were brought to the little sufferer and laid down for ever by her bedside. God used her wonderfully in intercession for others, and lists of those in sickness, sorrow, and trouble were brought her. In answer to her prayers many have felt His touch, and have received great blessing through this little channel.[6]

This also is a significant passage as well as being prophetic. It shows that Dorothy already had an awareness of the nature of her acorn, a vision of what God was calling her to be and to do, and had an affinity with "those in sickness, sorrow and trouble". From this time she also seems to have had the gift of touching lives through her prayer, or more correctly, acting as a channel so that it was Christ who touched their lives. Much had been given her in the acorn vision and was strengthened through her suffering, which in this period of her life was used very greatly by the Lord to prepare and equip Dorothy for His service. At a time when her contemporaries were growing up through their teenage trials and traumas and discovering what the world and life was all about, Dorothy was undergoing the "hidden" years, years of silent growth. It was a period of listening, of coming to herself; it was the time when she learned that obedience which was to be the hallmark of her life. Later she was to say that obedience was greater than sacrifice. This was the testimony of her "hidden" years. As others were learning to make relationships and meet people from very different backgrounds, the young Dorothy was forging her relationship with her Lord. It was the time of purgation, when the catharsis of suffering pruned this delicate fruit to bear a rich harvest. The times of silence and solitude, of music and laughter, of devoted companionship and of desperate aloneness, all contributed the rich fertile soil from which the small acorn might become the mighty oak. The hidden years were the opportunity for a profound listening to the Divine Will, the time of preparatory retreat. It was a time when her spiritual eyes were being focused (symbolised by the squint that righted itself just before her healing) so that her vision would be clarified. It was a time when all her spiritual antennae were sharpened, crowning the gifts of instinctive awareness and spiritual sensitivity which she already possessed. And it was a time when she discovered St. Teresa, whose life bore such a similarity to her own. If this was the time of her purgation, then we must now turn our attention to the remainder of the mystical quest.

Notes

1. Dorothy Kerin, *The Living Touch*, p. 149.
2. Evelyn Waterfield, *My Sister Dorothy Kerin* (Mowbray 1964) pp. 24, 25.
3. Also among her reputed ancestors was St. Keiran, who, it is said, was the first man in Ireland to give his life for his faith in Christ.
4. See Dorothy Musgrave Arnold, *Dorothy Kerin: Called by Christ to Heal* (Hodder and Stoughton, 1965) p. 4 ff.
5. Dorothy Kerin, *The Living Touch*, p. 50.
6. Ibid. p. 51.

5 THE ROAD TO UNION –
THE MYSTIC WAY

If we define mysticism as the direct intuition or experience of God, and a mystic as someone who to a greater or lesser degree has that experience, then it can be argued that Dorothy was within that tradition. Of course we must look more deeply into the whole mystical tradition and this we shall do. After all, every human being has a capacity for God in that we are His creatures and He is our Creator. In some human beings this capacity shines out with a colourful richness and vivacity. But what makes a mystic?

The word *mystic* has almost become a pejorative word in the religious vocabulary, almost a dismissive comment about someone regarded as off-beat, not in the mainstream, even unorthodox. Nothing could be further from the truth. Of course there have been some who have acted rather like the eighth-century prophets of the Old Testament who sent warning shots across the bows of the Church or leadership of their day, usually with good reason, but Christian mystics throughout the history of the Church have acted as its soul, recalling it time and again to its task of being truly the Church, the Body of Christ on earth. St. Francis of Assisi (1182–1226), for instance, provided a new dimension to the spiritual life of the Church. He and his followers have continually brought a renewing richness to the Christian consciousness, have been a prophetic sign, and have contributed a Christlikeness to the Church's spiritual quest. John Ruysbroek (1293–1381), who was brought up in

Brussels, expressed the desire "to be by the grace of God a life-giving member of Holy Church".

Mysticism, then, represents the very heart of religion and the Christian mystic down the ages has contributed much to the Church's spiritual life, in many instances fanning dying embers into a living flame once more. In fact the Church has been renewed time and again by the fresh and refreshing contacts of its mystics with God. They have been called the eyes of the Body of Christ. Frequently they have supplied that prophetic element in the life of the Church. They have been living witnesses to God's life-giving presence in and with His people. They have made their fellow Christians aware of the grace and mercies of God. In this way they have contributed to the corporate life of the Church by showing what Christian spirituality can be, for their prayer always issues in action. What then is its secret?

For most of us, the unseen realities are a matter of belief: for the mystics they are matters of knowledge, of first-hand experience. At one instant in their life, or in a number of "showings" that may have been experienced over a period of days or even years, they are given a vision of God; they realise Him as a living Presence within and around them and because of this experience in their life, their whole existence and outlook is transformed. Frequently such an experience transcends their powers of expression: "I beheld the ineffable fullness of God, but I can relate nothing of it save that I have *seen* the fullness of Divine Wisdom, wherein is all goodness," wrote Angela of Foligno (the first period of her visions ended in 1294). St. Catherine of Genoa (born 1447) wrote "If I could only show you a tithe of that Love in which I dwell." As we read their writings we are taken out of ourselves and become aware of another dimension of life, so beautiful and so true, that it transcends our powers of expression and even theirs. But one thing is for sure: they are trying to give us a glimpse of the Reality they have seen and experienced. For the time being, "we see but a poor reflection as in a mirror", but one day, "we shall see face to face", as they have seen (1 Cor. 13:12).

Dorothy, as we learned from the record of her healing and other "showings", was one of those who saw "face to face" and that experience alone places her in the Christian mystical tradition. In her address at St. Martin-in-the-Field, from which I have already quoted, Dorothy had declared, "I have seen Jesus; I have heard His voice; I have felt His touch, and I know that Jesus Christ is the same yesterday, today and forever."[1] The fact that she *saw* and that she *knew* places her firmly in the true tradition of Christian mystics and promises that our deeper search for other similarities with the lives of the great mystics may be rewarding.

In works on mysticism, there are regular references to the *mystic way*, a formula first used by the Neoplatonists but then taken over by the spiritual writers of the Christian Church. It describes in general terms the stages of development in the life of a mystic, though they should not be applied too literally or vigorously, for everyone is different and in no one are the stages so clear cut. The first stage is *purgation* which refers to the detachment from earthly interests and the gradual purification of character and alignment of the will in harmony with the will of God. The second stage is called *illumination*, when, the will surrendered, there is a "peaceful certitude of God" and deeper perceptions of life's true values, as when Angela of Foligno perceived that "the whole World is full of God". These two stages are not always separated for frequently further illumination leads to a greater awareness of the need for the "purgative Way", a term used by St. John of the Cross (1542–91) for the gradual spiritualisation of the mystics' life of prayer.

The final stage is called *union*. Hitherto the mystic has aspired to a life filled with the Holy Spirit and so lived in the presence and love of God. Now "he finds himself immersed in it, inspired and directed in all his actions by the indwelling love of God".[2] This is the zenith of the consecrated life, the spiritual marriage of the soul, a union with God that

51

persists amidst the busyness of life. In many of the mystics this final stage of union was expressed in a period of dynamic activity, for which amazing energy and powers of endurance were supplied to achieve goals far beyond normal human endeavour.

Without keeping too rigidly to the divisions or to the time spent at each stage of development, it is important to note how Dorothy's life contained the elements of progression and therefore how closely she follows in the mystical tradition. The first stage of the way (purgation) was, as we have seen, in the years up to her healing and was a path of suffering. Her healing, which was an experience of supreme revelation, began her second period (illumination). The third period (union) comprised her active life in Ealing and Kent and her missions abroad. This, of course, may be forcing a pattern on to a life that was full of surprises – because God is a God of surprises, and we must not expect His special servants to run on tram lines. A more simple division might be twofold – her passive life which would include the first two mystical stages, and her active life from 1929 onwards.

This latter twofold division links her life more closely to that of St. Teresa of Avila (1515–82) on whom Dorothy may have modelled her spiritual life and with whom she felt a distinct affinity. St. Teresa's life naturally falls into two distinct parts. During the first she lived in comparative seclusion in her convent, but made great progress in the interior life. The second period was marked by a seemingly ceaseless energy that enabled her to found and reform religious houses, based on a steady and inward assurance of union with God. A comparison with Dorothy's life reveals a natural likeness between their first periods of spiritual development, both of which included visions and revelations, while the second period includes, for each of them, intense activity, which included the building of lasting memorials. "Work! work! work!", wrote St. Teresa in a memorable passage concerning the object of her soul's union with God.

Dorothy probably had read her words and lived them out in the active periods of her life.

The similarity with St. Teresa does not end there. For both, their life of prayer brought about a flowering of personality for in prayer they were frequently in the heavenlies. This was the spiritual sustenance which undergirded for each of them an active career that was strenuous by any standards. St. Teresa engaged in that work "in a spirit of unfailing common sense, of gaiety, of dedicated love,"[3] and the same description would come to mind, word for word, in the case of Dorothy. Both were also equally flexible and versatile as regards the spiritual and practical sides to their nature: each one could turn instantly from talking of finance, or examining architects' drawings, or cleaning the house in a thorough manner to deal with sensitivity and wisdom with some tortured soul. Both could also glean their inward joys even from the long, hard journeys or experiences which they did not relish. All these experiences gave to each of them a courage and a refreshing freedom in the undertaking of their work, and an ability to communicate through the written word so that even today their spirit reaches out to modern readers who find a blessing in their writings.[4] In each case their lives achieved the spiritual maturity which other mystics have called the "spiritual marriage", or "transforming union of the soul with God", and Dorothy would have agreed with St. Teresa that "the object of the spiritual marriage is work".[5]

Dorothy's life and spiritual experiences also bear resemblance to those of other mystics. The German abbess St. Hildegarde (1098–1179) was the first great figure in the long line of women mystics. Her personality and accomplishments would be remarkable in any period of history. She was a writer with great intellectual power, of weak bodily health, yet skilled in medicine. She wrote a complete guide to the nature and properties of herbs, and was deeply interested in politics, denouncing laxity and corrupt practices in the Church. She corresponded with – and often rebuked – the great men of her day and was something of a poet and musician; in later life she travelled widely. Dorothy did not have all these accomplishments, but her life closely resembled that of St. Hildegarde in many respects. Despite their very full lives, both remained first and foremost contemplatives whose outward actions were always initiated by inward commands, which both learned demanded instant obedience, though St. Hildegarde learned the hard way. Twice illness overtook her when she did not respond to the inward voice and she was only healed when she later obeyed the command she had received. Dorothy, as we have seen, learned to obey in her first stage. Once they did obey, their sources of power manifestly lay beyond this world.

The greatest similarity between the two women was that from early childhood both were clearly marked out as unusual children. Dorothy preferred to talk about the angels, and they were a very real part of her life. In her serious illness when she asked her sister to sing "Abide With Me" and she was unable to do so, they both heard it sung by the angel choir. Hildegarde wrote in later life:

From my infancy until now, in the 70th year of my age, my soul has always beheld this Light; and in it my soul soars to the summit of the firmament and into a different air . . . Its name, which has been given me, is "Shade of the Living Light" . . . Within that brightness I sometimes see another light, for which the name *Lux Vivens* has been given me . . . When I see it all sadness and pain is lifted from me.[6]

She first experienced this "Shade of the Living Light" when three years old and at five began to understand the visionary world in which she lived. During her childhood she had constant visions and premonitions of the future which were accompanied by continuous ill health. Here is the strong link with Dorothy who wrote: "Especially have I to thank God for giving me spiritual joy and a feeling of His Presence

54

ever with me, which I had ever since I can remember anything."[7] Possibly we see in both these lives reflections of the paradoxical mystery from the life of another great mystic, St. Paul, whose visionary and hyperactive life was constantly accompanied by his thorn in the flesh (2 Cor. 12:7). There is a golden thread running through the lives of all the mystics down the ages which links them to each other because it first binds them to their Lord.

Before we go on to chart Dorothy's progress in the second stage of the mystic way, the period of illumination, there are two more Christian mystics, both women, to whose lives Dorothy's bore a special similarity. St. Catherine of Siena (1347–80) also received vivid religious impressions as a child, and before the age of sixteen decided to consecrate her life to God. After her mystical marriage experience in 1366, the culmination of her solitary life and absorption in God, she obeyed the Divine Voice which told her it was time to pass on to other souls the grace and certitude she had received. She immediately left her cell and devoted herself to nursing, comforting and converting the sick poor of Siena. This is a similar act of obedience to Dorothy's in 1929 when she went out to heal the sick, comfort the sorrowing and bring faith to the faithless. It is worth noting the similar content of their call and the result in both cases, for their peaceful and unselfish presence always ministered to others Christ's healing for both body and soul. They were also gifted with an unerring intuition concerning both heavenly and earthly things. In all probability this was given to them at the most important revelation of their lives which by a coincidence happened to both of them at the age of twenty-three. For Dorothy it was her healing. For Catherine it was a trance which lasted four hours and her friends supposed her dead, as Dorothy's family supposed about her on that eventful Sunday night. Catherine herself always held that her soul had left her body but was sent back to minister to other souls:

The salvation of many souls demands thy return, and thou shalt no more live as thou hast lived hitherto, nor have henceforth this cell for habitation, but shall go out from thine own city for the good of souls. I shall ever be with thee, and shall guide thee and bring thee back. Thou shalt bear the honour of My name and witness to spiritual things before small and great, layfolk, clergy and religious; and I shall give thee words and wisdom none shall be able to withstand.[8]

Totally fulfilled in the remaining ten years of Catherine's life, this would also have been a correct prophecy for Dorothy's. From the "cell" of her sick bed she went out for the good of innumerable souls, eventually away from her city to Burrswood and from thence abroad, with words and wisdom which changed and healed the lives of many, both small and great. Like Catherine, Dorothy too could be called "the mother of thousands of souls", among whom were the small, faithful and hard-working band of disciples which both women had gathered round them. Above all, both had a profound experience of God, which sent them forth to His work in unquestioning obedience. Both would have endorsed St. Teresa's saying that "to give our Lord a perfect service Martha and Mary must combine". Although in the lives of St. Teresa, St. Catherine and Dorothy there was a particular "Martha" period and a particular "Mary" period, each one in her own way blended these two essential elements of the mystical way together in perfect balance throughout their lives.

The other mystic has already been mentioned in relation to the "showing" of the hazelnut, comparable with Dorothy's acorn. Julian of Norwich (born c. 1343) was endowed, like Dorothy, with a singular beauty of character and a breadth of Christian spirituality which could include in one sweep both the transcendence and humanity of her Redeemer, rendering the sudden change from earthly duties to the heavenly realities a natural transition. Like some Gothic cathedral she combined the sense of mystery and sheer beauty with the robust earthiness of common life. This was especially true for both of them in relation to the sufferings of Christ. They both had the gift of unifying their *sumpatheia* to the mysteries of the Passion with a natural homeliness and gaiety. The way of the cross was a very real part of their lives.

Before her "showings" Julian's prayers were filled with a desire to know the Passion of Christ in such a way as would enable her to be at one with His life through grace. She asked for the mind or memory of Christ's Passion, so that she could experience the Passion in the same way His mother and closest friends did at the foot of the Cross. She also wished to come near death so that she might, after her healing, live better: "I wanted His pain to be my pain: a true compassion producing a longing for God. I was not wanting a physical revelation of God, but such compassion as a soul would naturally have for the Lord Jesus, who for love became a mortal man. Therefore I desired to suffer with Him."[9] Her prayer for a mortal illness was answered and during her suffering she received the visions. In her dark room light from the crucifix was visible, while an interior light flooded her soul during the showings.

For Dorothy also, the Cross and the sufferings of the Passion were a reality. In the same year as her healing (1912) she had seen many visions of the Blessed Virgin Mary, and in the November saw her holding a large shining cross which she placed on Dorothy's knees and said: *Always by prayer and faith, but this must come first.*[10] This was to be fulfilled in many ways and at many times during the remainder of her life. Within the next few years she received the stigmata and had out-of-body experiences, finding herself transported to minister to the dying in no-man's-land between the opposing armies of the First World War. This is to anticipate the next chapter, but it is also mentioned here to emphasise the thesis of this chapter, that Dorothy Kerin trod the mystic way and is in the direct line of Christian mystics who have contributed to the pilgrimage of the Church down the centuries by ensuring that the presence of Christ was central to its life and mission.

Notes

1. Quoted in *Dorothy: A Portrait* by James Davidson Ross (Hodder and Stoughton, 1958). See also Chapter 2.
2. Evelyn Underhill, *Mystics of the Church* (James Clarke & Co. Ltd., 1925) p. 27. I am greatly indebted to her writing in this section of my book.
3. Ibid., p. 173.
4. St. Teresa's writings were, of course, of greater significance, but both still nourish souls.
5. "The very object of her soul's union with God was, as she said in a memorable passage, 'Work! work! work!'" Evelyn Underhill, op. cit., p.176.
6. Ibid., p. 76.
7. *Fulfilling*, by Dorothy Kerin (Hodder and Stoughton, 1952), p. 11.
8. Quoted in Evelyn Underhill, op. cit., p. 157.
9. Quoted in *Revelations of Divine Love*, Mother Julian of Norwich, (Hodder and Stoughton, 1987) pp. 7–8.
10. See p. 30.

6 THE ROAD TO UNION –
THE VIA DOLOROSA

The day before Dorothy died in 1963, the feast of the conversion of St. Paul (the first Christian mystic? – who also saw the risen Christ in a flood of light), she said to those at her bedside, "Mine is the Way of the Cross". The Via Dolorosa was to run through her entire life, through her times of suffering, through the visions that followed, especially when our Lady laid the shining cross on her knees, and now into this final period of preparation for her ministry which combined the elements of purgation and illumination on the road to union. As the lives of all the mystics have shown, this period is usually accompanied by indifferent health and much suffering. Dorothy's life was no exception and although her final healing occurred at the beginning of this period, her spiritual experiences were such that she still suffered from heart troubles, headaches, unexplained haemorrhages, fever and depression. All this she bore with the fortitude of St. Paul with whom she could say, "I have been crucified with Christ and I no longer live, but Christ lives in me" (Gal. 2:20a).

Throughout her life she constantly offered this suffering on behalf of others and seemed to have a gift of taking into herself the sufferings of others. Again, with St. Paul she could say, "Now I rejoice in what was suffered for you, and I fill up in my flesh what is still lacking in regard to Christ's afflictions, for the sake of his body, which is the Church" (Col. 1:24). She always prayed that Christ would use these sufferings and setbacks on behalf of those for whom at that time she had a burden of prayer. This constant act of intercession on behalf of others was well summarised in one of her prayers:

> By the bruising of my whole life,
> Strengthen me with sympathy for every wounded soul;
> And let my prayers be a balm for the wounds of thy children
> That they may be healed.

It was, however, a very hidden part of her spirituality and very few, if any, knew of her sufferings during her lifetime, let alone the use to which she put them. And as we have learned from the lives of all the mystics, God also uses the suffering of His servants to create in them the Christ-like character and the total dedication of their life to Him, so that they can be His instruments, reflecting His glory and passing on to others the vision by which they themselves have been inspired.

For Dorothy, this was to be the period of her life when she had the space to build on the firm foundations granted to her in her healings and visions and when she came to know her Lord more fully by walking the Via Dolorosa. As Angela of Foligno remarked in a celebrated passage, "The Love of God is never idle, for it constrains us to follow the way of the cross."[1] This creative time in the wilderness was to occupy the first of the three periods of seventeen years between her healing and her final healing in death. Throughout this and the other two periods she was always conscious of the fact that "the love of God is never idle".

Dorothy was led to her spiritual director by a friend. She had tried to make her confession to one or two priests, but they had declined to hear it, possibly out of humility, for they would immediately discern the spiritual depths of Dorothy's character. Her friend became concerned that Dorothy was receiving invitations to speak from Theosophical societies and Spiritualist groups, and told her cousin, the Reverend Dr. Langford-James. He had read *The Living Touch* and was deeply impressed by it, but still wondered whether its writer might be of the true faith. His two-hour meeting with her at the invitation of his cousin convinced him that she was indeed a loyal member of the Church. When he asked her about making her confession she told him how one priest had declined because he did not wish to stand in the way of the Holy Spirit. He suggested she should go to another and promised to give thought and prayer to the matter.

After days of prayerful consideration, Dr. Langford-James decided to offer his own services, but in his letter stated that he did not see himself as her regular confessor. Dorothy replied, "I know I ought to come to you. Don't *you* know? Have you not seen?" She had twice seen a vision in which our Lady had led her to him. When he questioned her closely about the visions, he was convinced by her answers. And so began a relationship which, if difficult at times, was to be formative for Dorothy's progress in the spiritual life and which, because of her director's gifts, would lead her on a path of discipline along the mystic way, and so prepare her for the great ministry to which her healing and subsequent visions had called her.

Dr. Langford-James was well qualified to become the spiritual director of someone so advanced in the mystical way as Dorothy and to guide her on the path to union. Grounded in the classics, he had read theology extensively. Furthermore he had made a special study of mystical theology which equipped him with the valuable gift of discernment to assess and stimulate the progress of his charge. Contemporary portraits show him as having an ascetic type of face, a sensitive mouth and piercing blue eyes. Behind his features lurks a strong will. He was mercifully possessed of an irrepressible sense of humour and a keen wit. He and Dorothy both had a gift of spontaneous rhyming and vied with one another in the composition of limericks. He was also a fine conversationalist and an accomplished musician. It can surely be said that he was "ordained" to cross her path: he was given to her at this moment by the Giver of all good things. After a trial stay, not without serious misgivings on Dorothy's part because she thought it would be too much for Mrs. Langford-James, she was persuaded to move in, since living in a vicarage, as she did on and off throughout this period, would give her much more opportunity for constant and devoted prayer. Before this she had been attempting to live the life of her family by day and pray and see to her already vast correspondence at night.

Besides Dr. and Mrs. Langford-James, their household also consisted of two elderly sisters, who were deeply religious and became devoted to Dorothy. Dorothy was concerned about disrupting their lives and felt that they were all too busy for her to make any demands on them. Dr. Langford-James reminded her that our Lord had accepted sacrifices from others during his earthly life and she must do the same. That night she saw the crucifix he had placed in her room shining with light. The next day she asked him to interpret this "showing" and, reminding her of their conversation the day before, he pointed out that the crucifix was the symbol of sacrifice and that possibly this was an assurance that she should accept the sacrifice he and his household were prepared to make on her behalf.

Her director's parish was St. Mark's, Bush Hill Park, Enfield, and the vicarage was to be her home for the next years of her preparation and was to be the hallowed place of her deepest experiences of the Lord's presence. Soon after she moved in, the first of these took place in the Blessed Sacrament chapel at the top of the house. It was her sanctuary where she spent many long hours in prayer, her upper room where Jesus frequently "stood in the midst". On this first occasion she had been praying for some time when her director went up at 10 p.m. and found her rapt in contemplation. He left a note to say he would wait up for her. He went up an hour later and again at 1 a.m. to find her in the same situation, oblivious to the things of this world. He stayed for a further hour, praying she might be taken out of her prayer for he was afraid of the strain on her physical endurance. She then came out of her prayer and left the chapel, but on the way out turned and said, "How can I leave Him here all alone?" Her director reassured her, "He is not alone. His angels are guarding him". From the first he was thus shown the advanced stage of contemplative prayer to which his pupil had already attained. This was to be the period of illumination which would reach its climax in the union of spiritual marriage, equipping Dorothy to fulfil her vocation to bring healing, comfort and faith to all in need.

Such a spiritual odyssey is never without its perils. A short time after this occasion Dorothy had a satanic attack. While getting ready for bed she turned round and saw the Devil in the guise of a beautiful angel, but with dark eyes that possessed a horrid and evil gaze. She had been thinking of something our Lord had said to her in a vision and the Devil told her how presumptuous it was for her to think so much honour would be accorded to her and threatened to kill her there and then. The result of this encounter was a severe heart attack and haemorrhage from the lungs which left her exhausted. She then told her director how she had prayed to have the privilege of sharing some of our Lord's sufferings in his Passion.

This experience was the beginning of the positive answer she received to the prayer she had made and is reminiscent of Julian of Norwich who prayed as a girl that she might have an illness at thirty years of age which would bring her a closer understanding of the Passion. The actual experience of Dorothy is also akin to that of St. Thérèse of Lisieux (1873–97) who had a satanic attack during the vigil preceding the dawn of her day of profession, when she was made to feel as if her vocation was nothing but a dream and that she was quite unsuited to the Carmelite life.[2] She was fortunate to have a very sane novice mistress who quickly reassured her. Dorothy was equally fortunate in her director.

There was a sequel to this encounter which occurred while she was preparing to make her confession in church. Suddenly she was aware of the Devil standing beside her and saying in a jeering way, "I will never leave thee nor forsake thee," the words spoken to her by Jesus after her healing. Her director entered the church at that moment and with his powers of perception instantly discerned something was wrong. He summoned Dorothy into the sacristy, but the Devil followed her. When Dr. Langford-James was unable to beat back the attack with holy water Dorothy reminded him that the Devil feared the crucifix. He turned to the sacristy crucifix and commanded him to depart. They then went to the Blessed Sacrament chapel where Dorothy's full confession was the instrument of final victory.

Dorothy was naturally concerned when these events seemed to initiate a new phase in her life, marked by feelings of desolation of a greater intensity than she had previously experienced. Her director reassured her that this was the inevitable accompaniment of certain stages on the mystical way of life and prayer, and although God did not necessarily ordain these experiences He used them to deepen the spiritual life. With such encouragement she was able to keep the light of her vision in her sights and bear the continuing of these "rebuffs" with patience. The next part of her sufferings was to be so intense and yet so sublime as to mark her out as one of the Lord's special flowers, the daisy that was trodden under foot and yet plucked to be part of the Victor's crown.

A journalist, James Davidson Ross, asked her in later years if she would put on paper the story of her years of preparation from her healing in 1912 to when she began her ministry in 1929. She did this in a letter from Fiesole, dated May 18th, 1958, and it seems appropriate to quote it here:

This is inevitably a difficult task, so much happened during those years that I find it impossible to convey in writing or word. Those years were filled with a consciousness of

64

the living presence of our Divine Lord, wherein I was permitted to see many of His mighty works and to Know that the power of Jesus, used in His ministry along the shores of Galilee during His pre-Resurrection Life, are the same yesterday, today and for ever.

Worldwide interest was aroused when the facts of our Lord's Living Touch upon me was published and for a time life became a bewildering succession of demands of every sort and from every place. There was little opportunity for listening in solitude for God's guidance. It was at this time that I met in the house of a friend the Reverend Dr. Langford-James, who was urged to invite me to his home, where he hoped the necessary peace and quiet, of which I was in sore need, should be found. We were both convinced that this was in God's pattern for me at that time. I accepted this invitation gratefully and went to stay at St. Mark's Vicarage, Bush Hill Park, with his wife and himself. This visit continued for the next thirteen years. Dr. Langford-James became my spiritual director from whom I accepted a rule of life.

During those years of preparation, needed for the fulfilling of the purpose of our Lord's Healing Touch upon me, which in my prayer I was constantly made aware of, I was given all the time necessary for prayer, meditation and solitude.

Dr. Langford-James, a learned theologian, directed my spiritual reading. To him I owe a great debt of gratitude for the help of his vast knowledge and access to and use of his library.

During those years of waiting and preparation the thing I thank God most for is the fact that, by His Grace, I was helped to discover the great secret of obedience. This secret I believed to be the foundaton of the supernatural life, without which we cannot abide in God's will.

In visions and dreams He revealed to me many things in His pattern for the future. As these plans unfolded and have continued to unfold through my life, I humbly and thankfully affirm that I never consciously disobeyed Him. All that He has asked me to do in faith for Him has been done through His power, thanks be to God.

That which was once faith has now become knowledge and I know of a truth that where God guides God provides; and never in any instance has work embarked upon through what I believed to be His command, failed to come to fruition . . . the cruse of oil has never failed and the barrel of wheat never wasted.

Notes

1. Quoted in Evelyn Underhill, *Mystics of the Church* (James Clarke & Co. Ltd., 1925) p. 108.
2. *The Story of a Soul*, Chapter VIII (translated by Michael Day, Clarke Books, 1973). The likeness to St. Thérèse does not, however, end there: see Chapter 7.

7 THE ROAD TO UNION – THE STIGMATA

Suffering seems to have been the normal accompaniment of sanctity throughout Christian history. Because their Master suffered, those who chose to follow His *Way* (one of the original names of the Christian Church) chose particularly to be close to Him in His suffering. The martyrs are an obvious example of this closeness to our Lord in His Passion. St. Ignatius of Antioch begged the Christians in Rome not to deprive him of the honour of being eaten by the lions that he might gain the palm of martyrdom. And there are examples of this in every century and in every Christian country. The first martyr on English soil, St. Alban, boldly exchanged clothes with the priest who was being pursued and gave himself up to certain death.

There are also martyrs who endured prolonged and considerable suffering, much of which went unnoticed during their life on earth. St. Thérèse of Lisieux was one who asked to suffer in order to identify more closely with her Lord. He answered her prayer, but none knew the depths of her suffering, because she welcomed each agony with a smile and a prayer of joy for this "gift" of her Saviour. She had begun her discipline by constant mortifications in which she sought out the more difficult way by continuous little sacrifices. She passed her favourite sisters by and sought out those who were difficult to like and get on with. In these and many other "little ways" she prepared herself for the acute sufferings of her illness. She knew she was desperately ill, but remained at peace in her heart, "God has always helped me, leading me by the hand since my childhood, and I rely upon Him now. Though I shall endure the extremity of suffering, I know He will be there with me." When advised to walk in the garden by the Infirmarian, she obeyed, knowing a rest would do her more good. Each agonising step she offered for a missionary. "I have always forced myself to love suffering and to welcome it joyfully", she wrote. "Can a victim of love find anything her Spouse sends terrible? . . . My sufferings are very intense indeed, yet nevertheless I am extraordinarily at peace. All my desires are realised and I am full of confidence." She even saw her suffering as a proof of God's goodness. "How very good God must be," she once said, "to give me strength to bear all I endure."[1]

Dorothy could have identified with that uncomplaining and courageous declaration. During her long years of suffering prior to her healing, her mother testified that she had never complained, but maintained a lively trust in her Lord and Saviour who sent His angels to guard and uphold her and to minister to her in her suffering. And now that she had been healed by Christ, she was yet promised the "rebuffs" which she was sure to know might well involve more personal suffering.

The encounter with Satan she had recently experienced left her with a damaged heart. On the vigil of the Feast of the Immaculate Conception (7th December) 1915, she experienced excessive pain in her heart. On the day of the feast the pain was more intense and by the afternoon she had again taken to her bed. While her director gave her the laying on of hands, she experienced what he described as the most terrible attack of pain he had ever witnessed. With his intuitive awareness he perceived it was no ordinary pain. It was especially acute in her left hand which seemed to be the focus of her agitation. He then saw a red mark gradually appearing on the back of her hand. Later on, she became more distressed and showed him the palm of her left hand where a wound could be clearly discerned.

Dorothy wondered if it was demonic, being so conscious of her sinfulness as to believe it impossible that God should grant her such a blessing. She asked her director to pray that God would heal it.

It says much for Dr. Langford-James that he maintained that it was the Lord's work and insisted Dorothy should be thankful and not attempt to interfere with the Lord's dealings with her. Dorothy at this point had no idea of what it might be because she had always imagined that the stigmata would be invisible. So she asked her director to pray that the wound would be removed in the night, not to avoid the pain which she wanted fully to suffer and experience, but because she could not bear that others should see it. Accordingly he prayed in this manner, but also prayed that if it were God's will, the stigmata might be given also in the right hand to convince her and reassure her that this was a visitation from her crucified Saviour and Lord. She then went into a deep sleep.

The following day, 9th December, Dorothy received the wound in her side and in her right hand. Her director was not in the house, but she reported to him later how she had been kneeling in front of the crucifix kissing its feet, when she experienced a pain more excruciating than the first, as though a knife were being stabbed into her side. She became unconscious and when she came round she found that not only was there a wound in her side but also in her right hand. Her hand was full of blood which later vanished without her washing it.

On the next day the wounds appeared in her feet, like the appearance of a round red mark on her instep. When her director inadvertently touched one of her feet the pain was so excruciating she found it impossible to show him the inside of her foot. On the hands, marks were clearly visible on both sides; on the back like the head of a flat triangular nail; on the palm, a round bloodless wound. By the Sunday (12th December) the first wound had begun to heal. Her director was determined that there should be some independent witnesses to this remarkable and miraculous happening. He was only able to overcome Dorothy's reluctance by claiming her obedience to what he considered was his God-given authority as her spiritual director. Her immediate response of obedience, freely given and for the glory of God, was perfectly timed so that opportunity was given to the witnesses to make their attestations. Perfectly timed indeed because all the wounds healed within two weeks from the time they appeared, though they could still be discerned after that.

Apart from Dr. Langford-James himself, there appear to have been eleven other witnesses who made signed statements, attesting the fact of the stigmata. They include a bishop, an archdeacon and four priests. The bishop's statement was signed "Cecil, Bishop in South Tokyo" and declared that he "was allowed to see those sacred marks of the stigmata" and felt "sure this thing has been granted for the glory of God". He asked Langford-James, to whom the letter was addressed, to "tell her again for me that she has blessed and helped a 'heathen bishop' just as he is going back to where faith has to do without some of the unconscious props of Home atmosphere". The bishop had only seen the scars for his letter is dated 5th August, 1916, so he witnessed them after they had healed.

Others did witness them within the week before they healed. Among them was the vicar of a neighbouring parish, who wrote on 13th December, 1915:

On Sunday, December 12th 1915, I was told by Dr. Langford-James that Miss Dorothy Kerin had received the stigmata. Dr. Langford-James asked me to come and see Miss Kerin, that I might see for myself the truth of what he told me. I did so, and saw distinctly the marks of the Wounds in both her hands and feet.

Cyril F. S. Adams, Priest.

A Mr. and Mrs. Widdows also wrote at this time, on 15th December, "for the strengthening of faith in all who shall read" that they had witnessed that very day the marks of the stigmata in hands and feet. Mr Widdows signed himself as a "Fellow Royal Inst. Brit. Archts."

The two attestations of most interest, however, which offer the profoundest insights, are from Father H. J. Fynes-Clinton, a well-known and much respected name in Anglo-Catholic circles, and Father Austen Taylor of St. Oswald's, Walthamstow. They are both of sufficient importance as to be quoted in full. Fynes-Clinton's account was written about a year later from notes he made at the time, while Taylor's statement was written on the day he witnessed the stigmata, just a week after they had appeared, and so is the first to be quoted:

> St. Oswald's Presbytery
> Coppersmith Lane,
> Walthamstow.

I, Austen Robert Taylor, clerk in Holy Orders, and priest in charge of the church and district of St. Oswald, Walthamstow, in the county of Essex, Master of Arts, and member of Jesus College in the University of Oxford, make the following statement: On Wednesday, December 15th, being the Octave of the Feast of the Immaculate Conception of our Blessed Lady, I was summoned by telegram to St. Mark's Vicarage, Bush Hill Park, where Miss Kerin is residing. When I arrived there, I was taken to Miss Kerin's room. She told me that Our Blessed Lord had particularly told her to send for me, that I might see with my own eyes the Most Holy stigmata of His Passion with which He had been pleased to mark her; that it had been borne in upon her very plainly that I was in trouble; and that it was His Will that I should take courage from this signal favour.

She then allowed me to see and examine her hands. In both there was a Wound right through the palm. In one the colour was a much deeper black-red (the colour of clotted blood) than in the other; in the darker one something like a nail head seemed to be coming away. Dr. Langford-James, who was present, then obtained permission to uncover the feet. There, also, in both feet showing through from the upper side to the sole, were the Wounds, in that part of the foot which is flexible just below the arch. The Piercing of the Feet seemed to have been in a slanting direction towards the toes and not just through the shortest way. I particularly noted this, which surprised me. I was not shown the Wound in the side that I was told had bled somewhat, and had been extremely painful, until our Lady Herself came and placing Her Hand upon it had removed it; on Sunday, December 12th, I think I was told this had occurred. I talked some time privately with Miss Kerin, was allowed to touch and kiss the Sacred Stigmata, and then withdrew.

Austen R. Taylor,
15th day of December, 1915.

From the Reverend H. J. Fynes-Clinton, 27 Finsbury Square, London, E.C. 28th November, 1916:

In the Name of the Father, the Son and the Holy Ghost. Amen.
I depose that on Thursday, December 16th, 1915, I having previously been informed by my friend, Father R. L. Langford-James, of the reception of the Stigmata by Dorothy Kerin, and that the Stigmata in one hand came visibly to him as he watched, went to Bush Hill Park, Enfield, and visited Dorothy Kerin in St. Mark's Vicarage.

I saw the Stigmata in both hands and feet. They appeared as distinct wounds, apparently passing right through, being visible both on the backs and on the palms, of a size as though made by an instrument of the thickness of a pencil. There was discoloration as of a half-healed wound, and in one hand at least there still appeared some exudation.

72

There was also in one wound a small projection of flesh, more darkly coloured, as though caused by something projecting from the wound.

I remarked especially, as Father Langford-James asked her to show me the Stigmata, that this appeared to cause great shrinking. I then had a long conversation with her, for nearly an hour, and noted especially the following. She appeared to be endowed with a deep humility; and told me that she shrank very much from the showing of the mark to others: but that she obeyed in the matter, and said that after all, it was "He, not me." She was evidently still suffering, and spoke of having prayed that she might suffer, if it were God's will, on behalf of others. She said that previously to this event, after which Father James had explained it to her, she had not known that the Stigmata of St. Francis had been visible to ordinary eyes, but thought that they were only "spiritually discerned". She spoke of her great pain, and above all of the awful pain of entering into the Sacred Dereliction, yet she felt perfectly happy, she said, as it was His Will and for Him. After she realized that the Stigmata were visible, she had prayed that if it were God's will, "she might have the suffering, and others the marks". She felt the pain of showing them so much.

She then told me that when the pain in her feet began she had "felt impelled, quite apart from my own will" to offer the wounds in her feet for the Catholic League.

I was much impressed, indeed more deeply than I have ever been in speaking to any other person, with her simplicity, humility, her patience and spirituality. The whole atmosphere seemed full of the spirit of prayer and Divine Love. She was lying down, appearing very weak, and suffering, but radiant, though tranquil, and quite calm and entirely natural.

I have written this from notes that I put down at the time; and quote in marks from her words noted down soon afterwards.

73

I am absolutely convinced that the Stigmata are super-natural, and the visit was a profound spiritual experience to me.[2]

Signed: H. J. Fynes-Clinton, Priest,
Nov. 28th, 1916.

The preceding attestations leave us in no doubt that Dorothy was a recipient of the stigmata. Although being a stigmatic has never been a cause for canonisation, the fact that Dorothy was among their number marks her out as a person of profound spirituality. She had prayed, like Julian of Norwich and many other stigmatics, that she might share the pain of her Lord's Passion and her prayer was answered. Pain she had in abundance, especially during the period of the manifestation of the stigmata. The whole experience left her totally exhausted and she only regained her strength by Christmas. But the pain was to recur from time to time, just how frequently we shall never know. It was apparently exacerbated by trials and presumably by the "rebuffs", which Dorothy had been promised in the vision of her vocation, and which were with her until the end of her life on earth. Iris Moody, a secretary to the bishop of South Tokyo's Mission, who also was a witness to the stigmata on the eve of the conversion of St. Paul, six weeks after their manifestation, had noticed that the scar on her side, "in the form of a Latin Cross about five inches long with the arms in proportion", was "perfectly healed up, but the scar was standing out, perhaps a third of an inch, like a weal". Later Dorothy told her that "the condition of the Wound the first time I saw it was due to the effect of a trying interview she had had that day with some people of spiritualistic beliefs and practices. They had said many things that had hurt her, and she had felt great pain in the Wound while she was with them." One is led to wonder how often this pain and possible inflammation of the wounds occurred in the difficulties of her subsequent life.

A vision that was given to her on the day after Christmas Day, the feast day of the Protomartyr St. Stephen, does not altogether reassure us in this matter. The account of the vision exists in her own handwriting because she had been asked by her director to record it:

> On this night my soul was moved by the Holy Spirit to pray. In my prayer, I beheld the Holy Family at Bethlehem: the Divine Infant lying in a manger, watched over by St. Joseph and His Blessed Mother. She bade me "draw nigh and behold THE LAMB OF GOD". As I gazed, adoring my little Saviour, our Lady lifted Him out of His nest and put Him into my arms saying "Share also my joy". O unspeakable rapture of delight! The Holy little Head pillowed Itself against my breast, and the tiny baby hands caressed me. He lay in my arms cooing with glee as babies are wont to do. As I held Him, He grew heavier and heavier, until His weight became too much for me. Then our Blessed Lady took Him back and the vision passed. The King asked in my soul then: "Little Beloved, lackest thou anything?" And I answered, "No, Lord."

Rightly she agreed that she lacked nothing for she had been given privileges greater than is normally the lot of Christ's followers on earth, but the bearing of her Saviour and the showing of Him to those she would meet did become "heavier and heavier," especially when they did not have eyes to see and ears to hear. The stigmata and the regular visions that were given her after her healing marked her out as someone whom the Lord had richly blessed and whose life would bring abundant blessings in the future to the people who met her and to the community in which she lived.

Notes

1. *The Story of a Soul*, Epilogue (translated by Michael Day, Clarke Books, 1973).
2. These letters, of which the author has seen the originals, and the

other quotations, concerning the stigmata in this chapter, are to be found in Dorothy Musgrave Arnold's *Dorothy Kerin: Called by Christ to Heal*, Chapters 4 and 5, but see especially Johanna Ernest's *The Life of Dorothy Kerin* (Dorothy Kerin Trust, 1983) in which facsimiles of the originals are reproduced.

8 THE LORD'S LEISURE

It has been a matter of comment before now that whereas priests may undergo only three years preparation for thirty years or more of ministry, Jesus himself spent thirty years in preparation for just three years of ministry. His reversal of our time scale should make us pause and ponder. The question has been asked in regard to Dorothy as to why, after the blessings of her healings, her callings and the stigmata, she did not embark at once on her life's work to which she had been so clearly called. The years following the manifestation of the stigmata, however, provided the necessary period for the deepening of her spiritual life, during which she learned to "tarry the Lord's leisure".

These years began with the desolation of the soul which is well known to those experienced in the spiritual life. As she settled down to the normal routine of parish life, she became the centre of some malicious gossip that hurt her greatly. This kind of setback she was able to turn to good, as she had frequent cause to do in her later life, by offering it in union with her Lord's sacred Passion. In addition to mental anguish she also knew physical pain. She confided to her spiritual director that whenever she meditated on the Passion, and always at the consecration during the Eucharist, she felt intense pain in all the five places where she had received the wounds. These experiences were felt with deep desolation and undermined her physical well-being. Together with her long nights of prayer, the expenditure of energy while she worked in the house and parish during the day, and the desire to please everyone which was still with her in these early days, they left her in a state of exhaustion. With regard to this last point, Dr. Langford-James noted in his journal that only gradually she learned to be more discerning in regard to her demanding friends. She had been endowed with noticeable beauty and charm, set off by a ready wit, a naturally happy disposition and a voice which produced musical cadences and kept her audiences enthralled. She was a magnetic personality which both sexes found attractive. She was in fact a very human person and remained so until her dying day. Like St. Catherine of Siena, similarities to whose life have already been noted, it could have been equally said of Dorothy: "Everybody loves Catherine Benincasa because she is always and everywhere a woman in every fibre of her being." Here were gifts that would make some personal relationships difficult and Dorothy had to learn the hard way. Her director remarked that she had been prone to the fault of "sloppiness" which she mistook for charity. But he then went on to say, "She has really learned very well, and will do better."[1]

Her exhaustion was, however, a great cause for concern and she returned to Paignton for a holiday. Dr. George, who had attended her after the mugging she received, was able to examine her again. He found there was nothing wrong with her organically, but that she was in a state of exhaustion and had to take care to build up her strength. She wrote "home" that there was fairly good news on the physical front but not on the spiritual. She fell to wondering if she had given her Lord a rebuff. Earlier that year she had had a vision of our Lady who was holding a blue rope, doubled with three large knots, one white, one blue and one black. At the suggestion of Father Fynes-Clinton, her director had then spoken to Dorothy about taking private vows but she was very reluctant to take such a course of action. Had she thwarted the Divine Will, she wondered. In the letter she continued by saying, "I feel that He cannot come until I have done what He asked. I long to do it, and am sorry to keep Him away by my rebuffs. It sounds presumptuous to say He is longing to come back, but I believe this is so."[2] How frequently the expression of intention unlocks the closed door in the spiritual life. This statement by Dorothy in her letter seems to have done that for her. On her return Dr. Langford-James noted that it seemed as if the long period of desolation was over. Possibly some of the desolation had come upon her because of her disinclination to follow the leading of her vision of the knots.

In an interesting study of dreams, Russ Parker summarises his findings concerning biblical visions and dreams in this way: God speaks to us in waking life and then continues to communicate through dreams which intensify in feeling if we ignore the message. The final stage of the process is the physical or emotional stress that comes when we repress the truth from ourselves.[3] This was one of the few occasions on which Dorothy hesitated in her obedience and the hesitation itself may have been responsible for her period of desolation. She certainly had misgivings concerning the vow of chastity because she had a deep love for children, especially for babies. From a chance remark in her early days – "if I ever married I should want fifty (children)" – it was obvious that her maternal instinct was strong. Her holiday in Paignton seems to have given her the necessary space and distance from the pressure at home, possibly even from her director, and she seems to have concluded that the privilege of holding the child Jesus in her vision had once and for all satisfied this longing and so she was ready to go ahead with the threefold vow of poverty, chastity and obedience. The relief of having made this decision was obvious to her director on her return. She confirmed him in this opinion when she related how she had been able to resume her life of prayer and had experienced an ecstasy in which she had enjoyed full union. This was in the form of a vision in which she had been totally absorbed into the Sacred Heart and wounds of Christ. No longer was she conscious of her own body but seemed to be at one with her Saviour's body. Her own description of the experience, recorded at the instigation of her director, is important in that it throws light on her future ministry as well as highlighting the privileged states of prayer which were given to her. It also tells us something of the desolation she had experienced before the vision:

I cannot put into words the utter desolation, the indescribable ache, and longing, for the *realization* of the King dwelling in my heart. There can be no desolation like it, hell itself cannot be blacker than these past months in which my divine Jesus has hidden Himself, and taken away all spiritual consolation. I have failed Him so badly, in hopelessness, grumblings, and despair, and have indeed deserved that He should never more reveal His divine nearness to me, His faithless servant. But He has not rewarded me as I deserved, with hell. He has come out of His House, and ravished my soul with delights, embracing me in His love until I ceased to be and there remained nothing save JESUS in His Majesty reigning and possessing *all*. The "little house" shook and the King burst out of it and seized me to His Heart, saying "little beloved". I asked Him: "My Jesus, why have you left me?" And He said, "I have never left thee, I have hidden in the secret of thy heart. Reproach me not that I have given thee the darkness of Gethsemane. I was there with thee. For thy comfort, know that every tear and cry wrung from thy heart for me, I have counted as drops of blood from MY heart. Come, little beloved, into the garden." And from the shelter of His Sacred Heart (for I was *in* His Heart) I saw a Cross, firmly planted in the ground, the top of it I could not see for it reached up into heaven. The Cross was marked with spots of blood, out of each spot – I saw a soul reposing, then, the spots became steps, up which the souls mounted. The King showed me much more which I cannot write.[4]

This vision and "ecstasy" is the true line of the Christian mystics and describes a state of the soul not given to many.

It followed a period of extremely painful desolation which is also in line with the mystical experience. It also had its prophetic side. The Cross was always "firmly planted" in her life and the "spots of blood", indicative of immortal souls, represented the countless thousands her life and ministry were to touch in the future and, indeed, were already touching.

This ecstatic experience stands as a watershed in her life of preparation which followed the stigmata. For some time afterwards she saw the figure of Christ on the Oberammergau cross come to life and stand out every night. This was a beautiful crucifix Dr. Langford-James had placed in her room, having obtained it some years previously on a pilgrimage to Oberammergau.[5] It seemed that the way had now been prepared for the taking of the threefold vows and she took them on the feast of the Epiphany, 1917. Imploring the aid of our Lady, together with "Blessed Raphael, the Angel of Healing and of St. Teresa", she undertook the Rule of Holy Chastity in which she vowed to abstain from "any act or purpose with the end of marriage" and to consecrate "my whole being to God, my heart with all its affections and my body with all its powers and desires". In the Rule of Holy Poverty she undertook "to use all my moneys under obedience to my director, making necessity and charity the rule of my expenditure . . . and using all that is given to me as lent by God for his greater glory". The Rule of Holy Obedience was expressed by an undertaking to obey her director in all things lawful and by consecrating her will wholly to God.

To many it may seem strange that someone so blessed by the ecstatic experience of union with her Lord should have undergone the constricting discipline of taking her vows. But such a discipline can be of great support and lend stability to the periods of desolation that inevitably follow. It is somewhat like the discipline of the daily office to which all priests are subject. The celebration of the Eucharist and the experience of contemplative prayer may bring a priest

81

abundant consolations, but when they are denied and he experiences periods of dryness, the recitation of the daily office is always there as the firm foundation of the spiritual life to enable him to tarry the Lord's leisure. In all probability the vows were to stand Dorothy in good stead during her frequent terms of desolation.

All this heralded a period of great development in her life of prayer, interspersed with further ecstasies. In this period she obviously had the ability, perhaps gained, but more likely given, to engage in out-of-body experiences when in a prayerful state. She was able consciously to leave her body at night in order to minister to those for whom she was praying in their suffering. Her brothers were at the front at this period of the war and frequently she found herself in no-man's-land during her nights of prayer, ministering to the wounded and the dying. There is also a reference in a letter to Dr. Langford-James, who was ill at the time. Dorothy blamed herself for the demands being made on him through acting as her director and assured him of her prayers. She continued, "but I long also to give you some strength back. I shall ask Jesus tonight to let me come to you whilst you are asleep. You remember, it did make you feel better before; you told me so!"[6]

Dorothy also suffered from more exhaustion during this penultimate year of the war, owing to frequent air raids. The target was the small arms factory in Bush Hill Park. The raids caused much damage to property and the loss of many lives. All this was severely stressful to Dorothy's sensitive nature. During one of the severest air raids the whole family assembled in Dorothy's room and they asked her to pray for them. She prayed aloud until shrapnel began to hit the house, at which point she asked her director to give them all absolution. Once again she saw a great light shoot from the crucifix as he did so and this time it was also seen by Beatrice, the maid. To others in the room the figure appeared larger than it was, and all were conscious of the Lord's presence with them, which they took to be an assurance of His protection. The stress of the air raids continued to take their toll, however, as did her nights spent in prayer for all those including her brothers, at the front. Her "visits" to the front particularly over-taxed her.

More ecstasies were also given during this period, the first around the time of the anniversary of the stigmata. The ecstasy apparently lasted throughout the night and at 5.45 a.m. Dorothy found herself at the foot of the Oberammergau crucifix. She could not recall how she came to be there, neither could she remember having seen anyone or anything, but she awoke with a knowledge of indescribable joy.

These times of ecstatic happiness were usually followed by periods of desolation, such is the ebb and flow of life, and especially of the spiritual life. Dorothy had reason to be grateful at such times that God had given her such a discerning director. He himself had learned much from the spiritual writings of Father Baker who counselled directors to have very great patience and "to tarry the Lord's leisure" with regard to their charges. Painstakingly he encouraged her to keep the full spirit of the rule, even to the finest detail and to eradicate her faults one by one. Her natural wilfulness and zest for life had made the rule of obedience hard to follow at times. The rule of poverty frequently militated against her love of beautiful things and her standards of excellence. This latter came to a perfect reconciliation in later life as she saw that such a standard was in fact the offering of glory to God. There can be very few who have found the rule of chastity easy to follow. Dorothy was an extremely affectionate girl and was loved by all. This made it all the harder. But there can be little doubt that in this matter she was helped by our Lady. Not only had the Virgin Mary given her an example of chastity to follow; not only did she pray for Dorothy as Dorothy certainly believed; but she also appeared to her, especially at key times in her development, and led her each time to a greater love.

Notes

1. Dorothy Musgrave Arnold, *Dorothy Kerin: Called by Christ to Heal* (Hodder and Stoughton, 1965) p. 46.
2. Ibid. p. 40.
3. Russ Parker, *Healing Dreams* (S.P.C.K., 1988) p. 12.
4. Dorothy Musgrave Arnold, op. cit. p. 41.
5. The cross now stands in the Oratory of St. Luke at Burrswood.
6. Dorothy Musgrave Arnold, op. cit., p. 44.

9 THE ROAD TO UNION – DEIFICATION

A debt of gratitude is due to Dorothy's director for his insistence that she recorded many of her visions and ecstasies. But for his insistence we should have been deprived of knowing about one of the most formative visions which Dorothy experienced. In this she was shown the state of her soul and was then given the experience known by the mystics and in Patristic theology as *deification*, or the complete transmutation of the self in God, given to chosen souls and possibly a foretaste of the end-time when God is "all in all".[1]

This will be the third attempt I have made of trying to tell you about my last visit to the garden. It is so very difficult, nay, almost impossible to tell you in words what happened there, for in the kingdom of the garden there is no language, save that of the Divine Heart, which you know so well does not consist in words. I have asked the Holy Spirit to help me and if He wills it so, then I shall be able to share with you in some degree the unspeakable joy and pain that came to my soul in those moments of seeing. You know, Father, how unhappy I have been for some time, knowing in my heart that I have done so badly with the difficulties that have come lately, and how ill I have used the graces that the King has given me! Well, I was in my prayer (which was taken up with these thoughts) when I found myself in the garden (I have not been there for some time). There was a difference there. It looked fuller,

and there was more scent, but something felt quite new. I
could not understand. Then I saw our Lady in it (she has
not been before), and knew she had been working there.
She came to me, and you remember I told you about that
wonderful smile when she gave me the baby Jesus to hold?
Well, it was the same, but it passed and she looked sad.
I think she knew how bewildered I was about things for
she took my hand and led me to the different plants. Her
tears were still wet on some of them, and her caress was
on others. When they had all been visited I was alone.
In the corner of the garden, I saw a little heap of weeds,
the ones our Lady had pulled up, but there were others,
some quite near the plants, and as I looked at them, it
was given to me to see my life since the King made the
garden. He showed me every sin and imperfection which
had produced these weeds, the small ones came out and
were added to the heap, but the others would not yield;
bit by bit they were creeping towards three of the King's
best loved plants, and one little tendril had started to
clutch the stem of the HOPE plant and the weed was
fear. The same with the CHARITY plant, only the weed
had not quite reached it. That weed was *judging*. Then
the FAITH plant, the weed was not so near this, but was
creeping on. That weed was *despair*. As I saw these things,
the Holy Spirit showed me everything that had been done
by me to produce weeds, which have pierced the Heart of
Jesus. I was so truly sorry that I knelt down and confessed
it all to the King, and oh! Father, it is impossible to tell
you the joy and the peace which came into my soul after
I received absolution. Then the King opened the door of
His little House, and came out. He took me to the other
side of the door, and showed me the other plants. He *had*
been pleased with them. The OBEDIENCE plant had got
some new flowers (there were no weeds by it!!) and two
were big ones. Then the "Lily" plant, that had also some
new blooms, and how do you think they got there? It was
through Beatrice, and now I am so thankful for that time.

Then I saw a new plant. It had blooms on it. It was the tree of pain borne for His sake. The flowers were red like rubies and hung down like great red hearts.

Then He showed me about the last one, and clasped me in that unspeakable love embrace and drew me into the little house. I dare not try to tell you in words of those transcendental moments for it would be impossible. But I can tell you this: that in that space there was nothing but GOD, and, oh! Father, in that divine embrace I was God, for I was *in* God, nothing else existed. You will not be afraid of my saying this, for you will know that I dared to say it, because there was no "me". When the King put me from Him, I saw that all the weeds had gone from the garden and my heart was breaking with thankfulness. I have promised the King that I will be more watchful over that garden in future, for He loves it and means it to be so fair a place. I must tell you now, dear Father, how sorry I am for my lack of obedience, and all the difficulties I have made for you. You have been ever gentle and patient with my wilfulness and sinning, and the little progress I have made. I am indeed ashamed of it all, and was horrified to see what sad havoc it had made, as I know how it will pain you, but I had to tell you. It is almost too much to bear alone, and you will also share the joy of knowing that the King has renewed it all. I am very, very happy; so happy that I almost dread the possibility of forgetting those moments of real sorrow. Help me to remember them always, dear Father, *for that sorrow is the remedy against weeds.*[2]

Probably St. Paul knew something of this experience of deification. It is also consonant with the dictum of St. Athanasius (*c.* 296–373), "He became man that we might become God." For St. Augustine (354–430) it was manifestly part of his experience: "I heard them saying to me from on high: 'I am the food of those grown up; grow, and you shall feed on me; neither shalt thou, like bodily

87

food, change me into thee; but thou shalt be changed into me.'"[3] St. Richard of St. Victor (d. 1173), one of the great spiritual masters of the Middle Ages, was also familiar with the state of union and deification which he called "the third degree of love", when the human mind is "ravished into the abyss of the divine light, so that the soul, oblivious of all exterior things, is altogether unaware of itself and passes completely into God".[4] In this "third grade of love", though the self is divinely penetrated, it retains its personality which, far from being diminished, is enhanced and furthered on its journey to wholeness. It is the experience to which the mystics are led through their mortification and dedicated life of prayer, but it is no human achievement. Like all prayer, union and deification are the gift of God alone, and instead of cutting them off from the rest of humanity, send them out as creative and inspired servants of Him who wills all to find salvation.

These mystical states of prayer continued to the end of Dorothy's life. Her friends frequently noticed she was "elsewhere". The following Easter was another time when she became truly blessed in prayer as she watched by the Cross in Holy Week. She was taught the true meaning of *com*passion. On Maundy Thursday she watched with our Lord in Gethsemane, being told to watch with Him until His hour came. She spent the whole of Good Friday in the chapel into the early hours of Saturday morning. She related to her director how she had seen the whole of the Passion; that our Lord had kept her close to His cross all the time; that He had spoken to her; that she had actually seen the divine desolation and the piercing of the Virgin Mary's heart. She also told her director that her wounds were extremely painful throughout the ecstasy and that "when they killed Him, I felt I could have died myself". On the Friday of Easter week, the first weekly anniversary of the crucifixion, the wounds were open throughout the day. In her prayers during the night at this time she was praying that if she loved the Lord well enough, He would allow her to bear the pain in her side. She had been counselled that love for Christ did not consist in feeling but in the direction of the will. This was taken into her prayer and the pain increased until late one night, when her director came to see how she was, she exclaimed in great joy, "Father *I do* love him". The pain immediately left her.

Throughout this period Dorothy did not enjoy good health. The doctor put it down to the very damp area surrounding the vicarage in Bush Hill Park, and this may have taken its toll. Her director was convinced that much of it was caused by her compassion for, and total empathy with, the suffering being endured at the front during the war years by the soldiers of the contending armies. Her out-of-body experiences, mentioned already, were painful in the extreme. She experienced the horror of those left to their fate in the barbed wire entanglements and water-logged pot holes of the desolate no-man's-land between the opposing armies. Such experiences must have eaten into the soul of one so sensitive.

It will be noted, however, that the yearning to be alongside suffering humanity and to be an instrument – "a bit of pipe" was her favourite expression – of the Lord's healing balm for others, was ever more deeply ingrained into her being during those formative years of preparation. Throughout this time she never ceased from intercession and mostly kept in contact with those for whom she prayed through correspondence with them or their families. She was able in this way to help many whose lives had been shattered by the war, many of whom, including priests, had lost their faith as a result of their experiences. In her times of prayer she was sometimes given a vision or showing of those for whom she prayed. The consequence of such a vision was frequently the news of their recovery. During the last year of the war, Dorothy was constantly cheered by news of miraculous healings in answer to her prayers. It was fitting that the anniversary of the stigmata at the end of that year was marked by an appearance of her Lord who showed her

His wounds. Despite a resonance of pain in her arm, she experienced a day of supreme happiness. "Blessed are the eyes that see what you see" (Luke 10:23).

A move into the country proved a welcome respite after the war and was formative to Dorothy's future development. In 1919 Dr. Langford-James accepted the living of Thruxton, near Andover, in the diocese of Winchester. The church, in a sylvan setting, was a small medieval gem. The rectory on the other hand was Victorian, without electricity, mains water or telephone. With an attractive garden, the whole scene was a pleasant change from the noise of Bush Hill Park and the family soon settled down to life in the country. Dorothy took her full part in the life of the parish, the usual duties of the rectory family of those days – Sunday school teaching, magazine delivering, sacristy duties, visiting the poorer cottages and getting involved in the Women's Institute. All this was a timely and necessary counterbalance to the rigours of her spiritual life and was an essential preliminary to her life "on the plain". Indeed she found it a most helpful preparation for the next stage of her life – her active ministry. She also engaged in more exercise which must have brought health-giving fresh air to her lungs. She was presented with a bicycle and revelled in her rides in the countryside which affirmed her in her love of all created things. She also undertook a large share of the gardening and her well-known dislike of seeing weeds trespassing in a flower garden may have originated from the days of her gardening duties at Thruxton. Later on at Burrswood there would sometimes come a pause in a walk as Dorothy bent down to extract an interloper, saying "I cannot abide weeds". Did they remind her of the vision recorded earlier in this chapter when she was shown the mystical garden of her soul?

Another and final part of her preparation occurred at Thruxton. She experienced the blackest of desolation, worse than she had ever known previously. The wounds disappeared and she never had joy in her prayer, but only

90

pain. She told her director that at the beginning this dull night of the soul was so black that she thought she would go mad. She felt with an increasing intensity that she was no longer loved by God and that she was justly forsaken by Him. St. John of the Cross calls such desolation "this blessed night", and from his own experience was of the opinion that it was given to darken the mind in order to irradiate it with light in everything, and to humble the soul in order to raise it up and enable it to "press on towards the goal to win the prize for which God has called me heavenwards in Christ Jesus" (Phil.3:14).

It may be no mere coincidence that St. John of the Cross, who, like Dorothy, knew at first hand the dark night of the soul, also like Dorothy lost a much-loved father in childhood. In the course of an interesting study,[5] David Auerbach puts forward the theory that the dark night of the soul was for St. John of the Cross an expression of the loss of his father in early childhood. A more simple explanation may be that some of those who have known such a traumatic bereavement cast themselves totally on the mercy of God and then find themselves completely loved and blessed when the darkness has been healed. Be that as it may, for the time being Dorothy was in the grip of this dark night, with no sign of the Lord's presence. Neither was it helped by the situation in the parish. Dorothy was extremely popular among the villagers – it was they who had given her the bicycle – and especially among the children who helped to keep the church in perfect order. Sadly the same could not be said of the Rector who was unpopular and whose Anglo-Catholic ways were the source of discontent. This added to Dorothy's pain and desolation, all the more so since it seemed she began to lose the sympathy of Mrs. Langford-James. It was a deep hurt to Dorothy's sensitive and naturally affectionate nature and to the loyalty she felt towards her director. From this time onwards, it seems that their relationship deteriorated: Mrs. Langford-James especially felt Dorothy should spend more time on domestic duties.

91

To add to her darkness, Dorothy received the wounds back again in hands and feet, together with the pain. Although the wounds were smaller, her director noted that she had to use no less than four handkerchiefs in an attempt to staunch the blood, and also that she had difficulty in walking. Further he noted that "no ray of light came" as the pain and the darkness continued. Her Lord, who had always been so close, now seemed so far away. The advent of the influenza epidemic that was raging across Europe made matters worse and left both Dorothy and her director in deep depression.

It was not until the summer of 1921 that the darkness lifted. She wrote a letter to her director, who was away at the time, in which she gave him the joyful news and told him that our Lord had come to her and said,

> Arise, my love, and come away,
> for lo! the winter is passed
> and the rain is over and gone . . .

Later she told him that the Lord had come with such power of love that she could hardly bear it and that He had told her He had never really been away from her and all this time she had been held securely in His Sacred Heart, but it had been necessary for her to experience this desolation. Like her Lord, she had experienced such suffering for the joy that was before her in perfect union with the heavenly Father.

The four years at Thruxton were crucial to Dorothy's personal, social and spiritual development. Her personality developed as she attempted to balance out the demands of the spiritual life which were ever with her and which were always her priority, with the demands of daily living and of taking her part in the life of a rectory and parish in the country. The environment for this was ideal and morning by morning the beauty of the countryside spoke to her of the love and care of her Creator. She was at the same time involved at first hand in the lives of ordinary people, among whom her capacity for enjoyment, her empathy and compassion, her sense of humour and intuitive awareness of the needs of others found a ready response. Despite some incipient signs of tension in the life of the rectory family, her personal and social life underwent positive development during the Thruxton years.

By far the most significant factor in Dorothy's development during this time lay in the spiritual dimension of her life. It was in Thruxton that she reached the zenith of her mystical journey, experiencing the darkest of dark nights of the soul, which led to her Lord's assurance that the act of union she had experienced in ecstasy a few years before was still a reality in that He had her enfolded in His Sacred Heart. True to His promise He would never leave her or forsake her, whatever "rebuffs" she would encounter or receive. These years in fact became the bridge years between her preparation, of which they were a formative part, and her ministry. But the bridge was not yet fully crossed.

Her director accepted the living of Edgbaston, Birmingham, in 1923 and so, once again, she shared a move with the household. Her life in the new vicarage was to be the final part of her preparation. One facet of her life had grown and was to continue to grow over the years and that was her correspondence. She was diligent in letter-writing and always had a large mail bag, attending prayerfully and carefully to each letter. Another increasing demand was her life of intercession, especially as more and more people in need turned to her for help and guidance. And as the word implies, she did indeed stand before God on behalf of those for whom she prayed. She was a most powerful link for her fellow human beings with the healing power of Christ. Always her life of prayer was her priority and, by the close of this time of preparation, her basic discipline and regular times of prayer were fixed. This "ground bass" enabled her to improvise a sweet melody of prayer in the higher clef of her life. It gave her the ability to turn to her Lord and commune with Him at any time and in any circumstance. This was one of her most precious gifts. Everything was submitted to the Court of Heaven. She had the ability to switch off from a pressing task or interview and give herself the necessary silence and space to hear the voice and directions of her Beloved. The prayer of the young Samuel – "Speak for your servant is listening" (1 Sam. 3:10) – must have been in her heart many times in the course of a day. Frequently it went unnoticed, but those who received her counsel knew that what she said was a word from the Lord.

The whole secret of her spirituality, however, lay in the blessings accruing from her mystical experiences. The spiritual marriage, or transforming union, meant that she could never be separated from her Lord again. St. Paul knew this blessing: "I have been crucified with Christ and I no longer live, but Christ lives in me" (Gal. 2:20), and so did many of the great mystics.

St. Teresa of Avila described it in these words:

> In the Spiritual marriage, all is different:
> the Lord appears
> in the centre of the soul,
> not in an imaginary,
> but an intellectual vision . . .
> In an instantaneous communication
> of God to the soul,
> secret and sublime,
> the Lord is pleased
> to manifest to the soul
> the glory that is in Heaven,
> to its intense delight.
> The spirit of the soul
> is made one Spirit with God
> in a union of two
> who cannot be separated any more.

And again:

> The little butterfly of the previous Mansions

now dies,
because Christ is now her life.
As time passes,
the soul clearly understands
that it is endowed with life by God . . .
It never moves from its centre
nor loses its peace,
which is Christ . . .
The things the soul bears
may cause it distress,
but the centre of the soul
is not touched or disturbed;
there the King dwells.[6]

It is worth noting that the title of one of St. Teresa's chapters in this same section is: "Our Lord's aim in granting this favour; Martha and Mary must walk together". Dorothy was soon to leave the vicarage and her spiritual director, for whom she would always entertain feelings of affection and gratitude, to set out on her own life's work, the secret of which, true to the mystical tradition of the Church, was the integration of the two strands of the Christian life of which Mary and Martha are the apt symbols.[7] *Laborare est orare* is complemented by the equal truth *orare est laborare*.

Notes

1. 1 Cor. 15:28.
2. Dorothy Musgrave Arnold, *Called by Christ to Heal* (Hodder and Stoughton, 1965) pp. 49 ff.
3. *Confessions*. Quoted in ibid. p. 51.
4. *Of the Four Degrees of Passionate Charity*, edited by G. Dumeige (Vrin, Paris, 1955).
5. David Auerbach, *Surviving Trauma: Loss, Literature and Psychoanalysis* (Yale University Press, 1990).
6. St. Teresa of Avila, *The Interior Castle*, Mansion VII, Chapter 2.
7. Cf. Luke 10:38–42.

Part III

Her Ministry

10 DOROTHY AND HER MENTORS

"Martha and Mary must walk together", and, like St. Teresa's, Dorothy's ministry kept these two aspects of life in Christ perfectly in balance. Indeed "in balance" would not go far enough as a description, for the two were completely integrated in her life and work. Her prayer life would not have been complete on its own had it not issued in a total dedication to the task set before her many years previously in her vision at Dr. Ash's home in Portman Square. The product of her life of prayer was continuous and unremitting hard work. Indeed her colleagues always said that when they dropped exhausted they knew Dorothy was still at work, having worked even harder than they had during the day.

Similarly, her ministry and life's work would have been unimaginable without the long hours of prayer, sometimes at night, always in the early mornings, and the constant prayerfulness of her life during the day. The life of prayer sustained the life of work and the work was taken back into prayer. The life was one: Martha and Mary knew a perfect blending in her life. That was why it was so rich and full and an inspiration to others. The two parts were so fully integrated that her vision was in total focus – on her Lord Jesus Christ. He was her omega point, as Teilhard de Chardin, her contemporary, would have said. Christ was the fixed point to which her life, work and prayer were evolving in perfect harmony.

This perfect blending of the two aspects of life – to use a well-worn phrase, they were the two sides of the same coin

– was shown in many ways and not least in her sense of humour and her attitude to children, who speedily discern the unintegrated or disintegrated life, the unreal or the untrue. Dorothy was a born mimic and used to have her family and friends in paroxysms of laughter with her anecdotes from her journeys. She was especially good at cockney, and a trip on the top of a London bus was always a quarry for some humorous tale. She also had the gift of seeing the funny side of things and so lightened many a load. She joined in the family pranks as a girl and was usually the ringleader. She exuded the notion that life was essentially fun. She never allowed her patients nor her staff to take themselves too seriously. She was in a league of her own at organising parties and meals of celebration, especially at the Church's festivals. All this was relevant and integral to her work and was a gift that she brought to her ministry. All her patients were immediately lifted by her presence: her personality throbbed with life. Her staff, and very soon her patients, knew the source of that life, though she never disclosed it ostentatiously. It came, of course, from the "Mary" side of her which only went to underline the measure of integration which she had attained. One of her chaplains knew the source of this gift full well.

Her joy, her mirth, her tenderness are the Joy, the Mirth, the Tenderness of One who pours His own gifts into her, and through her, so that they may bless the folk whom He sends to her. If He were to leave her – He will not of course, because He promised not to – Her Joy would vanish at once, and I do not think that even joy would remain![1]

For Dorothy, the prayer of St. Paul that he might know the power of His Saviour's Resurrection as well as the fellowship of his sufferings, was amply answered (Phil. 3:10).

With children Dorothy was most at home. They adored her. She was one of them. She had become as a little child because her great desire was to enter the Kingdom of Heaven. It may well be that she was so good with children because she had been given such a full foretaste of the Kingdom's banquet in her early life on earth. She had their vision of the vast, unending life and world in front of them, a vision she never lost and constantly inspired in others. She had a complete affinity with children and never begrudged the time and trouble she gave to them. After all, she was to adopt nine of them herself, all the same age! But there were constant instances of her rapport with children prior to this. Her sister records one such from the Thruxton days. On arrival at Thruxton it seemed "dead" to her sister, an empty and musty-smelling church, an overgrown churchyard, an inconvenient vicarage and a lifeless village. That was soon to change when Dorothy had been around for a few months. On her next visit Dorothy and Dr. Langford-James met her sister, who was surprised to see a knot of excited children with them, also part of the welcoming party. All the way through the village, women and children came out of the doors to wave and another group of children lined the path to the vicarage gate. On expressing delight at such a change from the first visit, Dorothy told her sister to wait until Saturday. Evelyn ("Bid" to Dorothy) related the story in these words:

We were up betimes but not as early as the children. When we went to the gate there stood all the children of the village. They had baskets of primroses and violets, all done up in neat bunches. They were armed with brooms, brushes, dusters and furniture polish. We proceeded to the churchyard, which was transformed. The weeds had gone, the grass was cut, the graves were covered with flowers. Then into the church, which had completely lost its musty smell. The children laid their flowers in the font and set to work to sweep, clean and polish the church, singing all the while. "We do this every Saturday," they told me. They each had a special job to do, and it was a heart warming sight to see such lovely team work. When Dorothy had inspected and passed the cleaning we all, under her supervision, proceeded to decorate the church. Dorothy flitted about, her little feet scarcely touching the ground, and that most endearing set of children followed her around, putting a bank of flowers here and another there, until the church was a vision of delight and the fresh scent of primroses and daffodils pervaded the air. That memory will stay in my heart as long as I live.

Dorothy was a veritable Pied Piper with children and animals, they all approached her with the certainty of a welcome and complete understanding . . . Dorothy had accomplished such a transformation in bringing the church and village to life, she had opened up for the children a world they had never known and she was intensely happy.[2]

This talent Dorothy also brought to the service of Christ – the vision, clear-sighted and totally trusting, of a child. The hours spent with her Master ensured it became truly a Kingdom vision. There must have been many children over the years to whom a similar vision was imparted.

Zest for life and sense of humour, and a total affinity with children, were but two of the talents which she brought to her ministry. There were others too, and none more marked than her total obedience to her Master, learned through the years of suffering and preparation. All these things pointed towards this integration of the Martha and Mary elements. Two more talents, however, call for special mention: her love of beauty and excellence, and her deep perception of the heart of people and things. These were talents also given to her spiritual mentors and guides as tangential energies to their own focus on the person of Jesus Christ, giving them a basic affinity with their spiritual ward.

All through her life Dorothy followed the principle that only the best is good enough for God. She lived this out in her life of prayer and obedience to her Lord and it was the source and inspiration for her *modus vivendi*. The principle permeated all her dealings with people and the things of this world. Every person with whom she came in contact was so vitally significant and made to feel so because they were God's unique creation and He had seen that everything in His Creation was good. Each person had to be served and ministered to as if it was Christ himself.

It was the same with material possessions. She had renounced them completely and she was always short of money, trusting that for those whom God guides, he also provides. But when she was furnishing God's house or a room that would be used by one of "Christ's poor", or one of her houses that would be used for the glory of God, nothing but the best was good enough. She bitterly complained that too frequently God was given the "shoddy left-overs". For her such a notion was unworthy. Her knowledge of God and complete trust in Him led her to adopt the highest standards. Her houses had, therefore, to be full of flowers, supplied from her well-loved and tended gardens, standards that are still maintained at Burrswood. Beauty and excellence, marshalled by due order, were part of the air she breathed.

This led to her having a deep perception of people, for she saw the beauty and glory of God at the heart of all things and she had gazed into that heart. Many thousands of people came to see her in the course of her ministry which was now to begin in earnest. Some would only have ten minutes alone with her, but in case after case those minutes were life-changing. She had the supreme gift of being able to get to the heart of the matter. Her prescription for Gladys Modin's sister-in-law,[3] after standing at the foot of the bed for ten minutes, was a typical example: "You need loving", she said, and in her care the patient was bound to receive that medicine.

All these were some of the talents she brought to her God-given ministry, indicative of the measure of integration of "Martha and Mary". And although she could outdo most mortals in the guise of Martha, frequently leaving her fellow-workers exhausted while she continued to work, she had also chosen the good part of Mary, and her long vigils and frequent referrals of all she undertook to the Master ensured that that part would never be taken away from her. "She knows; she has been there", as one of her chaplains said.

These were also the gifts she found in her spiritual mentors, with whom she seemed to resonate at once. If they were fortunate to have her as their charge, she also was blessed to have them as counsellors and guides and as intercessors who would be faithful in lifting her life and ministry before the throne of grace. In the course of time she was to have only three, but each was given to her for a particular period of her life. We have already met Dr. Langford-James, who, with his scholarship and knowledge of the Christian mystics, was able to interpret to Dorothy the stages of the life of prayer and mystical knowledge she underwent, as well as being able to complete her education, of which she had had little because of her illnesses. He was able to guide and fill out her reading. He also had two other attributes, music and mountaineering. He was a Bachelor of Music and a gifted pianist, and his wife was an accomplished violinist. Evelyn Waterfield recalled that a performance of the Kreutzer Sonata by them was the crowning glory of a wonderful Easter Day she spent with them at Thruxton.[4] The beauty of music was a necessary part of Dorothy's life, for she had grown up with it thanks to her mother and grandmother. It was to fulfil a continuing need as a source of beauty that spoke to her of the angelic music she had heard, and she encouraged the performance of good music in all her homes. Dr. Langford-James was also a member of the Alpine club and took Dorothy climbing and walking from time to time. This appealed to her need for adventure which stirred her sense of fun and excitement in daily living. It also encouraged her to see wider visions.

Dr. Langford-James was "a man sent by God" to Dorothy to guide her progress during her years of preparation. For most of the fourteen years Dorothy was with him, he had faithfully kept a spiritual diary of her progress and had constantly sought, by prayer and reading, to be in a position to act as counsellor and guide to one who was privileged to see and know the life of the Spirit as she did. His final entry in the journal is enlightening:

I have just read through consciously, for the first time, all the notes I have made about Dorothy. In the light of experience, it now seems to me I expected too much of her vitality when she first came under my care. Her vitality is so wonderful, and she is so utterly unselfish in concealing so far as possible the fact that she is ill, that one is easily deceived. I had the fear of letting her give in too much to the physical. And also there was the fear, that she shared always, of her being regarded as an invalid, an idea against which she always protested vigorously. It is quite certain that some mistakes have been made by me. One can only plead that one has tried one's best to avoid them. At the beginning, of course, one had to go by what one read in books of possibly similar cases. As one has gone fourteen years now – and one's relations with Dorothy have really been of father and daughter from constant association with her – one has gained invaluable experience which has helped me, I think, to avoid mistakes . . . The acid test of course is the fruits of good living. *Dorothy's power has not diminished, in fact it has increased.*

One "mistake" may have been to place his ward under simple vows of poverty, chastity and obedience, but this was all part of the heavenly Father's plan and, as will be seen, was mightily used for good in pointing Dorothy to the next stage of her pilgrimage.[5]

When she began her ministry, she was to feel the blank left by leaving his vicarage and company. Mercifully the vacuum was filled almost at once. Philip Loyd, who had recently been consecrated bishop in the diocese of Bombay, had been told he must meet Dorothy by one of his missionary workers who had been restored to health through her ministry. When he appeared on the doorstep it was Dorothy who opened the door. They felt a mutual understanding immediately and from that moment Dorothy knew he had been sent as her soul friend and spiritual guide. Philip was tall and of aristocratic bearing. Eton and King's, Cambridge, had been followed by Cuddesdon, but from the age of fifteen he knew he was destined for the priesthood. From the first his Christian character was marked by a living relationship with Jesus.[6] Dean Eric Milner-White wrote of his fellow undergraduate and Christian companion,

> Philip's supreme contribution to this (scholarly) society was one of character. His eminence here was clear from the first: it shone. He knew, as few undergraduates do, both his foundations, which were profoundly and sensitively Christian, and his direction, to Holy Orders. From the latter he derived the strength of settled purpose; from the former his extraordinary sympathy and grace. He spoke through his charm, and you knew he lived in the eternal world.

He gave his best years to India and was about half way through his ministry in that country when he met Dorothy while on furlough. From that moment there was a spiritual bond between them. They appreciated the same things, especially the love of excellence and beauty. They had the same sense of humour and often vied with one another to find amusing rhymes. Above all there was a bond of prayer that must have been a tower of strength to them both through some of the dark days that were to come. Philip celebrated the Eucharist for Dorothy on the fifteenth of every month and wrote to her the same week. This particular bond, through our Lord's own Sacrament, was there from the first. On arriving back in India he wrote,

I don't know when I have had such a happy Mass as in the wee Chapel that morning, and it was largely because at the first sight of you, when you opened the door to me, I knew that the Lord Jesus had given me, as I said, a new sister. And then wasn't His Presence wonderful at the Mass? I suppose there is nothing we priests lament more than our coldness in celebrating the Holy Mysteries. Little Sister, pray for me.[7]

Other letters began like this: "I must write to you before I go to bed. You had your Mass this morning: this time you had to share it with fourteen simple villagers whom I confirmed at 9.0 a.m. . . . How are you, Dorothy dear? And how is the money coming in? I do so often think of you and pray for you." Or they ended like this: "God bless you little Sister, and give you back your health and strength, and may the Lord Jesus flood your heart with His peace and fill it with the desire of beholding His Face." Such was the man who would be her spiritual guide, bringing her new inspirations and sharing her decisions, truly a companion, if not in person then in the Spirit, for the next twenty-two years.

Dorothy was equally fortunate in her third spiritual mentor who was to see her through her life and ministry. Cuthbert Bardsley came to Burrswood to meet Dorothy and she invited him to be Warden of the Fellowship, announcing it in the Whitsun newsletter of 1954. He was to give the next twenty-six years of devoted service to the Fellowship and to the Community, even throughout his busy years at Coventry. At the time the *Croydon Advertiser* discerningly noted, "He has the lifting power of a cheerful spirit and the drive of an intense enthusiasm." Another observer saw the marks of his motivation, "single-minded, deeply converted and, above all, a truly Christ-centred person." Two of his expressions were "Think big" and "Expect great things from God". Throughout his ministry he was deeply concerned that evangelism should be at the centre of the Church's thinking and strategy and he saw the Church's ministry of healing as integral to that proclamation of the Good News. One of the finest preachers in his day, he also had a real understanding and commitment to the sacramental life. He was truly a man of prayer, dedicated prayer. It was easy for Dorothy to resonate with a Christian leader of this calibre, especially since both of them from time to time could find themselves maddened by the lack of vision of the Church they both loved and served so devotedly.

Just after they met, Cuthbert Bardsley gave evidence to the Archbishops' Commission on Divine Healing (July 1954). The evidence he gave then was similar to that which he gave in a letter to a friend many years later and shows how fully his approach to the ministry coincided with Dorothy's:

1.   There are very different kinds of "healer". The best are those who humbly acknowledge that God alone can heal and that he *will* heal in his own way at his own time. The less good are those who claim to have healing powers in themselves and do not refer to God. This is dangerous and arrogant.

2.   I dislike intensely the title "faith" healer because it gives the impression that healing is dependent on our faith. That is not so.

3.   I prefer the title "The Church's Ministry of Healing" which seeks to bring God's healing to the *total* man – his soul, his mind, his body. And the body is the least important of the three. God wants to heal the *soul* to remove fear, distrust, and anxiety and to help the sick person to trust in God absolutely.

He also wants to heal the *mind*, the person, from all that afflicts the mind – resentment, jealousy, vindictiveness, and to bring peace of mind.

He also wants to heal the *body* which often begins to be healed when the soul and mind are cleansed.

All this is the Church's Ministry of Healing brought through prayer with counselling, the laying on of hands and anointing with Holy Oil. In all this the Church humbly acknowledges that God is the healer and that he will heal in his own way, at his own time.

Summary: I distrust many so-called "healers" just as I distrust large, often emotional healing services and meetings. I prefer the one-by-one quiet encounters with sick people, in which we do not demand a particular kind of healing but leave to the Lord to heal as he will and when he will.

It is important to surround the healing ministry in a volume of prayer.

To this end, I have always sought to have the backing of a group of praying people who bring one's healing ministry to God in prayer. At Woolwich there was a large book located just inside the church entrance – the church was always open – so that people could come in through the day and insert requests for prayer in the book. Their names and the bare outlines of the needs of the sick were then taken by a prayer group into the crypt of the church where, once a week, the members of the group met for prayer, not least for me in my healing ministry.[8]

Such was the third of her soul friends who was to guide her and be her confidant for the remainder of her ministry and, after her death, guide the Community through that traumatic time, enabling it to maintain her vision and continue the ministry she had handed on.

With such talents, and with such men of God to come alongside her in God's own good time, Dorothy was now ready to embark on her full-time ministry and to that we must now turn.

Notes

1. Frank Drake in *Thy Son Liveth* (Hodder and Stoughton, 1959) p. 53. See also Chapter 1, p. 16.
2. Evelyn Waterfield in *My Sister Dorothy Kerin* (Mowbray, 1964) pp. 50 ff.
3. See Chapter 13, p. 139.

4. Evelyn Waterfield, op. cit. p. 52.
5. Dorothy Musgrave Arnold, *Dorothy Kerin: Called by Christ to Heal* (Hodder and Stoughton, 1965) pp. 64 ff.
6. A member of the sanctuary party at his consecration noted that the Holy Name was emblazoned across the morse of his cope.
7. This and other quotations from letters are taken from Dorothy Musgrave Arnold, op. cit., pp. 90 ff. For the main part of the information about Bishop Philip Loyd I am indebted to his biographer R. P. Stacy Waddy in *Philip Loyd: Missionary and Bishop* (Mowbray, 1954) including the quotation from Dean Milner-White.
8. *Cuthbert Bardsley: Bishop, Evangelist, Pastor* by Donald Coggan (Collins, 1989) pp. 199 ff.

   I am also indebted to Lord Coggan's excellent biography for the other details about Bishop Cuthbert Bardsley.

11   EALING

A common experience among those whom the Holy Spirit
is constantly urging forward seems to be that for a year or
two before a major change of direction occurs, there is a
period of waiting and expectancy, during which the "tent
pegs" are loosened. Dorothy experienced such a time at
Edgbaston where the Langford-Jameses had moved after
Thruxton. She knew she was being prepared to strike camp.
She had constantly over the years longed for this time, when
she could follow the call she had been given and be used in
the service of humanity to the glory of her Lord. She also
knew well enough, from her Master's example, that the years
of preparation were necessary to a fulfilled ministry and that,
according to the dictum of the spiritual life, the blessing was in
the waiting. But now the time to "launch out into the deep"
and let down her nets was at hand (Luke 5:4).

It was all brought to a head by a proposal of marriage,
which, together with the whole circumstances surrounding
it, was used to clear her vision. Throughout the years of
preparation, Dorothy was committed to an ever-increasing
correspondence, which continued to grow during her years
of ministry. Among her correspondents at this time was an
American priest who was involved in the healing ministry
and came over on a visit in 1929, with the intention of
proposing marriage. This he did in the vicarage garden.
After she had heard him out, she shook her head and told
him, "It cannot be, because I have vowed to live my life
in God's service in holy chastity, poverty and obedience."

Realising the finality of her decision, he went to accost Dr. Langford-James in his study and told him how wrong it was to have caused his young ward to take life-long vows and to imprison so precious a soul, who had been given such a charismatic gift, within the four walls of his vicarage.

Dorothy Musgrave Arnold, having related the story, commented that "the disappointed suitor returned to the USA, having done, beyond doubt, what he had been sent by God to do."[1] In fact it was not long after this that Dorothy, deeply grateful as she was to the Langford-Jameses for their hospitality and care of her for fourteen years, felt it was the time to go and told them of her conviction that God was now calling her to serve Him in the world. She went to live with her mother and younger brother in Ealing and almost at once began her ministry. Once again she had received a vision of what she was called to do and immediately responded with obedience. She used to say of her responses to the Divine Command and their sequel, "I leapt over the precipice into His arms." Another leap came hot on the heels of the first, and so it went on.

Her ministry began in 1929 and many things occurred in that same year. The opportunity of renting a house in Culmington Road presented itself, which could be made into an excellent place of resource for the many who were already coming to seek her out for counsel and help. There was never any money available at once, but Dorothy always believed in and "lived" the vision she was given and so it invariably worked out. It is the putting of the first foot forward that is the hardest step, but that very act enables things to happen. So she did step out and in a short time there were the necessary finance, furniture and fellow workers. Her first home of healing, named St. Raphael, after the archangel of healing, was opened in the autumn of 1929. As always the chapel, situated at the top of the house, as at Bush Hill Park, was the pivot and focus of the work, where Dorothy would spend long hours by day and by night. It was licensed by Arthur Foley Winnington-Ingram,

Bishop of London (1903–39), who became a very good friend, interested in and supportive of her work, while the Bishop of Southampton (Bishop Boutflower) blessed it. It was regularly used to give visiting priests an altar. It was probably about this chapel that she wrote the following devotional poem:

> A little Room up a winding stair,
> Blue walls, white altar, flowers are there.
>
> Kneel and pray – wait and pray,
> In stillness listen. Hear Him say:
>
> Ye are my Friends. Feed my sheep;
> Feed my lambs, O, mystery deep.
>
> In the silence, I whisper, I love Thee, Lord,
> Accept my service, my Friend adored.

Kneel-pray-wait-pray-stillness-listen-hear Him, – these are the preliminaries and attitudes of contemplative prayer, the basic ingredients of a dedicated life "hid with Christ in God" (Col. 3:3). Gwen Williams was the first patient and wrote later of how it was through Dorothy's sheer and unfailing "obedience and love and gentleness, our Lord turned my unbelief into a breastplate of faith".

She continued:

In these early days, Dorothy was full of irresistible fun and laughter. She herself did not give the laying on of hands, and did not even drop a hint that she was a great woman of prayer – she just seemed to radiate new strength and spiritual wholeness, and drew one to our Lord. In appearance she was small, slender and ethereal looking. Her complexion was creamy with no colour except for her lips. She had very beautiful blue-grey eyes which were most striking. They shone with a spiritual light that

113

seemed fathomless, and their expression varied according to the moods and needs of those she was with. Sometimes they sparkled with light-hearted mirth and joy; at other times they glowed with the tenderness of compassionate love; occasionally their expression was sad as if weighted with the sorrows of the world; and on occasion, they could blaze with righteous indignation. Her eyes were the genuine windows of her soul . . . Always I have felt the love of our Lord through Dorothy.

One of my most treasured possessions is a most beautiful old silver cross, with a crucifix on one side, and our Lady and the Child on the other, in a blue case lined with white, which Dorothy gave me before I left. She told me she had worn it next to her heart for some time until it rubbed her too much, and she could bear it no longer. One day she had taken it with her when she went to visit a mental patient, and a light shone around it and the patient was healed.[2]

The demand for places at St. Raphael's soon grew and began to be overwhelming. People from all walks of life and from all quarters came to seek her ministry. She was lost in thought during one of her walks with the faithful Bruno, her extremely intelligent and lovable dog known as "the brown verger" from his regular attendance in chapel, when she felt herself drawn to a large, derelict house which she must have passed many times in her visits to Walpole Park. One day she pushed open the gate and as she stepped into the drive, a vision came to her that this was God's house, prepared by Him for some work He meant her to do. As she left the grounds she distinctly heard "The Lord is King" and with these words throbbing in her whole being she went home, straight up to the chapel, and asked to be shown the Lord's will. The answer came directly and strongly, "Get it for Me." Her gift of obedience was, as always, ready in response.

Many people, when they see Burrswood today, ask if Dorothy was very rich. There was never any money – in the bank – and that was so in this case, from the very beginning. But the process of implementing new visions was invariably the same and it is instructive for Christians in any generation. First she prayed that the Lord would give her a sign. The "fleece" in this case was a prayer that it might be made possible to pay off the debt that still remained on St. Raphael's. The sign came on the third day when a friend wrote to her, "I have received some unexpected dividends, and feel that God asks me to send it to you. I have no doubt you will find some good use for it." Her first prayer was answered. The second step was to consult two of her close friends. Philip Loyd, recently consecrated as Bishop of Nasik, was still in England on furlough and she asked him to visit the house with her. The bishop later told her that he had intended to bring his common sense to bear upon her to prevent her making so rash a commitment. But as they went from room to room in the silent house, it seemed to him that our Lord was claiming it for His own and showing him the rooms filled with people waiting to come. As they knelt down, they both broke into the words of the *Gloria in excelsis Deo*. The other friend also came in the same frame of mind, but similarly felt it was all waiting, "waiting to be cared for and filled and used for such service as our Father should make known by his Holy Spirit, to be carried out in the Name and in the strength of His beloved Son."[3] These were the second signs.

The third stage was to put a foot forward in faith, and this she did by making a definite offer to buy the house. The owner was sympathetic to her work and reduced the asking price from £5,000 to £3,700. Obviously more money would be needed to put it right and furnish it. There was no money, only the certainty of God's will. It is at that point that God has room for manoeuvre! Gifts began to flow in and to complete the sum the bank advanced £500, to be repaid before Christmas. The gifts were large and small and among the latter was the gift of a Jubilee florin (now a 10p piece) given by a poor woman who gave it in thanksgiving. She prayed her "most treasured possession" would be blessed and multiplied a thousandfold. Dorothy always had the coin on the altar in each of her houses.

In the meantime the house became ready for occupation and was blessed and opened on 25th October, 1930, by the Bishop of Woolwich (Bishop Hough). He laid his hands on Dorothy for the blessing of the work and told her quietly afterwards he had seen the house next door joined on and that in God's own time this would happen. Dorothy then told him that indeed it was true and she knew that in God's own time all the houses in Mattock Lane would be part of this work. But by the end of the following month there was only £80 towards the bank debt of £500, a large sum in those days.

To add to her troubles – "rebuffs" always came to her after a step forward had been made for the Kingdom of God's sake – Bruno, her "brown verger" and beloved companion became dangerously ill and she nursed him day and night for forty-eight hours. As he lay in her lap, she was pondering on how the money might be forthcoming when she heard the voice she knew so well, "Fear not, I will provide all thy need". Immediately Bruno stood up and wagged his tail, his own form of thanksgiving for his sudden recovery. They both went to chapel to join their thanksgivings together. She knew then that this was a test of her faith and went to her desk, wrote out the cheque to the bank, dating it with the date of closure, and placed it on the altar. Joy was in her heart and she slept soundly. This was the fourth stage towards the implementation of her vision in which, as so frequently is the case, God transformed what seemed to be a rebuff or negative element into something wholly positive and affirming. The final outcome was no longer in doubt. The money came in gradually during the first fortnight of December. The last gift of £20 arrived from an unknown benefactor on the final day, completing the £500 exactly, and enabling the cheque to be posted on time.

God's timing is always perfect and His promises are sure, provided we keep within His will and obey His slightest command in total trust. Dorothy's trust was so honoured in the beginning of her very own home of healing, her first Chapel House. Before we leave this story, however, there are two lessons to learn: the first is that at some point a foot has to be put forward in total trust and faith. Once she had the first two assurances that this could well be within the will of God, Dorothy did just this by making an offer for the house even when she had no money. When you have nothing, the only course left is to trust God, but this she did in a positive way. She took the initiative. The other lesson we learn from this story is that when God is seen to be at work we must expect even greater things. He has far larger plans for us than our small request and "is able to do immeasurably more than all we ask or imagine, according to His power that is at work within us" (Eph. 3:20). The matter in hand was large enough, humanly speaking, with the whole of her future and credibility at stake, but she saw beyond the present crisis into the counsels of God and had even further and greater visions of His will for her life of service. It was this gift of being so immersed in the sure mercies of God that Dorothy had in abundance, enabling her to be one step ahead, with a larger vision of the divine horizon. It was the same gift that Archbishop Garbett saw in Mother Margaret, the founder and first Prioress of the Order of the Holy Paraclete, Whitby, and that has manifestly been present in the lives of such holy women as St. Teresa of Avila and her namesake in this century, Mother Teresa of Calcutta. Never were such people of vision more needed in the Church of Christ on earth today.

The work that began with such a vision was blessed from the first. As people began to hear of miracles of healing, the news brought many, too many, to her door. Referring to the period 1930–40, Dorothy wrote, "God's wondrous power was made manifest in countless blessings and acts of healing."[4] Her colleagues witnessed to the signs of the Kingdom which occurred again and again – "The blind receive sight, the lame walk, those with skin diseases are cured, the deaf hear, the dead are raised, and the good news is preached to the poor" (Matt. 11:5).

At this period in her life, though this was not always to be the case, Dorothy was supported by the Established Church. The Archbishop of Canterbury himself (Dr. Cosmo Gordon Lang) "had given Dorothy his blessing and commissioned her, in the name of the Church, to go out into the world to proclaim the message of hope entrusted to her by our Lord Jesus Christ".[5] He had also given her permission to lay on hands, although at this time she only ministered to patients in private.

The first chapel in which Bishop Loyd and Dorothy had knelt had proved inadequate in terms of space. Her own Bishop of London blessed the new chapel in Chapel House and gave her permission to have the Reserved Sacrament. It was a rare privilege in those days in the Church of England to be granted permission to reserve the Sacrament. It meant a great deal to Dorothy, not only in terms of personal devotion, but also for pastoral reasons because the Sacrament was readily available to the sick in her care. On hearing about it, Bishop Loyd wrote to her at Epiphanytide 1933, "I am so glad about the Tabernacle; how lovely! When shall I kneel before it with you? I just simply don't know."[6] Her local parish priest, Father Barrett, Vicar of St. Barnabas, Ealing, gave her his fullest support and as much time as his parish duties permitted. He used to celebrate the Eucharist once a week in the chapel and at times he took healing services. Ruth Farr recalls that he "would say Mass once a week with great devotion. He was a shy, rather withdrawn bachelor. To hear him say Mass was moving and impressive, for he brought to it reverence and a sense of reality that was unforgettable."[7]

Dorothy was also well supported by the medical profession. She had been fortunate to secure the services of Sister Rose Friend, who came to see Dorothy, having been told they must meet. On one of her weekend visits after their first meeting, she contracted pneumonia, but "on the third day I had the laying on of hands by the Chaplain (Father Barrett) and was instantly healed".[8] Sister Friend was to become Dorothy's lifelong companion and personal assistant (some called her "the bodyguard") as "Jummie", giving her years of devoted service. Dorothy had also been fortunate to find Dr. Helena King, known to her patients as the "beloved physician". Dr. King remained alongside Dorothy's work for many years. Both of these ladies were going to be needed by Dorothy herself before long.

There was one further body of supporters without whom Dorothy could not have been upheld to do her work and survive the many difficulties she had to face in the course of her ministry. This was the Chapel House Fellowship, now known as the Burrswood International Fellowship. It started with a letter to all of Dorothy's connections signed by Bishop Loyd and Lord Daryngton. The only obligation of membership was – and still is – to say regularly the Chapel House Collect (the Prayer Book collect for the sixth Sunday after Trinity). The letter also asked members to share, as they were able, in the financial burdens of the work. The response was immediate, in prayer and money, and the fellowship was born, remaining the strong support and stay behind her ministry and later behind that of her successors. Dorothy knew its strength and was always so grateful for its loyal and unfailing support. Perhaps the collect chosen – though it was the collect of the week at the time Chapel House was acquired – says much about Dorothy's own spiritual life and affections:

O God, who hast prepared for them that love thee such good things as pass man's understanding; Pour into our hearts such love toward thee, that we, loving thee above all things, may obtain thy promises, which exceed all that we can desire; through Jesus Christ our Lord. Amen.

Dorothy had not been long in Chapel House when she was faced with an important decision. Its resolution was to have a lasting effect on her work and ministry. It arose over the question of fees, which at the time were left to the patient's discretion. This obviously could not go on, because only a fraction of the costs was being met. A Harley Street specialist had been sending her patients and one day she discussed the problem with him. He immediately advised that she should register Chapel House as a Nursing Home and charge normal fees, adding "Chapel House is far too valuable to us to allow anything to interfere with the work being done there". She took this advice to the Lord in prayer and it was borne in upon her that this might give her the opportunity of actually seeing more of God's poor, since if she was sure of a regular income from statutory fees, she would then be able to see others who could not afford to pay. She made the decision to register Chapel House and her work and ministry took on a new dimension; a new vision was opened up as a further healing began to be experienced – that between the Church and Medicine. This was to be one of her aims, as well as of her successors, from that day on. The list of sponsors she obtained for Chapel House underlined this coming together. It included the Archbishop of Canterbury and the Bishop of London as well as Bishop Loyd, Father Barrett and Dr. Langford-James. It also included no less than four Harley Street specialists and Dr. King. The remainder look like an entry from *Who's Who*, but the essential point should not be lost: it was a genuine attempt to repair some of the broken bridges between the Church and Medicine. A decade later, Lang's successor at Lambeth, Archbishop William Temple, was to take a nationwide initiative to the same end in founding what is now the Churches' Council for Health and Healing. In fact both initiatives proved to be bridges too far ahead as there were very few other people to cross them at that time. Fifty years on the position is very different.

Dorothy continued to preach what she practised and from now on she stressed time and again how "these two instruments of God's healing power" should work in harmony together. During her ministry and certainly in the Ealing days when she seemed to have a hot-line to Harley Street – or possibly it was the reverse – she promoted the co-operation between the healing professions.

From the moment Chapel House opened it was full and always had a waiting list. Although she had a staff of trained nurses, this was an era before bursars, estate managers and even secretaries. The running of the whole enterprise, though assisted by devoted colleagues, placed an immense strain on Dorothy. To this was added the demands of the ministry to all who came, not only the residents. Her correspondence increased so rapidly that it became a burden and a strain. Catching up with it meant further inroads into her sleep, already shortened by her discipline of prayer. Meals were not regular and only taken when time allowed. It is hardly surprising that such a burden weakened her immune system, she caught a chill and developed pleurisy. Dr. King and Jummie knew why they had felt a strong call to work alongside Dorothy: she now needed them for her own sake.

She was extremely ill, in a total state of collapse and probably it was only the devoted nursing of Jummie that saved her life. Dr. King was deeply concerned and called in a specialist. He asked to be left alone with Dorothy as he delivered his verdict: "You will have to make up your mind whether you wish to live and continue your work. As things are, you cannot live for longer than two or three months. If, however, you promise to do exactly what I tell you, it is possible for you to pull through, but only on this condition. Now I shall leave you to make your decision." During the half hour he left her, she took the whole matter to the Lord in prayer and saw the doctor's demand as a matter of obedience to her Lord. She gratefully accepted the conditions, the first of which was complete immobility for a month. As always she saw ahead and used the illness positively. Instead of asking the "Why me?" question endlessly, she saw it first as an opportunity to place her total trust in the Lord and to

121

recall His promise time and time again that He would never leave her. Then she saw that perhaps our Lord wanted her to deepen her understanding of pain and suffering and human weakness and helplessness. So she accepted her illness as "something to be shared and thrown into the common pool of suffering, and offered perhaps in some tiny way, as a drop in the filling up of the cup."[9] A further blessing in Dorothy's eyes was that call of Helena King and Rose Friend to the work of Chapel House.

On the human plane things were not good. The patients left, the place deteriorated and there were bills to pay. But God used this time. Dorothy was shown many things in prayer and discerned how God was teaching her lessons that could be learned in no other way. She thanked God for it. In 1936 Bishop Loyd was home again and spoke at a small gathering to give thanks for her recovery. He said:

> There is nothing like thanksgiving for keeping up faith. We have to admit that, although the Lord has led Dorothy through many hard times, He has sustained her in them . . . And so I want to leave this message with you. Dorothy asks for our prayers, that she might be sanctified and filled with the spirit of faith, and love, and Holy discipline, and that there might be no obstruction to this channel of the blessed life of our Lord.[10]

One is left to wonder what toll this took of Dorothy's vision as well as of her physical strength, and whether Philip Loyd's final request for prayer on behalf of Dorothy was inspired by his inner knowledge of her true state. Did this illness constitute a crisis in her life? Did it at all dim her vision? In all probability it knocked her slightly off course for a time by its very severity. It may even have darkened temporarily the brightness of her vision. It showed that her life subsequent to her initial healings was prone to suffering which could be extremely severe. The total commitment she had to her call and the energy with which she followed it was bound

122

to place undue strain on the strongest of physiques. Her salvation was her deep communion with her Lord and the disciplined way she kept her tryst with Him. Her trust in Him was total and even if events for a time knocked her sideways or dimmed her vision, because of her life in the Spirit, she had amazing and speedy powers of recovery, both physically and spiritually. This was a case in point. She did get back to work very quickly, but she had been very ill indeed and had had plenty of time to ponder on her life and calling. But as at all times she kept her life of disciplined prayer at full stretch – even during her illness she had continued her intercession – and was soon one step ahead once more, dreaming dreams and seeing new visions.

Chapel House filled up again and soon there was the same pressure on space. With perfect timing, one of the other five houses in Mattock Lane came up for sale. It was bought, furnished and then blessed by Bishop Boutflower as St. Gabriel's, to accommodate those who did not need actual nursing. The archangels were still looking after her – first St. Raphael, now St. Gabriel. It was not long before the next "archangel" came into view and Dorothy's prophetic vision again found fulfilment. "St. Michael's is for sale," she told her mother, who thought she was "quite mad to attempt anything more." Yet within a week it was made possible with the help of two friends.

A further vision of momentous consequences was given her on the day of its blessing: she became "conscious of children's feet and the sound of their laughter . . . this happened subsequently again and again."[11] Dorothy decided to move into St. Michael's with her mother and keep it as a house where people could come and be quiet or make a retreat.

It took some courage to leave Chapel House and most especially the chapel where she had been used to finding sanctuary at all times of day and night with her Lord. There she had faced all the trials and difficulties and surrendered them. There she had witnessed miraculous outworkings of the Lord's healing power. There she had worshipped the Lord in the beauty of holiness: it was in fact a very beautiful and numinous place. On one side of the altar, draped with blue curtains, there was a figure of our Lady nursing the Child Jesus, carved for her by a nun from Wantage; on the other a statue of the Sacred Heart; above, the flickering sanctuary lamp denoting our Lord's Presence in the Tabernacle. This "beauty of holiness" was the very place where she could be truly at home and relaxed as she waited for her Host in her long vigils. This was the inspiration that kept her vision undimmed. It was also the chapel where she had seen other visions. One night her Lord came to her while she knelt by the altar, waiting for His guidance before taking a momentous decision. She became aware of His Presence as He laid a baby in her arms, saying, "Nurse this child for me." The weight of the child became heavier and heavier so that she could scarcely hold her any longer, but in her heart she felt "complete satisfaction". As the vision passed she expected the baby to be still in her arms, but then it was borne in upon her "that this was something that God held for the future". She locked it in her heart. Three years later it was to be fulfilled.

The chapel would, of course, still be available to her and remain central to the whole complex and to the healing work being undertaken there. But she did feel the change acutely, almost as a bereavement, and only finally moved after her Lord had given her the assurance while she was actually walking from the chapel to St. Michael's, "I will go with thee." She was able to record in due course, "The Holy Spirit filled St. Michael's; it was a happy, joyous place. All who came to it knew that God had set his seal upon it and had blessed it."[12] It was not long before St. Faith's was added, making four down and three to go of the houses in Mattock Lane. But there were storm clouds on the way that would make it even harder to hold to a healing vision for the human race.

124

Notes

1. *Dorothy Kerin: Called by Christ to Heal* by Dorothy Musgrave Arnold (Hodder and Stoughton, 1965) p. 64.
2. Ibid. pp. 74f.
3. Ibid. pp. 76 ff. The story is also told by Ruth Farr, in *Will You Go Back?* (Dorothy Kerin Trust, 1970) pp. 40 ff.
4. Dorothy Kerin, *Fulfilling* (Hodder and Stoughton, 1952) p. 88.
5. Ruth Farr, op. cit. p. 46.
6. Dorothy Musgrave Arnold, op. cit. p. 94.
   The Tabernacle is a locked safe on the altar, or on the gradine behind it, in which the Sacrament is reserved for the sick. An Aumbry, which serves the same purpose, is placed in a wall adjacent to the altar. A white light denotes the fact that the Sacrament is reserved.
7. Ruth Farr, op. cit. p. 46.
8. Ibid. p. 83.
9. *Fulfilling* p. 46, cf. Col. 1:24.
10. Ibid. p. 49.
11. Ibid. p. 55.
12. Ibid. p. 56.

12   HER MINISTRY IN WARTIME

Like many others, Dorothy had known in 1938, if not before, that a supreme tragedy brooded over humankind. Frequently an acute desire to be alone came over her. This was made possible by the acquisition of a small cottage in Berkshire, affectionately named the Ark. Here she was able to find the stillness and solitude she craved. Her innate mystical sensitivity led her to give more and more time to being with her Lord, in "deep mid-silence open-doored to God", as the storm clouds of strife mounted in Europe. It was a time of recharging her batteries in preparation for the testing time of the war years, a time in which she was constantly reassured of the divine protection and eternal presence.

Here was an instinct she in fact shared with the Master Himself. At the beginning of Mark's gospel, in the middle of a section describing intense activity – healing and exorcising, travelling, dealing with immense crowds and impatient disciples – we read the words: "Very early in the morning, while it was still dark, Jesus got up , left the house and went off to a solitary place, where he prayed" (1:35). Henri Nouwen, commenting on this verse and on solitude as the secret of life, says: "In the centre of breathless activities we hear a restful breathing. Surrounded by hours of moving we find a moment of quiet stillness. In the heart of much involvement there are words of withdrawal. In the midst of action there is contemplation. And after much togetherness there is solitude. The more I read this nearly silent sentence locked in between the loud words of action, the more I have the sense that the secret of Jesus' ministry is hidden in that lonely place where he went to pray, early in the morning, long before dawn. In the lonely place Jesus finds the courage to follow God's will and not his own; to speak God's words and not his own; to do God's work and not his own . . . It is the lonely place, where Jesus enters into intimacy with the Father, that his ministry is born."[1] Dorothy would have resonated with this moment as she went away to the peace of the Berkshire countryside to imitate her Master and keep His company.

Solitude is, of course, not an end in itself. Its true purpose is communion. Saints go into the desert for love of God and to enter into deeper fellowship and communion with Him. And this can be true for us all, whether it be an hour of prayer or a lone walk on the hills. Solitude increases our intimacy with the Christ of solitude. The second reason for solitude is again communion – with other people. We go "into the desert" to improve our relationship with others, not to lose them but to find them, not to shelve our responsibility but to learn to help them more. Solitude is necessary for us if we are to be useful members of society as well as better servants of God. As Thomas Merton said, "Solitude is as necessary for society as silence is for language and air for the lungs and food for the body."[2]

Dorothy's need for this solitude was the greater because she discerned the world crisis and its consequences as being far-reaching. She had shared the immense suffering and slaughter of the First World War, finding herself in mystical compassion on the battlefields of Flanders. The loss of life was beyond telling; the terrible disablement of men a constant reminder. Another major war could well unleash a chain reaction of constant belligerence, total mistrust, victimisation and violence which could destroy peace once and for all. If she saw this, she was too near to reality for comfort. Her instinct knew that the Devil was best pleased when good people did nothing. Her answer was to seek total solitude with her Lord to plead with Him and intercede for

His world. Her time spent alone with Him was for the healing of His world and His people, as well as for His servant.

Dorothy was in fact at the Ark on that Sunday morning, 3rd September, 1939, when Neville Chamberlain announced that we were in a state of war with Germany. Exactly a week before she had been shown three symbolic visions. On the first occasion, during the journey from Chapel House to the Ark, she saw a large, fiery red cross. The second vision was seen while she was resting. Again she saw the red cross, but in front of it was a dove with wings outstretched, and with a deep wound in the heart whence flowed a stream of blood separating into drops of gold. On the third occasion she saw the same red cross but this time the dove was hovering over it with its wings outstretched once again. It seems that Dorothy interpreted the vivid symbolism of the vision as not only a premonition of the suffering to come, which it clearly was, but also as an indication of the divine protection and eventual victory over evil. When the sirens sounded on that very first day of the war, as they did all over the country, Dorothy telephoned Jummie in Ealing and said with a clear voice which sounded serene and confident, "Tell them all 'in confidence and calm shall be your strength', and give them my love." And then after a pause, "He has spoken and told me, *Be not dismayed*".

Precautions naturally had to be taken and she was ordered by the local A.R.P. authorities to build a shelter for the patients. Once again, nothing but the best would do – her standards of excellence even extended to air raid shelters! A comprehensive shelter was built under the front lawn, "very comfortable and complete with telephonic communication to the house." Little wonder it was known as the "Dorchester" and despite some horrific nights when bombs were dropping and sirens wailing, nightly processions were the occasions of much fun and laughter, especially when a dignitary of the Church, who was staying the night, rushed to the shelter with a meat dish perched on his head. Dorothy's description of her own plight shows her humour and resourcefulness: "I

128

must confess to dismay when I heard that my presence in the shelter was insisted upon. This to me was the last straw. Shall I ever forget the snores? In every key and tone they seemed to be, and after a few nights I armed myself with a long stick, which did valiant and able work in silencing some of the nightingales."

There were nights – and days – when life was not so funny. Sometimes the shelter became flooded and Dorothy and Marina had to bale out the water between the volleys of gunfire and falling shrapnel. Frequently that part of London as well as the East End was alight with blazing fires and searchlights combing the sky for enemy raiders, together with the deafening noise of the guns and falling bombs, but "seldom did fear raise its head amongst us, thanks be to God".

There was one night, however, when she sensed that Chapel House was threatened. One of the guests who was having a sleepless night in the shelter heard Dorothy in her fitful waking periods reciting the Jesus Prayer continually. As a general rule Dorothy was not given to praying aloud in this way. This, however, seemed to be a matter of urgency throughout that night. Towards dawn the awaited bomb came and though it fell only fifty yards from Chapel House and made a huge crater in the park, the blast was minimised and little damage done. There were other times too, in war and peace, when she would have an urgent premonition or gift of knowledge and continue in prayer until the danger was past or the crisis resolved. Her response of prayer at all these times demonstrates the fact that she knew who was the giver of that knowledge and responded to Him in prayer.

Considering the damage done to their houses and the fact that none of the staff or patients received a scratch, it was, Dorothy said, a clear case of angelic protection. In fact those who had been evacuated to the Ark pleaded to come back: they preferred danger and disturbed nights with Dorothy to peace in the countryside. This enabled the Ark to be sold, which helped the exchequer. Although somewhat battle-weary, the whole community came through the war unscathed in fulfilment of Dorothy's prophetic insight on the first night.[3]

The time of solitude in preparation for those wartime experiences, as well as keeping her community in good heart and safety, also ensured her vision was not dimmed by outward difficulties. Two parts of her vision were fulfilled in these years. The first was the coming of "the sound of children's feet and their laughter". It was three years since the vision when our Lord had said to her, "Nurse this child for me". The first, a war orphan, arrived and was baptised in the Chapel by Father Barrett, who also acted as Godfather. She was called Anne. It became a time of great joy for Dorothy. Seven months later it was revealed to her that there would be eight more, five girls and four boys in all – all babies. This was in 1941/2. Dorothy encountered great opposition and some resentment but she used to say that this was a small price to pay for so great a blessing. Although this would probably not have been allowed by law today, she was merely obeying "the Law of the Most High". There was no further question about it: her Lord had spoken; she obeyed. But she did legally adopt them, which was possible then, and so they took her name. To Dorothy they were "a perpetual and ever-increasing revelation of new fields of wonder and joy". They helped to keep her young and renew her vision and certainly gave her a new zest for life. She saw them as symbolic of our Lord's plan, as children of the new Kingdom. Perhaps it was her staff who were the heroes and to them we must now turn. They were the second part of the vision in those years.

Dorothy undoubtedly had the gift of choosing staff with powers of endurance and stickability! This was inspired and fed by a devotion to her. Nearly all of them remained at their posts not only throughout her life, but also throughout their own. Their devotion to her, of course, made for difficulties between them and this is nothing new in community life. The fact that Dorothy's own life was so totally Christ-centred and truly and wholly dedicated to the work of the Kingdom made it all possible, even if there was frustration at times in having to live up to such high standards.

During this period of the war she had five devoted colleagues, who, with the nurses and daily helps, saw the work through. Presiding over the kitchen was the indefatigable "Bocky" (Miss Caudwell) who came of Lincolnshire stock and joined the staff at the beginning of the war as cook. She worked all her waking hours and continued to do this at Speldhurst and Burrswood, where she is still in her kitchen at 6.30 every morning. Marina Chavchavadze was of Russian royal stock and escaped with her family at the Revolution in 1917. She came first as a patient before the war, but then stayed on to give a lifetime's service. She helped Dorothy with writing, entertaining and supervision and is still continuing to write today. Mary Carr (Nanny) was Dorothy's personal maid who became nursemaid to all the children, a job at which she excelled and to which she gave her all. There was one tense moment in the war when Dorothy had one of her premonitions and shouted to Mary to get all the prams in at once. There was no alert on at the time, but almost at once a bomb dropped, jettisoned by a fleeing enemy raider, and the shrapnel landed where the prams had been a moment before. Jummie we have already met. She, too, had been a patient, but with her nursing qualifications stayed on to be Dorothy's right hand. They were devoted to each other, but there were times when Jummie could be over-possessive and over-protective, something with which Dorothy found difficulty in dealing. For Jummie, to work for Dorothy was the fulfilment of life for, as she wrote,

it is very wonderful working in a house that is verily God's, realising so often that He is undertaking all things . . . So many sense His presence and during the war years it was so often asked, "What is it in this house that is so different?" . . . You will understand what a revelation it has been to me to work in Chapel House as a trained Nurse. I can and do testify to the fact that the blind have seen, the deaf have heard, the lame have walked, crooked limbs have been straightened, and the mentally deranged have found peace and sanity, and in many instances have resumed their normal work . . . and this often, after medical skill has pronounced them "incurable".[4]

The fifth companion was Ruth Farr, whom we have already met through her short biography of Dorothy. She was the practical member of the team, a qualified electrician who knew a great deal about the building trade and so was immensely helpful in the Burrswood period. She had come to Chapel House, Ealing, as a patient and had three months to observe Dorothy and all that went on around her. She was puzzled about Mrs. Langford-James, by that time also a patient, who would spend hours in the chapel. On coming out, she would stridently say she must see Dorothy and ask her forgiveness. Without a word being said, Dorothy one day summoned Ruth and began to talk about Vivienne. Ruth's description of what followed is a testimony to Dorothy's gift of discernment and of knowledge concerning her patients, for she spoke of everything that had been on Ruth's mind. It is also revealing about Dorothy's own counsel:

"Poor Vivienne," she said, referring to Mrs. Langford-James, "she thinks that she has committed some unforgivable crime against me and, though I have forgiven her dozens of times, she still thinks she has to ask my forgiveness".

"It is remorse, I suppose", I said uncertainly.

"Yes, but it is not good, is it? Remorse can be a way of throwing God's forgiveness back in His face."

These few simple words suddenly let in a flood of light on me. I had been feeling remorseful myself. Dorothy went on talking about Mrs. Langford-James and explained the circumstances which had led up to her own sudden dismissal from that household. Even then she did not enlarge on how difficult Mrs. Langford-James had been to live with, or the fact, which came to us later, that her eccentricities had been both baleful and alarming at times.

"How is it that she is here now?" I asked wonderingly.

Dorothy explained that a rather extraordinary happening had brought this about. Fairly recently, she said, when the enemy bombing had been fairly widespread, she had been woken from her sleep one night by the sound of Mrs. Langford-James calling to her in great distress, saying: "Dorothy, Dorothy, help me!" Dorothy had telephoned through in the early morning to Birmingham and after discovering that there had been a raid in that area, she had journeyed up to the Langford-James's house in Edgbaston. A bomb had fallen close to the vicarage and, though all the occupants escaped harm, it was the very last straw in Vivienne's unhappy existence and she had begged Dorothy to take her with her to Chapel House.

I listened to all this with amazement and great relief and I was delighted when Dorothy went on to talk about the past. Suddenly she began to talk about the period in which she had taken simple vows. At this point she stopped and said with a smile: "I don't know why I am telling you all this".

If I had been more generous I would have explained that she had read my thoughts and that she was telling me all the things that I felt I needed to know quite desperately. As it was, I just smiled back at her and hoped she would go on. She did go on . . .

"You see, I was very young when I took those vows. I had only recently emerged from those wonderful encounters with the living Lord and I was naturally on fire with love for Him. If anyone had been able to convince me that to prove my love and gratitude for Him I ought to jump off a rooftop, I would have done it."

She gave a rueful laugh and went on: "As it was, my director convinced me that to prove it, it was my duty to take these vows; and so I took them. Of course, it was a mistake. It was all so totally unnecessary. Those pressures should never have been brought upon me. You see, the vow of Chastity was Dr. Langford-James's way of guarding me from any possibility of marriage. But I never wished to marry. It is true that I had a great love of children but there was the 'Daddy' part and that never interested me. As to Obedience, it is, as you know, something that I have valued above all things. God had already given me His commands and I lived only to fulfil them. Then there was the vow of Poverty. My conception of Poverty differs from that imposed on me then. I am nothing and I have nothing of my own; it is all His. All that comes to me must be used for His glory and, under His guidance, I am His steward and answerable to Him."

And then she added: "Of course, I am not bound by those vows now . . ."[5]

There seems to be no record of when Dorothy was released from these vows. Her uncompromising obedience in all probability meant that she would have felt constrained to seek official release and the Church's blessing if she was led to take such a step. It was ultimately something between her and God; it seems she wanted it kept that way and so there is silence on the matter. Speculation may be an unfruitful activity, but it would be interesting to know if her desire to be released from the vows had anything to do with the adoption of nine children. After all, she then became the "mother" of a sizeable family. Did this mean that all the vows came up for questioning? She herself, in the above passage, related how her view of poverty had undergone a development. There was bound to be a clash between the high standards she insisted on maintaining – "nothing but the best is good enough for God" – and her original vow of poverty. This would be exacerbated when she had to provide for nine children, whom she brought up according to the same high standards. Whatever may be the case, her conscientiousness, sensitivity and deep desire to obey God's will in everything may well have led to tension in this matter and so to an increase in her suffering.

Two more members joined Dorothy's permanent staff at the end of the war. Both were to be of immense help to her. Peggy Simpson came as a patient and was finally healed of an illness which affects the throat and which an operation, the first of its kind in the country, had partially cured. Marina Chavchavadze remembers Dorothy coming down from her room: she paused and quietly said, "He was there". The Speldhurst spring water sealed the healing. She became the driver, who often drove Dorothy through remote parts of the country, all night long if necessary, to visit patients. During all these times she had a great ministry of prayer.

All the companions were individualists and characters and none more so than Kathleen Burke-Collis. At seventeen, in order to get away from her stepmother, she applied for a job with a Norfolk family as chauffeuse. She got the job, although she had never driven a motor car in her life! It was Dorothy Arnold, the future biographer, who found her – in Switzerland, where she had just finished a job as governess to the Siamese royal family. "What can I do next so that I may give my life to God?" she asked. Dorothy Arnold replied she knew just the person who was a woman of God and who needed her. Kathleen became Dorothy's own housekeeper and looked after the children. She was fun and they loved her. The present author once asked her what was most difficult in her hectic life helping to bring up nine children. "Sorting out eighteen wellies", was the immediate reply. I also asked her what she thought about Dorothy Kerin. This time there was a long pause and a measured reply: "She was a saint." Such was the loyal and hard-working team who went with Dorothy first to Speldhurst and then on to Burrswood, to be joined by others in due course.

Before we leave London in wartime, however, it is good

to ponder for a moment the small but effective part Dorothy played in helping her country, indeed the world of nations, in time of war. No one can assess the part her prayers played in the return to peace and in the comforting of the battle-scarred and war-weary. In the First World War she had her out-of-the-body experiences, finding herself in the no-man's-land between the opposing armies, ministering to the wounded and the dying. Knowing the horrors of modern warfare, she would have ample material for her early morning intercessions. But there were also tangible acts of help to be carried out. There would be many like Mrs. Langford-James who, weary of the blitz and greyness of wartime Britain, would need comfort and pastoral care.

There were also combatants who sought her help. Air Marshall Dowding became a great friend in later years. He first came for help in the war, in which he was in charge of Fighter Command during the Battle of Britain. He could not live with himself having to send all these young men to their deaths, as he put it. He used to see them in his wakeful dreams. Dorothy was able to work through the whole trauma with him. He was known as "Stuffy" Dowding because of his brusque exterior. If only we knew, as Dorothy seemed to know, what went on inside people. Some, of course, are better at hiding it than others. There was also an Admiral, who worked in the War Office. He came to see Dorothy in Ealing. "Why have you come?" she asked. "I don't know, but it seemed to be told me that I should come and see you", he replied. She told him that they had better wait upon the Lord together to see what *He* wanted to tell them, and so they did. After some time Dorothy rose to greet someone who was entering the room. The Admiral could see no one and asked who it was. Dorothy described him, – a young naval officer, in uniform, wounded, etc., etc. "That is my nephew, who was lost at Narvik", he said. The nephew went behind his uncle and told Dorothy some of the German secrets he had learned. She told his uncle. The information proved to be of vital importance to the War Office.

There is no explanation for these things, but we are now wise enough to know that they happen. It would be wholly "natural" for a person like Dorothy, who was so near to her Lord and had herself been caught up into supernatural experiences, to be used in this way to give help to those in need. Was she not committed to comfort the sorrowing and bring faith to the faithless as well as to heal the sick? And the fact that these events concerned the immediate problems of the time, a nation at war, indicates that though Dorothy was attuned to the things of heaven, she also had her feet firmly on the ground.

Notes

1. Henri Nouwen, *Out of Solitude: Three Meditations on the Christian Life* (Ave Maria Press, 1974).
2. See my *A Healing House of Prayer* (Hodder and Stoughton, 1987) p. 176 where I acknowledge my debt to Robert Faricy, S.J. and his book *Praying* (SCM Press, 1983).
3. The story and quotations about the wartime experience are to be found in Dorothy Kerin, *Fulfilling* (Hodder and Stoughton, 1952) pp. 57–9.
4. Ibid. p. 45.
5. Ruth Farr, *Will you go back?* (Dorothy Kerin Trust, 1970) pp. 61 ff.

13 SPELDHURST

With her prayerful sensitivity, Dorothy always knew the right
time to move on. She never embedded her tent pegs in a
concrete base, until she discovered that Burrswood was the
"Promised Land" where her ministry would be continued.
Possibly the experience of war began to loosen them once
more and she may have entertained thoughts of the country
to regain some of the peace essential for her work, and also
now for the healthy upbringing of the children. It was a
similar instinct to that of Lady Elgar after the First World
War who knew her husband needed the idyllic peace of
a remote country cottage – Brinkwells near Fittleworth in
West Sussex – to bring fresh inspiration after the trauma
of war. In this case the result was Elgar's Cello Concerto.
For Dorothy there was also new inspiration, but the change
seemed to come by a circuitous route.

The very year that Dorothy moved into Chapel House
in Ealing, the Modin family moved into Etherton Hill in
Speldhurst, near Tunbridge Wells. It was a fine family home,
greatly used by the children, but was requisitioned during
the war. After the war the derequisition notice contained a
threat that if no other use was found for it in a month, it
would be re-requisitioned. Such is the jargon spawned by
bureaucracy. Gladys Modin and her father had moved back
into the cottage but the state of their dear old house was
appalling.

At that juncture, a relative asked to be taken to someone
who would minister true Christian healing. Gladys made

138

enquiries and two friends told her of the work of Dorothy Kerin. She telephoned and there was one bed vacant. She took her relative up to London, saw her safely to bed in her room in Chapel House and awaited the arrival of Dorothy, whom she longed to meet. When this small figure came in, she ignored Gladys's outstretched hand and went straight to the foot of the bed to absorb the signals from the new patient and listen for the word of wisdom from above. After a few minutes she prescribed, "You need loving". Gladys withdrew and on the way out said to Jummie almost as a throw-away line, "You don't know of anyone who wants to buy a house in the country, do you?" "No," replied Jummie, "we are very happily settled here." Gladys and her father had hardly walked in the door when the telephone rang: "Dorothy Kerin here. My secretary has just told me about your house being for sale. I know that I have to have a house in the country. May I come down and see it tomorrow?" Dorothy never let grass grow under her feet, but this also seems to tell us that she already "knew" it was time to move on and this was the kind of "word" she had been awaiting. Despite it being a drenching day and the house in a terrible condition, she negotiated an immediate settlement and began making plans. What had finally decided her was a sight of the house from the lawn, which nature had transformed into a hayfield. She exclaimed, "It is the house my mother saw eleven years ago, even the white shutters are there."

It was a minor miracle to get the whole house restored within and without, and as always Dorothy had arranged the date of dedication in advance. The trouble was that all materials in 1946 were either rationed or unobtainable. The chapel, which now is situated in the grounds of Burrswood outside Chapel House, was a case in point. Etherton Hill had no chapel and every room would be required for the enlarged family, but they managed to procure an old Red Cross hut which was no longer weatherproof. Could it be ready in time, all wall-boarding being rationed and no men available to do the work? But wall-boarding and some planks were found, the men's lorry broke down which confined them to work in the village, and so the job was done. There always seemed an inevitability about the completion of Dorothy's projects. There was also an accident during the restoration when a workman fell off a ladder and lay stunned and apparently badly hurt. Gladys immediately rang Dorothy in Ealing who calmly replied, "Yes dear: I saw him fall and he will be all right."

The dedication of Etherton Hill took place as planned. Philip Loyd, by now home for good and Bishop of St. Albans, did the honours. There were two other bishops there, including one from the Greek Orthodox Church, Dr. Langford-James in his Doctor's scarlet, and a vast number of clergy and friends. "After blessing the little chapel, which was hidden by trees at the top of a slope, the Bishop visited every room in the house and finally the gardens, praying that love, joy and peace might reign in this place."[1] Dorothy and her mentors were always thorough in their execution of the spiritualities. They believed the Holy Spirit demanded the utmost efficiency in His department.

Dorothy had a mutual understanding with Gladys from the first. In that sort of like-minded climate it is easier to have a clearer vision. Other things don't get in the way. Soon Dorothy saw that old Mr. Modin would not be with them for Christmas: that was in the summer. In the autumn his health deteriorated, but he had seen his family home once more filled with children and laughter. As she was watching by her father one night Gladys received a telephone call from Dorothy: "I'm coming down." On arrival – in her dressing gown, Bocky having driven her down at a moment's notice – she quietly said, "I'm going to stay with you", and sat in silence at the other side of the bed. Some time after three in the morning she said, "Quick, he is going." He opened his eyes – having been unconscious for days – smiled beautifully at his daughter and was gone. Such was the way she was able to care for her staff and patients. She was constantly in tune with the music of heaven.

The plan was that Dorothy would spend half her time in Ealing and half in Speldhurst, with the children at the latter. They all instantly settled down and loved it, slightly dreading the time when "Mummy" would have to be away. Often they were outspoken about it, especially in their prayers! Out of the mouth of babes . . . Dorothy herself knew that it was unsatisfactory and having to commute between the two wasted both time and energy. She wrote: "I felt torn at times with the longing to be in both places at once. There was so much at both ends that could not be attempted for lack of time. My energy was getting depleted. The chief desire in my heart was to do what God willed, but it was not easy to see what He might be asking of me".[2] She discussed the problem with Bishop Loyd and together they took it to the Lord, for, "He knows what He is going to do, and He will show us if we really want to do His will."

After prayer he said to Dorothy, quite prophetically, "Little Sister, I feel that our Beloved Lord may be going to ask you to give Him something that will cost you a great deal. But if He wants it, He will first give you all the strength and courage you will need. I know you will not fail Him. You will give Him all He asks, and in return He will give you Himself in the fullness of His Love."

"What do you think He is going to ask of me?" she questioned.

"I think He may be going to ask you to give up Chapel House."

She was shattered by the reply. For once she had not seen it and her bishop had acted as her eyes and seen the vision for the next phase of the ministry. She wondered still if the bishop had made a mistake. Again they went to pray, he taking her hand and saying, "Let us go and say the 'Our Father' together". They were on their knees a long time but as they rose Dorothy knew that she had laid Chapel House on the altar and her only wish was "Thy will be done". Despite this, there was no peace in her heart for some days, but the wise bishop wrote, "Leave it to God; if He wants you to give it up, there will be some sure sign and you will know."[3] A few days later, she was approached by the diocese of London as to whether they could make an offer to buy Chapel House for a diocesan house. Although this did not materialise it was taken to be the sign.

Dorothy began to look at houses in Kent and gradually went through the list, until she only had two left to inspect, both in Groombridge. As she had her hand on the key at the front door of Burrswood, she turned to Kathleen Burke-Collis and without even going inside said, "This is it: there is no need to look any further." The place was in a total state of devastation, as we shall see in the next chapter. But she saw it as it might be, and would be – a place where thousands would come for the healing touch of Christ. Here she would ignite a light that would never go out. She went to work with the necessary formalities, but then came one of those rebuffs, always timed when a move forward for the Kingdom was being made. To cut a long story short, the Middlesex County Council, to prevent the Chapel House estate being sold in individual lots to private buyers, threatened a compulsory purchase order. Dorothy agreed to sell it to them instead of to those with whom she was negotiating, provided there was an early settlement. The purchase price was much less than she would have received and was so long in forthcoming that a question had to be asked in the House of Commons to procure the money at all. By that time she had purchased Burrswood.

Meanwhile, life continued as normal at Etherton Hill. The stable-block was converted for accommodation and so was able to take those patients from Ealing for whom homes could not be found. The children were happy with Dorothy there full time and grew up steadily in the clean country air. They also had a healthy relationship with the heavenly Father, their prayers sometimes reducing the adults to laughter, at other times to tears. They learned to ride at an early age and Dorothy learned to cope with their accidents. One was particularly severe: Priscilla fell off her horse and fractured her skull. A passing ambulance probably saved her life. Dorothy did not allow her to be moved to hospital but had her X-rayed at home. Dorothy wrote that night,

I was kneeling by the child's bed, she was semi-conscious, and had complained of "a big headache". She was restless and feverish, and as I knelt by her side praying that God would touch her, I felt His power upon me, and laid my hands on her head. I was conscious of the Saviour's Presence. Later Priscilla opened her eyes and said, "Mummy, did Jesus tell you to do that? cause all fwee headaches have gone – all fwee of them."

She fell into a deep and perfect sleep, and in the morning there was no evidence of any injury except for a very bruised eye. She appeared to be quite well, asking for food and wanting to get up. When the Doctor came he was amazed and said that he had always hoped to see a miracle.[4]

The peace and beauty of the house and its gardens also impressed itself on Dorothy, tired after the exertion of the war years. She needed the stillness of the early mornings and the space and beauty of the countryside to refresh her soul and recharge her batteries after the noise and danger of war-torn London. She began to see visions and dream dreams once more and she was given what she called "an indescribable sense of expectancy". Indeed the unexpected was always happening, life was fun again and God gave her and the community continued evidence that He had His loving hand upon them.

During one of her prayer times in the early morning, as she looked out upon the garden clothed in its morning mist, she saw a "radiance of golden light" around the lily pond. As she gazed she saw it flowing out of the pool and cascading in diamond-like drops. She looked up and saw a stream of people, young and old, some on crutches, others being helped. They all came and drank of the water, whereupon some of them abandoned their crutches and others walked unaided. She knew the Lord was at work, healing His people. The vision passed but its memory was imprinted on her mind. Possibly God was showing her His plan for the future. She then went down to the pool and found there was a gentle flow of water emerging from the side. A new spring had started flowing whose source was traced to under the Chapel. She knew God would use this water for the healing of His people.

This in fact happened. At Bishop Loyd's suggestion, although he said she should regard it "as the secret of a King", Dorothy gave the healing water to some who came to see her at Etherton Hill (which had now been renamed Chapel House, Speldhurst, since the sale of the Ealing property) and they were healed. Peggy Simpson, who later on drove Dorothy to cases all over the country, was herself helped by the water. She wrote:

At Chapel House, Speldhurst, I had a further sign of God's wonderful love. I had been suffering from double vision for some time when Miss Kerin offered me to drink the healing water from the pool in the garden. This I drank in Chapel, and the same night, just as I was going to sleep, a glorious white light passed over my eyes and they were completely healed; and so my life now is full of light and joy where once was despair and sadness. I must end this testimony of God's great mercy and love with thanksgiving.[5]

As quickly as it had begun, it ceased to flow, although Dorothy thought that one day it would return. Possibly, however, the vision and the flowing of the spring had been a symbolic indication of a future time when the fruits of her ministry would be seen within the Church as an indication of its Lord's healing power, with consequent blessing for the sick, the sorrowing and the faithless.

Whether the water flowed or not, Chapel House, Speld-hurst, was a place of true healing and was an essential link in the chain. It was the bridge between Ealing and Burrswood, and yet more than the bridge. It was the place that prepared Dorothy and her team for Burrswood and equipped her with more staff who were capable, totally loyal and hard-working. Gladys Modin, whose father's home it had been, was a valued new member of the team. Dorothy put her in charge of her old home when the move to Burrswood took place in September 1948 and Chapel House, Speldhurst, continued to function under her leadership for another ten years. Dorothy paid her a glowing tribute in *Fulfilling*:

> I will not try to describe her selfless giving, not only of herself, but all that she has, and is. Her efficiency and tireless devotion to the work, to which both she and I believe God has called her, is one of the greatest bless-ings He has bestowed upon us, for which I am eternally grateful.[6]

Chapel House, Speldhurst, continued for the next ten years to take patients who needed more nursing. Dorothy would telephone Gladys when the pressure became too great at Burrswood. Once it was "Darling, do you love our Lord enough to have ---- ?" Another time " ---- must either go or you must take her. Can you have her?" Speldhurst was a most valuable resource to Dorothy and the relationships with the staff there were so helpful. She relied heavily on Gladys, especially for administrative purposes and getting things done. She referred to her as her bit of rock.

Kathleen Nest came on the scene at Speldhurst. Having nursed her mother for seventeen years, she was very run down and caught shingles. It was Gwen Williams who found her in Marlborough Cottage Hospital and arranged to bring her to Burrswood (against her will). Dorothy sent her to Gladys and there, with much divine help, she recovered and became Gladys's lifelong companion and for some years was an efficient bookings secretary at Burrswood. Her sense of humour and ability to mimic resonated with Dorothy's own talents in that direction. Marisa Filmer also first came as a patient to Speldhurst and remained, like Kathleen, as part of the working staff until retirement. It is thanks to her there are some valuable recordings and photographs of Dorothy.

Dorothy in the meantime was settling into Burrswood and to that momentous step we must next turn. Chapel House, Speldhurst, remained a "sheet anchor", and sustained the essential work at Burrswood, allowing Dorothy also to give necessary time to the children. In her total vision it had formed the bridge, enabling her to sacrifice the Ealing complex and its pioneer work in order to have space to see larger visions, to build greater facilities and so extend the work, even internationally.

Notes

1. *Fulfilling* by Dorothy Kerin (Hodder and Stoughton, 1952) p. 76.
2. Ibid. p. 77.
3. Ibid. pp. 78 ff.
4. Ibid. p. 84.
5. Ibid. p. 86.
6. Ibid. pp. 88 ff.

14 BURRSWOOD

In many ways, Dorothy had been as happy at Speldhurst as anywhere in her life. It had been a great relief to come into the beautiful Kent countryside after the rigours of wartime London. She was able to spend time with the children, enjoying life with them in their country pursuits; they all learned to ride at an early age. She had a good staff around her, her faithful Bocky in the kitchen, Peggy who looked after the horses, Kathleen and Mary who looked after the children, and now Gladys. She also had her capable staff still in Ealing, but then there had come the great happiness when they moved under one roof. She herself learned to ride, secretly, to give the children a surprise. It was a time to *be* and catch her breath before the next stage of her ministry.

She was equally happy during her first years at Burrswood, where she enjoyed the same freedoms, was able still to give time to the children and had enough leisure to take a leading part in reclaiming and beautifying the gardens. But as Kathleen drove Dorothy up the half-mile drive for the first time – it was actually more of a track and overgrown on each side – past the four ponds until the kitchen garden wall came into view, the timbered cottage (now St. Mary's), the apple store (now the offices) and the stable complex (now staff accommodation), they must have wondered to what they were coming. They had rejected the other house in Groombridge as rambling and unsuitable because of its bad condition. Now, as they approached the main house, looking

147

pretty derelict and with its surrounding gardens covered in
brambles, they could have been forgiven if they had turned
the car round immediately. But as Dorothy had her hand on
the key she turned to Kathleen to say this was the end of
their journey and gave three resounding knocks on the
door. The present house had been built between 1834 and
1838 in the gabled Elizabethan style by David Salomons, a
London stockbroker and banker, whose main interest was
public life. He later became the first Jewish Lord Mayor
of London and received a baronetcy. The architect was
Decimus Burton (1800–81). There was also an estate of
319 acres. The house passed to several owners in the course
of the century, but it was the Johnstone family, who owned
Burrswood between 1906 and 1919, who were responsible
for designing and planting the beautiful gradens, of which
rare trees are a feature, and who imported truckloads of
bulbs from Holland. They employed fifteen gardeners and
people came from all over Kent to the open days.[1]

Dorothy could immediately see that this was the place,
even more than Etherton Hill, which her mother had told
her she would one day have as a home to which the many
sick, sorrowing and faithless souls might come to have their
several needs supplied. As she toured the house, the vision
grew of how she could make it "something beautiful for God
to use". She walked through the house on to the terrace
and saw first the magnificent trees, and then beyond them
the little river Grom which had accompanied them on its
winding way from Groombridge, disappearing eventually
under a railway embankment to join the Medway. Then her
eyes went on up the Medway valley which descended from
Ashdown Forest, the latter forming a magnificent horizon
on which the winter sun would set. Just below the forest was
the spire of Hartfield Church, where A. A. Milne brought
up Christopher Robin, with all the associations of Pooh and
Piglet and their companions. It was their forest. The view is
especially beautiful in the early mornings and the evenings,
and Dorothy must have appreciated it as one of the finest

148

views in the south of England. Her gaze would frequently be fixed in that direction as she imbibed its inspiration. But meanwhile there was much work to be done. The whole place had been left as a jungle, with ammunition abandoned in the ponds and at the side of the drives. But this was *the place*. She bought it, at a reduced price because of its condition, on the 21st April, 1948, and arranged the opening for Michaelmas Day at the end of September. She always gave herself and her workers a target to aim at!

Throughout the summer, work went on in the house preparing it for occupation again, while at every available opportunity, Dorothy, Kathleen and Peggy came over to hack their way through the undergrowth and have bonfires. They also had the help of the head gardener from Ealing and some prisoners of war. Kathleen said that Dorothy worked harder than anyone: that was usually the case, for when after long and tiring days others dropped into their bed, they knew Dorothy would still be at it and again up early to keep her tryst with her Lord and tackle her correspondence before breakfast.

The move from Speldhurst took place in September as planned and Gladys was left in charge of the nursing home there. The house at Burrswood, which was able to accommodate Dorothy, the children, her staff and also six guests, was blessed a fortnight earlier than planned as Bishop Loyd could not come on Michaelmas Day. He dedicated the house and small chapel (now Bocky's kitchen) to St. Michael, nevertheless, and the house still bears the archangel's name and stands under his defence today. Bishop Loyd underlined the vision for the work in his address:

Chapel House at Ealing has been a place where for years God has done many wonderful things. His work will go on here, and for that purpose is the blessing of this house.

There are few places on earth where there is faith for God to do His mighty works, but here are people who believe that He can do them.[2]

Over the next years, in Dorothy's own words, "We realised the vision of Burrswood fulfilled."[3] By this she meant two things; first, it began to develop into a centre for the healing ministry, as Chapel House, Ealing had been, where people in need could come in an ever-increasing flow and find the presence and touch of the healing Christ. Second, the estate which had been split up into various lots – even St. Mary's cottage was owner-occupied – she managed to reclaim and bring back into "a complete whole again".

It was during these early years that Bishop Loyd spent a year at Burrswood because of an illness. When he was well enough, he was able to celebrate the Eucharist and minister to many who came. At one of the early Fellowship days he took the theme of Peace:

"Peace I leave with you, My peace I give unto you." It is of this peace which our Lord gives to us I wish to speak now; because during my residence here in Burrswood for over a year, I myself have had abundant experience of the bestowal of this peace, and have also heard many others testify to their sense of it . . . It is not the tranquility of remoteness from life and its burdens, from its trials and failures. We have our Dorothy whose life testifies to this. No, this peace is a precious gift which we receive from the Lord Jesus in the midst of our pains and distresses . . . Our Lord himself gained this peace by bearing the heaviest burden ever borne by man, the sin, the shame, and the sorrow of all the human race . . .

He then reminded them of the cross and resurrection and showed them how Jesus had bequeathed this hard-won peace to the disciples on Easter Day: "Peace be unto you . . . Receive ye the Holy Ghost." He continued:

But if this is so, if all the time Jesus is re-creating us, and making new creatures of us, by the in-breathing of the Holy Spirit, ought we not to take much more pains to be

quiet before Him, so that we can become more receptive
of this His gift of Himself and His Peace? This is what
the Lord Jesus has been saying to me this Whitsuntide, in
order that I may pass it on to you on this our Fellowship
Festival day. And it is only right that I should attempt to
do so, because it was here at Burrswood that He said this
to me, and it is the love and the sacrifice, and the prayers
of Dorothy and the Fellowship which do so much to make
Burrswood and Chapel House what they are.[4]

Bishop Loyd knew from his own experience as well as
from Dorothy's, that the cross must come first and the
Easter blessings were hard-won gifts from Christ. There
was, therefore, the greater joy in watching their bestowal,
especially that of the gift of peace, on all who came to
Burrswood. How frequently must this brother and sister
have identified with St. Paul: "If anyone is in Christ, he
is a new creation; the old has gone, the new has come" (2
Cor. 5:17).

For their own lives, the peace was not yet, and the cross
and more rebuffs had still to come. Bishop Loyd became
restless and in June 1951 decided he must leave, despite
being far from well. He was dependent on drugs to keep
his heart in reasonable shape. Two factors were decisive:
although he had been forced during his illness to resign the
see of St. Albans, he was determined to work again; and
then there was, by now, the question of the children, whose
constant noise had created a real problem for Dorothy and a
difficulty for her staff and patients. Eventually this was faced
and a God-given answer provided, but in the meantime
"Uncle Philip", as he was affectionately known by them,
felt he had to go. His last letters to Dorothy are instructive
and provide a prophetic insight into the joint vision they
shared for the work:

You are constantly in my thoughts and prayers, and I wish
I could do more to help you. But it is *you* whom God has

called to Burrswood, and to whom He has given it all, in order that you may give it all back to Him. And if He is to use your offering as He wants to use it (and the welfare and salvation of so many souls, old and young, depend upon it), then it must be a very costly offering, which the Beloved has stamped with His own Cross. So we who love you so dearly must needs leave you to make your own offerings in the way that God has appointed for you. But we are there in love and trying to help with our prayers: and I believe that God does use our prayers to support you and strengthen your faith, even at the times when you feel most alone – and yet not alone, because He is with you.

And you may indeed be sure that God's grace is sufficient for you, even as His strength is made perfect in weakness. You are not going to fail Him; and He will never fail you; and His purpose will be accomplished to the glory of His Name. In all our sufferings and trials let us endeavour by the grace of the Holy Spirit to thank Him sincerely for the means which He takes to effect in us the sanctification which we so greatly need.

He eventually decided to live in Bournemouth and wrote to her as he began to make preparations for the move:

This is Sunday evening, and there does not seem to have been any time till now to write to you. Now, I have a clear week before me, in which to get ready for my migration to Bournemouth. My heart is very full when I think of all that God has given me through Burrswood in the last year and a half. He has been so good to me, and has had such great mercy on me, and helped me so much in my great need. And I see so clearly that it was His loving plan and gracious will to give it to me through you and through the life at Burrswood. If I was allowed to contribute to that life while I was there, that makes it all the lovelier, and is one more sign of His Goodness and most loving Condescension. I just keep thanking God for such a priceless treasure which is all the more precious because so many others – according to their many needs – are allowed to share in it day by day.

In the Epistle for this last week (Trinity XXII) came the words "I thank my God upon every remembrance of you, for your fellowship in the Gospel . . . being confident of this very thing, that He that hath begun a good work in you will perform it until the day of Jesus Christ; even as it is meet for me to think this of you all, because I have you in my heart." So lovely and so true! And remember that the *good work* of which St. Paul speaks there to the Philippians is not the work of personal sanctification (tho' that of course is necessarily involved), but the "fellowship in the Gospel"; that is to say, the work of making God to be known to others, and glorified, and that chiefly by the common life – the fellowship – which we live together. That is the good work that is going to grow and grow at Burrswood. And oh, how confident I am of this very thing. And you may humbly and thankfully be very sure that the growth and growing effectiveness of this "fellowship" and "good work" at Burrswood is a very sure and certain seal upon your own personal life and work there; a seal by which He reassures you that you yourself are indeed responding to His call, and allowing Him to fulfil His gracious will and purpose in you. How wonderful and lovely this is, but how *costly*! as you know well enough, for there always has to be the "dying of the Lord Jesus" which we bear about in our body; for only so can His life abound in us, and through us in others. Read what St. Paul says about it in 2 Corinthians 4:7, 15.

He moved to Ellerslie Mansions, near to St. Peter's Church much to his joy, for there was a daily Eucharist and Reservation. His last letter was written on 31st December, eleven days before he died, in the possible hope he might be able to return to Burrswood:

I still get very little writing done: because the doctor keeps me fairly well doped, and I do a tremendous lot of sleeping. It is answering very well so far as my heart is concerned, and he is greatly pleased with that. Yesterday, he said that in a fortnight's time he hoped to be able to say where we were, and whether he wanted to keep me on here for the present, or whether he would send me over to you.

You know how gladly I shall come: and I am sure that God will show me what His will is, and with your help and prayers I will try to obey. You say that you felt I ought never to have left Burrswood: and indeed at that time you did show that that was your opinion. But I just don't think that I could then have made up my mind to another year there, without trying to go out and be a bit more active. For me it would have meant sinking into a kind of semi-invalidism; and I did not believe that that was God's will for me.[5]

His final journey was not to Burrswood in this life, but into the life of the world to come – on a Sunday morning. He had just got up to light the candles in preparation for the Sacrament brought to him by the parish priest. That morning the Sacrament was unnecessary: by the time the priest arrived, Philip Loyd was in the nearer Presence.

Dorothy missed him intensely, but threw herself into the normal routine of the ordered life which was the backbone of the ministry at Burrswood. A healing service was held every Thursday morning in the small chapel. It was not yet Dorothy's practice to minister herself unaided. She used to have a priest conduct the service and during the ministry he would place his hand on her shoulder while she ministered the laying on of hands. In this way she felt that there was a demonstration that the healing power of Christ came through His Church. "We are channels, bits of pipe", was her constant reminder of this truth to people who tried to place the credit for the healings on her shoulders. Usually

154

it was Father Gilbert, vicar of St. Thomas's, Groombridge, who was the priest in those early years. In fact, the village of Groombridge is divided by the river Grom, which is both the county and diocesan boundary. Father Gilbert's church was in Sussex and the Chichester diocese. Burrswood is north of the river and so lies in Kent and the diocese of Rochester, but Dorothy while living at Speldhurst had regularly worshipped at St. Thomas's and she naturally turned to its priest. He used to come on Thursdays to celebrate the Eucharist and take Communion to any who were unable to come down to the chapel. More and more used to come to the services of healing, held later in the morning as they are still today. After her early morning prayer, which usually she began before 5 a.m., she would deal with the correspondence and with the children, who were a constant and noisy presence in those early days. Then, except on Thursdays when Gladys brought some patients over to Burrswood for the service, she would visit Speldhurst. In the early days there was time for gardening in the afternoon, and Dorothy and Kathleen continued to expend their energies on reclaiming more of the wilderness. They would arrive back for tea exhausted. Then Kathleen would put the children to bed and Dorothy would visit her patients and finally the children to join in their prayers. In the evening the two of them would go for long walks.

The problem of the children was partially solved by sending them away to school, and very good schools they were. Mercifully they had extremely generous Godparents and there were always thoughtful benefactors. During his lifetime, Bishop Loyd had paid for their shoes. School holidays were still a problem for the staff, especially as Dorothy could not afford to take them away to a hotel. Parties and other celebrations took place instead, but of course this all led to more stress and strain for the staff and patients. The heavenly Father was, however, still watching over her. An answer to the problem would be forthcoming.

Before his illness Bishop Loyd and Dorothy had been

walking in the lanes close to Burrswood and paused to admire the beauty of Court Lodge. The Bishop asked if she knew its history. Dorothy replied, "I know nothing of its history, but I do know that one day it will belong to Burrswood." The Bishop then said, "If you see this, I am sure in God's own time it will be so. When this happens, I pray it may be a place of escape for you and the children." In fact, Court Lodge had once been the manor house at Udimore, near Rye. The medieval house was patronised by the Plantagenet kings, but this was a fifteenth-century replacement, a fine, four-square, timbered structure built round a courtyard, which eventually fell into disrepair. At the beginning of the twentieth century, the artist Lawson Wood bought it as "material" and transported it to Groombridge on the edge of the Burrswood estate. A detailed plan was made and each piece numbered and packed with care. John Clarke, the architect, re-erected it to be as near to the fifteenth-century structure as possible, including the plaster work. The gardens were designed in 1916 and a wing was added in 1919.

Some time later Dr. John Elliott, who had heard of her remark to the Bishop, told her the owner had died and that the house was on the market. In the silent watches of that night she knew for certain that God had a plan to reveal, and waited expectantly. The "silver" anniversary of the beginning of her ministry (20th October, 1930) was approaching and was to be marked by a "Quiet Day of Prayer". She asked the priest to pray that God's will would be revealed. The insistent answer that came from the voice she knew so well, was "Ask Winifred". Winifred was indeed a patient, but what should she ask her? She again waited, but events moved on. The watchful doctor told her to hurry her decision because others were interested. She went to view it and secured the first refusal. The price would be around £15,000. The enormity of what she had done came over her on her walk back down the hill and up the drive, and yet the reassurance came: "Leave it to me." She knew her Lord's plan was fulfilled and went to the chapel to give thanks. On returning to her study she found a note asking her to see Winifred.

Unknown to Dorothy, Winifred had been awaiting a court decision about the estate of a relative in Australia who had died intestate. She received the answer from her lawyers that very day. As Dorothy mounted the stairs, considering what she should say and why Winifred had called her, the answer came from her inner consciousness, "To see the wondrous works of God." She found Winifred bursting with excitement with the news that her relative in Australia had left her a large sum of money. She added, "I know God has sent it for you in order that you can have all you need." The vision Dorothy was given in the conversation with Bishop Philip Loyd was fulfilled. Dorothy was time and again assured of her maxim in this way, – "Where God guides, God provides."

Court Lodge was dedicated by Bishop Cuthbert (by now at Coventry) on St. Andrew's Day, 1955, amidst a large crowd of Fellowship members. Winifred Wade-Brown died peacefully in May of the following year and the little garden chapel at Court Lodge was dedicated later in that same year to St. Winifred in thanksgiving to her memory. The ceremony was performed by Bishop George Bell, the most famous of all Chichester's bishops in modern times, who would soon be thinking of retirement after an episcopate of nearly thirty years.

Dorothy valued the beauty of Court Lodge and regarded it as a special gift from God. When it was of no further use for the Lord's work and the children had grown up and were dispersing, it was sold and the money used to extend the facilities of Burrswood for the work God had given her to do. It was a happy interlude there and made a most beautiful home for her and the children. It is enhanced by fine gardens and a lovely view across the Grom valley. It was a place for seeing visions, but none of the lesser visions impeded Dorothy from following the major vision in total obedience.

Notes

1. I am indebted to Johanna Ernest for her excellent history of Burrswood, *This House named Burrswood* (C.U.P., 1989. Foreword by the Archbishop of Canterbury, patron of Burrswood.)
2. *Fulfilling* by Dorothy Kerin (Hodder and Stoughton, 1952) p. 88.
3. Ibid. p. 89.
4. Ibid. pp. 90–2.
5. *Dorothy Kerin: Called by Christ to Heal* by Dorothy Musgrave Arnold (Hodder and Stoughton, 1965) pp. 134–6.

15 BURRSWOOD –
"WHILE I LIVE, I MUST BUILD"

Dorothy's primary concern was always the building up of her tiny part of the Body of Christ and she knew that the only firm foundation was the life of prayer. She herself was the great exemplar while the staff and patients were all able to share in the fellowship prayers. The divine office was a regular feature of life and whenever a priest was available so was the Eucharist. She laid the foundation of a prayerful atmosphere and that prayerfulness lay at the centre of the care and love offered to the patients. This was one of the great lights she lit at Burrswood which has never been extinguished.

She also saw to it that both she and the staff had a wise counsellor and spiritual guide, with whom she could build the spiritual foundations and together in prayer discern the will of God for the work. We have seen how blest she was in the three men who gave her this essential help (Chapter 10). It had not been very long after her move to Burrswood that Bishop Loyd had died and now she must seek another guide, but who could take "Uncle Philip's" place? He had seen her through so much. He had been a true brother to her and shared her vision of a Church renewed through experience of the healing power of Christ. Who could follow him?

In Cuthbert Bardsley, Dorothy found just such a person. He was at the time Bishop of Croydon, possibly the foremost mission preacher in the country, with an easy presence that betokened a holy man of prayer. He also believed strongly in the call of Christ the Healer to "rebuild my Church". In him Dorothy found another like-minded soul with a similar vision to her own. With joy she announced his acceptance of her invitation to become Warden in the Whitsun Newsletter to the Fellowship in 1954:

> You will be thankful to know that the Fellowship is no longer a flock without a shepherd . . . The Bishop of Croydon has most kindly consented to be our Warden. This is immensely kind of him. We all know how full his life is and are therefore doubly grateful. The Bishop has warned me that he will not be able to take a very active part in the life and work of the Fellowship, but we shall have the support of his prayers, his understanding, his sympathy . . .[1]

As Lord Coggan comments, the warning proved to be ill-founded as he gave himself increasingly to the work and vision of Dorothy at Burrswood. Never for him the quick visit for a meeting: he would usually stay for three days, listening to the community and patients, befriending them, praying with them, giving them new hope and blessing them. As an extension of his own spiritual care he arranged for Father Geoffrey Curtis of the Community of the Resurrection, Mirfield, to come to Burrswood every two months for a day, in order to be available to the members of the community for spiritual counsel.

A measure of Bishop Cuthbert's commitment was that he not only served for the next nine years during Dorothy's lifetime but for a further seventeen after that, and with greater responsibility then, for he was both Chairman of the Trustees and Bishop Visitor. The doubts as to whether he would continue to be of service to Dorothy and Burrswood after his translation to the busy diocese of Coventry in 1956 were also ill-founded. Once Bishop Cuthbert had set his hand to the plough he would never look back (Luke 9:62). In his message to the Fellowship after his first visit (on the Feast of St. Simon and St. Jude, 28th October, 1954), he wrote:

160

The atmosphere of the house struck me most forcibly – an atmosphere of peace and harmony. It was a privilege to meet people who have experienced wonderful spiritual and physical healing through the work of the Fellowship. The light of God was in their eyes, and their hearts were filled with gratitude. The one supremely glorious thing about Burrswood is that Miss Kerin and her fellow workers believe in the Power of Prayer. They pray expectantly, confidently, and so must we. The Bible does not put forward arguments for the existence of God, the Bible takes for granted the existence of God, and lays claim to His Power, believing that His Power is available for all of those who really trust him. This was true of St. Simon and St. Jude, and it is true today of Miss Kerin and the Burrswood Fellowship.[2]

This was the spiritual foundation Dorothy gave to her building for Christ. Such a "building" was bound to attract notice. People who came were aware of "something different" about Burrswood. As Bishop Cuthbert discerned, the power of prayer was almost tangible and this kept the vision alive and in focus. People could see that Dorothy and her helpers had a purpose in life, fired by their mission from the healing Christ. It is hardly surprising that Burrswood began to attract more patients, and also visitors to its healing services. Spiritual building necessitated more physical building to accommodate the increasing flow of people. The move to Court Lodge in 1955 had undoubtedly helped by releasing several more bedrooms for guests and patients. Accommodation for extra staff had been built in 1952 (The Nest) and 1955 (the two bungalows). But more room was urgently needed, especially if the whole unit was to be brought under one roof. The necessary room would have to be found for the Speldhurst patients and staff. The only answer to the problem and to the fulfilment of the vision was to build. The year 1957 was to initiate a period of continuous building.

Once again Dorothy began by putting first things first. The

chapel of St. Michael was no longer large enough and so a new chapel was constructed on the ground floor at the west end of the house. It had acted as the old schoolroom, but with an extension westwards it enabled the growing numbers to be accommodated at the healing services. It was dedicated to St. Luke, the "beloved physician", on the anniversary of Dorothy's healing, 18th February, 1947. Bishop Cuthbert took Acts 3 as his theme, applying the healing of the lame man to Dorothy's own healing, and uttering a prayer that for many the new chapel would indeed become a "Gate Beautiful".

The dedication service led to a new vision which Dorothy wrote about in the Newsletter a month after the event. She referred to the Bishop's hope that for many the chapel would become a "Gate Beautiful" and then spoke of her vision:

> I refer to this particular sentence for the reason that already, as one peeps through the Gate Beautiful, one sees the ever-increasing goodness of God, stretching out and opening up new fields of service in this, His Ministry of Healing. I humbly believe that God has shown me that another prophecy of our beloved Bishop Loyd is now to materialise. We are to go forth in faith and build a new wing on to Burrswood and so consolidate the work under one roof. It is becoming increasingly difficult, as the work expands and grows, to convey and to administer God's gifts to those He sends to us for help. The fact that we now have three bases inevitably means wastage of strength and time. This God-given strength, I am convinced, must be conserved for the purpose for which He gave it. I believe this new venture of faith to be God's plan which has unfolded in the watches of the night with Him. I ask you all to make a matter of earnest prayer that God's will may be done in this, and that through His grace, we may go forth fearlessly commending the issue to Him.[3]

Speaking to the Chichester Diocesan Conference held at Haywards Heath a year or two later, Dorothy spelt it out in factual terms:

It was revealed to me in a vision that God meant all the work to be united under one roof. The estimate for the new building was £20,000. There was nothing at all for this, but there was the command of God to do it, and I am so sure of that Voice, that, in the face of the whole world, I would have gone forward fearlessly with that plan, because I *knew* in Whom I had believed. And so the work was started and in ten months the building was completed. At no time was any appeal made for funds, because there was no need, and now that house is built and fully occupied.[3]

And that indeed proved to be the case, but only after the concerted prayer of the Fellowship over Whitsunday. The Festival of the Holy Spirit became increasingly significant in the life and ministry of Dorothy and of her staff. It was always approached with great expectancy, which only seems right and fitting, but very special things happened, and this particular Whitsunday had that expectancy. She had written to the Fellowship:

I ask you, therefore, as a Fellowship, to join with me at our Whitsun Communion in prayer that we may be guided and kept in the way of His will concerning all that is done for greater effectiveness of His work at Burrswood, and that as we go forward in faith with the building of the new wing, God will make known His plan for providing all that is needed. He *knows* where the necessary money is to be found, and *I* know that if we do our utmost in offering Him our Love crumbs, He will weld them into a loaf – as He so often has done in the past. So let us go forward in the strength of the Lord, nothing wavering.[4]

The money was forthcoming and the new wing, known as St. Faith, to the east of the main building and adjoining it, was dedicated on 15th February, 1958, by the Bishop of Edinburgh, just a year after Bishop Cuthbert had opened up the vision through the "Gate Beautiful" at the dedication of St. Luke's Chapel.

The new building now made it possible for staff and patients to be under one roof and the following month the move from Speldhurst took place, and Chapel House was closed. In thanking God for the twelve years of loving care that had been offered to all who came to Speldhurst, and for the community life which had been lived out there (for the last ten years without her apart from her regular visits), as well as for the vital bridge it had made between Ealing and Burrswood, Dorothy added:

The move was achieved with unhurried smoothness and skill. Our thanks are due to Miss Modin, Miss Nest, Sister, Nurses and Staff who put all they had into this gigantic undertaking. Speaking for myself, I am thankful that the work that was under three separate roofs is now under two. Very soon, God willing, it will be entirely under one, for God has shown me that I must go back to Burrswood to take, under His guidance, the Captain's wheel, and steer, with His help, that little ship for so long as He wills.[4]

Even when one vision was being fulfilled, another was opening up and its implications began to come into focus. "Always one step ahead." And once when questioned about this by someone who tried to counsel her to have a rest and take breath after one such achievement, she quietly and determinedly said, "While I live, I must build."

Dorothy's present vision was threefold: to lay the foundations of a sound spiritual life and to build on a Christ-centred theology; to build new premises to accommodate the increasing flow of work; and the third part, now that the community was housed under one roof, was to build up the community into a true fellowship of the Holy Spirit. She lost no time in gathering her full staff together to address this matter and share with them her vision for the future:

Beloved Friends, we have met together to look at a picture, a pattern which I believe with every fibre of my being is a

164

pattern that our Lord Himself has made for us, and of which He will unfold to us the design as the days go by, provided we strive faithfully and selflessly to make of ourselves the instruments of His will. It is a wonderful pattern, and for a moment I want to take you back about a year ago when I put before you a plan which I believe our Heavenly Father revealed to me. I told you then that I did not know what the fulfilment of this might involve of sacrifice and hardship, but that what I did know was that without question I was going to follow wherever He called me, and, you remember, I asked you all, "Are you coming?" Without a moment's hesitation, you all answered, "I am coming!"

Now, it is through obedience that that building (St. Faith) has come into being, obedience to the heavenly command. I believe I have said this before. I cannot over-estimate its importance. I believe with all my heart that when our Lord commanded me, a dying girl, to get up and walk, had it not been through the grace of obedience to that heavenly command, nothing would have happened. I want you all to remember this, because obedience is the foundation upon which this work is built. Obedience was the secret of our Lord's triumph. It was not the Cross that was so important, but His implicit obedience to His Father's will. The human side of us does not always want to do God's will. Our Lord did not want to be crucified. He prayed, "If it be Thy will let this cup pass from me; not My will but Thine." That is the most revealing thing for our encouragement.

We are starting on this venture as a fellowship of friends, all dedicated to the service of our Lord. Every one of us in this room has been called to serve Him in this particular work. Without each other, it would be impossible to carry out His work, whether it is sweeping a floor or listening to people's troubles. It is our Lord who has given us each our particular work to do. You will see that as we embark upon this great adventure some wonderful acts of God will take place and I know that we go forward together in faith.

Of course difficulties lie ahead of us, but we can only face these difficulties if we face them as one solid company. If we are going to achieve our Lord's work, we must not ask ourselves how the new regime is going to affect us individually, but how it is going to affect the work, for that alone matters.

I am aware there has been a good deal of conjecture as to what is going to take place. There will be no difference in the policy of this house. Our Lord appointed a captain of this ship, and however unworthy she may be, that captain *was* appointed by our Lord. That captain has been placed by Him on the ship with her hand on the wheel, and so long as she is left there by our Lord, she has no right whatsoever to delegate her responsibility to anyone else.

I know that I can count on your love, your loyalty and your obedience, and so what I ask every one of you to do in the Name of God is to give each other some of the love and forbearance that you give to me. God has given us a wonderful opportunity to renew this venture, and I believe He has asked each of us to love each other. You know the hidden meaning of what I am saying. Harmony, peace and love must rule this family. Of course there will be difficulties, but if we are obedient to God's will, and forbearing to each other, we shall be given the strength to do what God has laid upon us. I do not know whether it will be more difficult for you here, or for those coming from Speldhurst, but I do know they have come to us with heart-whole desire and intention to give God everything they have. Their wonderful love and obedience are such that they send me on the knees of my heart. I know that each and all of you will face every difficulty and trial in the spirit of "How much can I give?" and not "How much can I spare myself!" That applies to me also, but with all your prayers, God may enable me to guide this little ship into safe waters.[5]

This gives an indication of the leadership Dorothy exercised over her community. Whatever else, it was centred in the ascertaining of, and the obedience to, the will of God. This was paramount in her life and thinking. She saw obedience as "the secret of our Lord's triumph", even relegating the Cross into second place after the Lord's total obedience to the Father's will. This was not to denigrate the Cross and all it stood for. It was primary to her life, and our Lady had told her it must come first. But the Cross was the outward symbol and inevitable result of the Lord's unswerving obedience to the divine will. To Dorothy obedience was the first step that always had to be made. The Cross might well follow as it did for Christ and may well do so for his followers. Dorothy knew all about that. But her vision of her Lord was always kept in focus by her unquestioning obedience to His every bidding. It was because her staff and companions saw this level of obedience offered to her Lord so clearly manifested in her life, that they wanted to offer a similar obedience to her as their leader. They discovered that she had the vision to see clearly where she was going because of this obedience and they gladly followed. More than anything else this was the unifying factor which now began to weld into one cohesive whole this community of individuals who had for ten years lived in two separate places. Whether total success was ever achieved in this matter is open to doubt. It was inevitable that there would be some demands for the attention of so charismatic a leader as Dorothy which would be more strident than others. It was also inevitable that the happiest members of the community were those who made no such demands, thereby allowing the edifice to grow under the quiet influence of the Holy Spirit, its builder and maker.

The building of St. Faith's and the uniting of the community under one roof – and Dorothy was not far away down the lane at Court Lodge – began the inauguration of a period of building that was to last for the remainder of her life. The swelling of the family meant that St. Luke's Chapel was not large enough and had to be extended. This time it was extended eastwards which meant the demolishing of the old staircase where the downstairs cloakrooms are now placed, and the building of the elegant circular staircase (a feature of her buildings) out of the main hall. The Russell brothers, the local builders whom Dorothy favoured for all her buildings, were put to their first difficult test and virtually remained on site from this time onwards. They became firm friends and although they never knew when the money would be forthcoming, they trusted Dorothy and became devoted to her and the work she was doing.

This "partnership in building" with the Russell brothers and their men began in 1948. At the first interview, Mr. Ted Russell noted how Dorothy was "a most unusual woman who seemed to know all about work and how to get it done". She had told him, "I want to see you; I do not want to see a foreman", and added, "We should understand each other, I do not want anyone with a bowler hat, I want workers."[6] On his second visit she told him, "Take care of yourself, as I have a lot of work for you to do." This he afterwards learned to be too true and always she would talk to him about the next project while he was still engaged on the last. When he mildly remonstrated about this one day, she replied, "Mr. Russell, God has only given me so long on this earth. I have a lot to do, and not much time in which to do it. I want you to do everything as arranged as quickly as you can."

Mr. Russell constantly noted how she was able to "see" what could be accomplished, always in advance of or despite his professional knowledge. She had wanted some oak panelling for the first chapel and had asked Mr. Russell to go and find some. To his protest, "But where?" She insisted, "You will find some, Mr. Russell, I know you will." He did, exactly the right amount and size, for £75 when the estimate had been £1,000. It was in place within two weeks. Even at that stage she knew the chapel would be too small and was planning another – St. Luke's. Then came the test mentioned above, the circular staircase. The Russell brothers' verdict was short and to the point: "Impossible". She smiled back and said, "Why, I have seen it there. I just will not accept your verdict." By now they knew her well enough to believe that what she had "seen" was true. It fitted perfectly in the place in which she had envisaged it. Mr. Russell commented, "Burrswood was steadily growing during all these building operations. Moving the stairway was just a small item in Miss Kerin's vision of the future."

The Russells' firm was kept busy in 1958. Hardly was the cement dry in St. Faith's, the staircase in place and the chapel extended, when the vision of a new Chapel House began to take place. This was to be the final move in bringing the whole community into one place. The new Chapel House would be home for herself, her children and her immediate staff. Work began in the September of that year, and, as always seemed to be the case, it was ready for dedication on the anniversary of her healing the following February. Once again Bishop Cuthbert did the honours. There is something that speaks of beauty, dignity and a quiet prayerfulness about Chapel House. Again, it has a fine hall and a semi-circular staircase. It is now used as the guest house and for training courses in the Christian healing ministry. The tasteful drawing room is a fine meeting place for the community and a very up-market seminar room for the training courses. It speaks of Edwardian elegance. Downstairs there are three bedrooms, one of which, "Acorn", was Dorothy's private sitting room, another the dining room, while upstairs there are eight bedrooms including the Dorothy Kerin suite, which contains her private oratory where she spent her night and early morning vigils, and also a room that used to be reserved for visiting bishops. Into their new home she and the children, now just grown up, moved in 1959 and Court Lodge was sold.

If Ted Russell was one man who could share her vision with imagination and courage, Frank Hammerton also came at the right time to join the team as head gardener. He also was a man of vision and knowledge, a gardener to his green finger tips. Dorothy always placed great emphasis on the beauty of the gardens as an integral part of the healing process. She had an eye for colour and flowers, as well as for design, that would bring together a therapeutic harmony. Frank Hammerton

169

was just the man who was able to see her vision and translate it into actuality. She adored flowers and knew how fortunate she was to have such a gardener, who could tackle a large kitchen garden as well as the acres of formal gardens. For his part, he told Eve Waterfield what a pleasure it was to work for such a wonderful employer and friend for sixteen years.

It was in this era of building that Dorothy Musgrave Arnold joined the community. A descendant of the poet Matthew Arnold, she had spent twenty years in China, had found Kathleen Burke-Collis in Switzerland and, brought to Christianity by Dorothy, was able to help her when she began her missions overseas. She also became her biographer.

Also in 1957 the Reverend Gordon Kenworthy had become chaplain and "his gaiety of heart, warmth of sympathy and unfailing concern for patients and staff" during his years of devoted service endeared him to all. He was chaplain when the church was built and dedicated and we must now turn to this climax in Dorothy's vision for Burrswood, which she saw as the oak that had come from that small acorn.

The vision of the church was given to Dorothy in her night vigils. She saw it clearly in every detail, so much so that when the plans came along she was able to correct them. In all probability this story is slightly "doctored", but one version went like this. Dorothy came down to breakfast one morning and said, "We are going to build the church now." "But we have no money," was the reply. "Yes, where the rose garden is," said Dorothy. "On our lovely rose garden?" they questioned. "Yes, and the architect is coming at 11 this morning!" Ted Russell in fact related how he was summoned to the rose garden one morning where Dorothy asked him, "How would you like to build a church here?" He was speechless; after a pause he asked "You don't mean *here*?" "Yes," she replied, "on the rose garden. God has said to me I must build a church here. He has told me to start it." His unspoken reaction was that this was far too big a job for his firm, but she read his thoughts. "You have nothing to fear, Mr. Russell. You are part of the Plan. I have seen you build it," she said and then added, "When you require some money, come to me. I have not got the money, but God will provide it. When will you get the turf up?" On his protestations about plans and not being competent to tackle such a big job she gently reassured him, "God will provide you with the knowledge and strength to build this church." His misgivings were allayed. He knew he could and would build the church, and so he did, in co-operation with the architect, Philip Beauchamp, A.R.I.B.A., and helped on chiefly by Dorothy.

In many ways it was a minor miracle in itself. They were given a glorious summer to start it. A quarter of a million bricks were delivered when the building trade was suffering an acute shortage. The builders were never held up for materials and deliveries came at exactly the right time. The money also flowed in regularly so they lacked nothing. And all the time Dorothy took a personal interest in every detail and was always "one step ahead". The workmen marvelled that she always remembered what she had suggested to them on the previous visit without taking notes and came back to discuss the implementation of the details the next time.

Dorothy herself laid the foundation stone on Michaelmas Day in thanksgiving for her healing and then one day she told Mr. Russell she had managed to fix the day for the dedication of the church! It was to be 14th May, 1960, less than eleven months after they had begun the work. As the date drew nearer, the number of doubting Thomases increased, but Dorothy was as calm as ever and knew it could be done. For the last three weeks they worked overtime and Dorothy herself brought out the refreshments every time, offering each man a personal word of encouragement. Ted Russell compared her to Churchill who managed to get the impossible done during the war: "We always considered Miss Kerin as having built it. We did the actual work," he said, "but she was the inspiration, and only Miss Kerin could have got the work done on time." To the undoubted power of her prayer she had also put at their disposal her gracious personality, her

171

untiring interest and her keen perception of the complicated job in hand.[7]

The Church of Christ the Healer was dedicated on the day as arranged by the Bishop of Coventry, assisted by the Bishop of Lewes. Dr. George Thalben Ball brought his choir from the Temple Church in London and played the organ. The chapel was free of any debt; the £30,000 which it cost had been raised. In fact no appeal was ever made for funds, but as people heard of the enterprise, the money was forthcoming. It came from people all over the world, and of every sort, mostly given in thanksgiving for the blessings they had received through Dorothy's prayers or ministry.

From the outside the church has Florentine characteristics with its neat lines and square tower, and Dorothy found most of the late-Renaissance interior furnishings in Florence. As one enters, the feelings of light and prayerfulness dominate and the usual reaction is to be still and silent. The attention is first drawn towards the sanctuary. The altar is of seventeenth-century design and came from the chapel of a princely Italian family. The panels on each side of it are of St. John the Divine and St. Catherine of Siena, probably painted in the workshop of Andrea del Sarto. The eyes are then led upward to an arresting rose window of Venetian glass. Its twelve fluted panes, representing the Apostles, point inwards to the central circle in which is depicted the head of Christ. Dorothy may well have placed it there as a statement that the whole work of healing must find its focus in Christ, and also as a reminder of the early days in Ealing where the rose windows at Chapel House were dear to her heart. It has certainly been the focus for much meditation and contemplative prayer over the years.

Above once again, the shallow barrel ceiling is finished in blue with gold stars, surrounded by a design of oak leaves and acorns, a reminder of her earliest vision. The whole church is indeed a symphony of blue and gold.[8]

The windows on the right, which is actually the north side, the altar being at the west end of the church, are of the four archangels, always part of her life and devotions: Michael, captain of the host who defeats evil; Gabriel, messenger from God of Christ's Incarnation; Uriel, sent to warn Esdras not to meddle with things beyond his reach; and Raphael, who restored to Tobit his sight and is patron of the Church's healing ministry. The windows were given by the family in memory of a patient, Hilda, whose heroic fortitude and shining faith had converted and brought everyone of them into full membership of the Body of Christ. There is also a beautiful Lady Chapel on the south side and a gallery housing the organ, and in Dorothy's day a choir, at the rear. Her memorial window, depicting the healing of Jairus's daughter, was placed on the south side as a thanksgiving for her healing which had several points in common with that of the subject of the window.

Two statues – of our Lord, carved in Oberammergau, and of our Lady – are placed one on each side of the church with stands for votive candles which are continually offered in prayer. The bell, cast by Taylor's of Middlesbrough, which sings out the service times and the Angelus, was the gift of Violet, Lady Ypres in memory of her husband who had died in 1958. Thousands have now answered its summons and will do so for the time to come. After the building of the church, Dorothy told Gladys, "I have lit a light that will never go out. Burrswood will continue for as long as time is." At the time of writing there is an increasing number of people coming from far and near to the four services of healing held each week in Dorothy's church. She had, after all, been under divine obedience to build while she lived. It was the Lord's provision through her for the needs of His people.

There was still more time and she continued to keep Ted Russell occupied. A cottage (The Nest) and two bungalows had previously been built for staff. Now she built a fine stone house for the chaplain (dedicated on 18 February, 1961). In the same year the Haven was built up the hill as the guest house, and also a Swedish log house (Little Sweden) the gift of the people of Sweden in thanksgiving for Dorothy's ministry there. The following year she built St. Luke's, a stone building overlooking one of the ponds, with a characteristically fine hall and semi-circular staircase. It was built for her eventual successor, Dr. Edward Aubert, a like-minded Christian and a physician whom she had met during one of her visits to Guernsey. He was a tower of strength to her in her last year, as Dr. John Elliott had been from the moment she arrived at Burrswood.

Even now the building programme was not quite completed.[9] She had put in motion the building of an extension to the Haven and the reconstruction of the drive. Both were completed after her death. There, was, however, building of another sort still to be done. She had seen that she must build "a city of refuge", a name she once gave to Burrswood. There were still people to whom she must minister and proclaim the power of Christ to heal.

Notes

1. See *Cuthbert Bardsley* by Donald Coggan (Collins, 1989) p. 203. cf. *Dorothy Kerin: Called by Christ to Heal*, by Dorothy Musgrave Arnold (Hodder and Stoughton, 1965) p. 141.
2. Dorothy Musgrave Arnold, op. cit. p. 142.
3. Ibid. p. 150.
4. Ibid. p. 151.
5. Ibid. pp. 152 ff.
6. *The Life of Dorothy Kerin* by Johanna Ernest (Dorothy Kerin Trust, 1983) p. 77.
7. See the account in *Dorothy Musgrave Arnold,* op. cit., Chapter 18.
8. See the description in *My Sister Dorothy Kerin* by Evelyn Waterfield (Mowbray, 1964) Chapter 12.
9. For a composite catalogue of Dorothy's building programme, see Johanna Ernest's *This house named Burrswood* (C.U.P., 1989) pp. 50–57.

16 "GO . . . AND TELL . . ."

With the home base being built and laid on sure spiritual foundations, and with the capable and dedicated staff she had trained, Dorothy was also conscious that her message was to the whole world. In 1957 she had begun accepting invitations to speak to gatherings outside Burrswood, the invitations for the most part coming from the clergy who would also ask her to minister to the sick in their parish. It obviously cost her something to do this for she confessed to a friend that the thought of speaking in public made her feel quite ill. Her addresses were on the face of it very simple, and yet those who heard them testified to them being words of power, spoken by one who not only believed but knew at first hand the "Lord of power and might" of whom she spoke.

In one address she asked,

> Why is it that today, in spite of the enormous advances medical science has made, our hospitals are full, our mental homes full to overflowing, and it is more difficult to get a bed in a hospital than it is to get a seat in a church? The reason is surely that we have failed to obey God's command. We have lost our vision. We have lost faith.[1]

The humble way such words were spoken would come as a strong challenge to a change of heart and subsequent renewal of vision among her hearers, especially the clergy. Now a new challenge to go outside this country "into all the world" was facing her. What was the Lord's will?

175

The word that she needed, and without which she would never initiate any new move, came in a vision she had in January 1959, when there was already enough transpiring on the home front to keep her busy for years to come. She had just taken on a nurse who was not an Anglican and, such were the rigours of those days, she was debarred from Communion. In the vision Dorothy saw a large banqueting hall all prepared for the guests. The guests were ready and waiting and she was among them, but she noticed a number of people at the side who had not been invited, among them the nurse. Then our Lord entered and everyone prostrated themselves in loving adoration. He then went to Dorothy and took her by the hand and placed her next to Him. But Dorothy saw He looked at her with reproach in His eyes. He told her that none of His committed followers should be excluded from His Sacred Feast. His eyes rested on the nurse; Dorothy then went and took her by the hand and brought her to the Table. When she related this to her staff she said she had been shown other things which she could not yet reveal.

It was in the spring of 1959 when Dorothy received her first invitation to visit Sweden. The tour was to be *ecumenical*, centred in Stockholm. She went off in May and spoke to packed churches – Lutheran, Methodist, Congregational, Free Lutheran and Baptist. Marina Chavchavadze and Violet Ypres accompanied her. They recalled how at one Lutheran church which was filled with 1,600 people her words (interpreted by a member of the Salvation Army) were received with an intense silence which grew deeper and deeper. A spiritual experience was given to two people who did not know each other. A white cloud, lit with flecks of fire, descended from the dome into the nave. They both heard a voice within: "I will enter into every heart that is willing to receive me." There were many subsequent testimonies of moral and physical healings from people who attended the service.

Dorothy seemed to be drawn to Sweden and she was

to make two further visits. In all she held healing services and spoke in more than eight major centres including Gothenburg and Uppsala, as well as Stockholm itself, on each occasion. The Swedes are a kind and hospitable nation: they opened their hearts and their homes to Dorothy. The Radio and the Press gave her wide coverage and many, many contacts were made and kept. By the time of her death she had ministered to a large number of grateful people in Sweden who gave the Swedish log house as a thank offering from their nation for her missions.

Her addresses were usually on a similar theme, varying the words and illustrations. Her opening and closing passages always produced the profoundest silences, touching the hearts of her hearers. The following is a typical beginning:

We have all met together tonight with one purpose and desire in our hearts, and that is that we may enjoy the intimacy of our Lord's presence. Let us pray that our hearts and minds may be alert to the sound of His Voice, because unless we can hear the sound of His voice speaking to us, there is no purpose, no point in our being here.[2]

And this was how she ended one of her addresses in Sweden:

Now it is a challenge to every Christian to bring back this gift of our Lord Jesus into the Church for that is its home, that is where it belongs. Our Lord Jesus said: "Preach the gospel, Heal the sick" . . . In England that glorious power has been allowed to atrophy. It has not been used and the enemies of the Lord have stolen the Church's fire. But though this glorious gift has atrophied, it is still a living power.

The need for Christ's healing is so great and, because many people have not been able to find it in the Church, spurious forms of spiritual healing have sprung up in our midst. We know that in many places spiritual healing has come into disrepute. There have been all sorts of abuses

177

and extravagances, but I would humbly suggest that you cannot make a counterfeit coin unless you have a real one to copy from. So let us all . . . who have heard this message from our Lord, go forth with a flaming torch of love and fearlessly proclaim this: the living Christ ever comes to heal and make whole. Thanks be to God.[3]

She was also insistent that people were prepared for the laying on of hands and knew why they were coming for the ministry:

I believe that some of you may be coming to receive the Laying on of hands. In so doing, let us be quite clear that we are obeying our Lord's command, and unless you come with faith believing you are going to touch the hem of His garment, do not come, because Dorothy Kerin has no gift to give you: she is only God's instrument. There is only one Healer, and that is our Lord Jesus Christ who uses human instruments to convey his gift. It is His power, His Living Touch, otherwise it is no use at all.[4]

A final quotation is from an address on her third Swedish visit, given to the clergy and ministers of many denominations, a truly ecumenical gathering, and it underlines her depth of feeling concerning the healing of the churches:

My heart has been so warmed and filled with the warmth of your welcome and obvious love, and the wealth of your prayers. As you know, I belong to the Anglican Communion, but what has impressed me most is the wonderful spirit of brotherhood and unity among all the denominations of Christians here, and this is really what the Holy Spirit has laid upon my heart – this need for man-made barriers to be broken down, and that we may permit the love of God to heal these wounds within His Church. You know much better than I do that Peace can never be in the world until we have peace and unity within the Church of Christ. The breaches in England seem to me

to be much wider than here in Sweden, because at all the
Services I have been privileged to attend, there has been
nothing but love and welcome, and one has been made
so conscious of the family and brotherhood of Christians.
I thank God for this, and that is the message I shall take
back with me to England. We have so much to learn from
you. May we be humble enough to learn it.[5]

After the first Swedish tour, Dorothy had to give her whole
attention to the building of the church and seeing that the
home base was indeed strong enough to stand her longer
absences. The nursing staff needed an anchor person. She
found Johanna Ernest, a fully trained nurse from the private
sector, and a month after the church was dedicated brought
her in, through some persuasive letter writing, as the first
matron. She was later to become bursar and archivist to
the community and still possesses a pastoral eye for those
who need special care. Her appointment left Dorothy more
confident of leaving some very sick patients in the nursing
home so that she could answer calls to take the message of
the healing Christ to other places.

Her further visits to Sweden were again marked by her
total self-giving, especially in interviews and visits between
the services; by packed churches – it was estimated that
20,000 heard her speak in the three visits and that in all
she ministered to 2,000 – and by a lasting response to
her message. At the final service a priest from the State
Lutheran Church had offered up a prayer on behalf of all
the clergy present in which he asked God's forgiveness
for them all for their neglect of His gift of healing. As
for Dorothy, she opened her heart to the Swedes: in an
address to the members of the Burrswood International
Fellowship and Prayer Group in Stockholm, she put into
words how much Sweden meant to her.

First, I want to tell you what you already know, and
that is what an enormous joy and pleasure it is to me

179

to be here with you again. As each year passes that bond of friendship grows stronger and stronger between Burrswood and Sweden. The little seed which our Lord sent me to plant three years ago has now grown into a sturdy plant, a plant which we at Burrswood love very dearly. I have often wondered why Sweden came so quickly and so surely into my heart, when, one morning quite recently, our Lord showed me why. It is because there have been so many wonderful happenings linking the work at Burrswood with Sweden. In the first place, it was a Swedish gentleman, Gotfrid Modin, who made it possible for me to start a house in Kent. It was Swedish money that helped me to educate those orphan children. It was Sweden that gave the first gift towards the building of that Church of Christ the Healer. And now, this group of Fellowship and Prayer in Stockholm is growing and being used mightily by God. It all makes one know there is some great significance in this: it cannot just be an accident that all these things have happened in connection with Sweden, and I believe in my heart that God has a special purpose for Sweden. I humbly believe that in this next year, 1962, we are going to see some mighty works of God. I believe that this little fire of the Spirit which has been lighted by your love and faith will flame into a great bonfire. Let us all pray that we may each one be alert to God's calling of us. We know the time is not far off when the Christ will come again in glory, and this we know is the hope of the salvation of the world.

We had that wonderful gathering last night together, and for my part I felt we were in the Upper Room with our Lord, nothing less. So many people have said they were conscious of His Presence; some heard His Voice, and some felt His Touch. What a wonderful privilege for us all! For my part, how undeserved, and as the work of the Fellowship expands, I am sure our Lord will lay new responsibilities upon us for more prayer, for more sacrifice, more service.

I want to tell you a little tonight about Burrswood, because you are so closely associated with it now – indeed you have all become a part of it. The work has now expanded across the oceans in many directions, and day by day it grows, and our Lord is working mightily within it.

As you know, the Church of Christ the Healer has been built, and is being mightily used and blessed of God. He is sending so many people in need that I think it quite likely that we shall soon have to enlarge the Church, because now at most Services the Church is full to capacity. The Chaplain's new house has been built and blessed, and the Chaplain is safely housed in it. The staff at Burrswood has had to be increased, and our nursing staff now numbers 8 nurses. A number of these nurses are having to be housed in patients' rooms, which of course restricts the work, and our next project must be to build a Nurses' Home, because those who serve the Lord should be comfortably and well housed.

Well, just before I left home to come here, I made the plans with our architect for this Nurses' Home, and I want to try and draw a picture of it. The site where it is going to be built is in a lovely little bit of woodland looking down on Burrswood. In the centre will be the little Swedish log house. It is going to have a shingle roof, and it will be painted in red with little white windows, and on each side there will be 3 more rooms and a bathroom with two little gables. The middle has two floors and the rooms on each side have one floor. In the middle house, there will be a member of the staff and a little sitting room. I thought of calling it "Little Sweden". It must be Swedish; it is the Swedish part of Burrswood. I want Sweden to be the first one to give a gift towards that – I do not care how little, but I want to say "Sweden has done this." Because there is no money for it at the moment, it is an act of faith. Well now, in the Name of the Lord, I hand that over to you – that really was my little secret.

If I were to embark upon telling you all the happenings

181

that have taken place, I should be here for many hours, but I want you to know that there have been some outstanding miracles of healing. There is one more thing to tell you. As soon as we have finished "Little Sweden", we have to build a house for a resident doctor, because there is a lovely Christian man who wishes to give the rest of his life to work for Burrswood. So you see, our Lord is making an enormous demand upon Burrswood. He is manning that ship with wonderful and worthy sailors, and we all count on your prayers. We know we have them, and we long to welcome you all to Burrswood whenever you can come there.

If I went on talking for a week, I could not tell you how dear Sweden is to my heart, and I thank God for your love and prayers, and I think we all have to thank dear Gunhild because she is the one God called to start this work in Sweden.

Between the second and third Swedish visits, Dorothy answered the call of two Swiss ministers to hold a short healing mission in Geneva. The practical, level-headed Swiss, like the Swedes, also took Dorothy to their hearts and again the churches were packed. She made a special point of addressing clergy and doctors in one church, but other people pressed in too, saying that any meeting or service held in church was a public occasion. People came from all over Switzerland, and even from France, to hear her and especially to be ministered to by her at the healing service in the Temple de Montbrillant. She also addressed large international congregations in the English church of the Holy Trinity and the Emmanuel Episcopalian church. One leader commented, "Her luminous presence has made a lasting impression and we would like to know more of her life and work."

The following year, again in the midst of the Swedish visits, she was invited by the French Reformed Church to speak in Paris. It was late May and the chestnut trees were still in bloom in the Champs-Elysées. It was also Whitsuntide. An article described one of the services – in the vast church of the Holy Spirit built by the Empress Eugénie during the second Empire:

Nobody seemed to know where the crowds came from that filled the great Church of the Holy Spirit in the Rue Roquepine . . . A woman was present in our midst . . . of whom above all we remember the tender smile so revealing of her immense love steeped in joy, (who) is neither a "faith" healer nor a pseudo-visionary, nor the follower of some obscure sect. She is a living member of the Anglican church, who was instantaneously healed in her girlhood of an incurable disease by our Lord Jesus Christ, from whom she received a mission to bring back to His Church the exercise of her forgotten ministry of Divine Healing. She underwent many years of preparation and waiting upon God before she exercised her ministry, which she has always refused to do outside the Church, or to limit it to one religious system or group. Without equivocation or ambiguity, she has everywhere proclaimed that the only Healer is our Lord Jesus Christ, the same yesterday, today and forever.

On Sunday, at a Service commemorating the Last Supper, with Pastor Grosjean standing at her side to say the Prayer, she made a moving appeal to the sick present to come with living faith to receive the Laying-on-of-Hands, so that through the Power of the Holy Spirit they might be healed of their physical, mental and spiritual sicknesses. At that Service, when some 250 people came to receive the Laying-on-of-Hands, I knew many would be healed and many were, and I had a vision of the thronging crowds that moved our Lord to compassion. I felt shaken by the unbelievable dryness of our Protestant Services, by their deadness and their inability to reach man in his hidden depths and so touch his life in its reality. In these days of Pentecost, I came to realize that the Church, so

183

faithful in preaching the Word, and in ministering the Sacraments, has deprived herself with inexcusable timidity from exercising the fullness of the Power conferred upon her by Christ, and which she alone can offer to the hungry and shepherdless crowds. This is a question open to lengthy discussion, around which theological arguments can rage furiously, but any such would be meaningless, for they would neither add to nor subtract from the authenticity of the spiritual experience of the hundreds of people who at this Service saw with their own eyes our Lord Jesus Christ manifest astounding miracles in their midst through the channel of His humble servant Dorothy Kerin.[6]

One of the "astounding miracles" referred to in this article concerned a woman who was in the long queue waiting for Dorothy's ministry. A strong urge came upon her to substitute for her own need, that of a friend who was blind, and she decided to receive the ministry on her behalf. Obeying her "prompting" she received the laying on of hands on her friend's behalf. When she visited her the next day to tell her about the service she found her friend had received healing at the exact time she had knelt vicariously for her. Her friend had at that moment experienced a piercing, burning pain shoot through her eyes. Nothing further happened until the morning when she awoke and could see. Her eyesight was at once good enough to thread the finest needle.

After the mission in Paris, a Roman Catholic who had attended the other healing service in the embassy church wrote to Dorothy. His letter illustrates how frequently she was able to impart to people a new vision of life:

I want to thank you for one of the greatest moments in my life. I have always believed living the way you do, walking about in such simplicity and goodness towards all who suffer was the reason for your being on this earth

– and yesterday in the British Church, I knew that LIFE had come through in your person, in front of me. I knew a better life could start in this world, and all my critical and sick mind opened to an illuminating love and understanding. I can never thank you enough for all this, and wished to tell you my love and gratitude for ever.[7]

By far the most demanding mission, because of its sustained length, was to the USA. There were many members of the Fellowship there and one of them organised and oversaw what was to be a tremendously rewarding yet extremely taxing trip. Dorothy sailed in the *Queen Elizabeth* on Michaelmas eve, 1961 and began her mission on the feast of St. Francis (4th October), always two important days in her spiritual calendar. The opening service was in New York's Marble Collegiate Church, in which famous religious leaders of the Old and New Worlds had given their message.

A Dr. Laurence Blackburn introduced Dorothy with these words:

"Ever and anon from the hid battlements of eternity, a trumpet sounds." This striking quotation might be interpreted to say, in terms of the experience we are to have tonight, from time to time there walk among men those who clearly reveal the Power of God and who by their testimony call us to a positive faith.

In almost the same breath, Jesus uttered the promise, "Ye shall receive power," and gave the command, "Ye shall be my witnesses." That promise and that command were not only to that day but also to ours.

Our primary witness is to what we have let God do for us. In a nation and a world surfeited with power, the people cry aloud for the conviction of a God Who is real, Who is near, Who cares. The world will never believe that God can mend our broken world until it sees that God can make whole a person in body, mind and spirit.

THE VISION OF DOROTHY KERIN

The one who comes to us tonight has achieved that power. Her life is a wonderful witness of gratitude in loving action. Great crowds have felt the impact of her spiritual power in Europe and in England.

I have heard her speak. I have visited her beautiful Burrswood. I have witnessed a Service of Divine Healing in her exquisite Church of Christ the Healer. I have felt the upsurge of power as she placed her hands on my head in prayer.

Have you ever seen a miracle? There is one among us tonight – walking, talking, witnessing. She is a living testimony to a living Christ, a gracious gentlewoman of England whom it is a privilege to introduce to America.[8]

From New York, she went on to Philadelphia and Washington, where she held no less than five healing services in St. John's Church (the Church of the President, opposite the White House). In expressing appreciation the clergy said, "The joyous faces of the people coming out after each service told their own story. You will long be remembered for the good work our Lord accomplished through such a precious channel as you are."[9]

From Washington Dorothy and her party travelled south to Richmond and Norfolk, Virginia. At the latter, there seemed to be special blessings, particularly a sweet resonance of the Spirit between Dorothy and the parish priest, whose prayer group had been praying for weeks that "our Lord would mightily use His messenger". Their prayers were answered and after the visit the parish priest wrote an appreciative letter in which he said:

You cannot know except through the Spirit how deeply moved and changed we are by the Power of Jesus through Miss Kerin. He reached so many people. The level at which He reached them was deeper than has ever been done before. The Peace of our Lord still lingers. How many have spoken of His Peace! We are grateful indeed for His mighty servant Dorothy Kerin. Please convey our deep gratitude to her for the powerful Love of Jesus we all experienced.[10]

From Norfolk they had a long drive to Baltimore where Dorothy addressed and ministered to the largest congregation of the tour, including a great many coloured people. The gift of tears among the 450 who received ministry was most in evidence on that evening. After this she moved on to Boston where she addressed the annual gathering of the Order of St. Luke keeping the festival of its patron. This organisation, which exists to promote the Christian healing ministry, is particularly strong in the USA, much more so than in this country. This time she ministered to over 300 people. The following morning she addressed a large gathering of the Boston prayer group, which was then a powerful body of intercessors ministering far beyond the state of Massachusetts. It was in this talk that she announced "God's gift to Burrswood", a brilliant young doctor who had abandoned his lucrative practice according to what he believed to be the call of God to come alongside her as the resident doctor at Burrswood. This was Dr. Edward Aubert, who was to succeed her in leading the community. Her vision for Burrswood was never far from her heart and mind, even when she was the other side of the Atlantic.

From Boston, the party moved on to Providence, after which she was given a welcome few days break in Newport and was able to absorb the beautiful colours of the North American fall. Doubtless this would recall the glorious autumn at Burrswood. Even in the solitude of the Episcopalian Church rest home Miramar on the shores of the Atlantic she was not "safe". She was asked to address forty-five chaplains of the US Navy who for a long time eagerly plied her with questions. After an all too short rest, it was time to return to New York, calling in at two more places on the way to meet and speak with people. The final service was held in the vast church of St. Bartholomew, and although everyone had expressed the hope of a return visit, Dorothy probably knew that it was the last time she would address the American public. She gave all she knew to the address and the ministry, because she felt so keenly, as did others who were there, the Presence of the Lord. Truly, as many commented, "Life will never be the same again." Such is the dynamic about-turn effected by the healing Christ, who mightily used His servant on that tour.

She arrived back in England four weeks to the day after she had landed in the States. She returned on the *Queen Elizabeth*, but even with the break this afforded, she came back physically drained. After all she was now over seventy years of age, and the itinerary and programme she had accomplished would have proved exhausting to many half her age, especially had they been able to minister at her depth and intensity. On all these tours abroad she had given others something of her vision, a vision for their life, which opened to them a new experience. Possibly this is the greatest gift so freely given by the healing Christ to Christians in every generation. Happy are those who are able to encounter such a channel of that new life experience as Dorothy Kerin.

Notes

1. From an address given at St. John's Church, Reading and quoted in *Will You Go Back?* by Ruth Farr (Dorothy Kerin Trust, 1970) p. 78.
2. *Dorothy Kerin: Called by Christ to Heal*, by Dorothy Musgrave Arnold (Hodder and Stoughton, 1965) p. 206.
3. Ruth Farr, op. cit. p. 79.
4. Dorothy Musgrave Arnold, op. cit. pp. 206 ff.
5. Ibid. pp. 207 ff.
6. Ibid. p. 212.
7. Ibid. p. 213.
8. Ibid. pp. 214f.
9. Ibid. p. 216.
10. Ibid. p. 217.

17 THE FINAL VISION

Humanly speaking, to take a year off, would have been a wise and sane decision on her return from the USA. But Dorothy seemed intent on tackling the mountain of work, especially correspondence which took punishing inroads into the night, as though constrained by some inner knowledge. Her tours overseas had been granted unnumbered blessings and will be seen as some of her greatest work. They extended the influence of the healing movement in a deep and lasting way, because she had seen and she knew the power and presence of the living Christ at work in her life. But these tours had sapped her physical energies, and the demands made on her by the mounting queues of people and correspondence meant that she saw less of her staff, who were her great resource at home. They suspected that she was driving herself too hard. Soon after her return she probably began to have heart murmurs. As the next year unfolded, it was known that healing services became a greater strain and that she might well have a heart attack before and/or after the service. She carefully hid this and went on with the work.

Almost immediately after her return, she went straight into the annual thanksgiving service, which for the first time was to be held at St. Paul's Cathedral in London. People came from all quarters of the globe to attend that service and Dorothy sat inconspicuously among her many friends and people she had helped in the congregation. In his welcome the Dean said:

189

BELOVED in Christ, we welcome you to St. Paul's Cathedral. We are met here to give thanks to Almighty God for the revival within our Church of the ministry of healing; in particular for the miraculous healing of Dorothy Kerin nearly fifty years ago, when she was at the point to die; for His employment of her to bring healing to the sick, comfort to the sorrowful and faith to the faithless, in our own and other lands.[1]

More large gatherings followed as her name and her message began to make inroads into a nation hungry for a deep spirituality and more purposeful vision. She spoke at healing services and ministered to people all over the country. She addressed the Methodist Conference, held that year in Manchester's Free Trade Hall, sitting beside Dr. Leslie Weatherhead. Her visit was said to be the highlight of that year's conference. She spoke at Eton College where the boys hung on her every word and gave her an ovation at the end. All that was in the last two months of 1961 after she returned from the USA.

Further visits abroad were projected for 1962 but in the event none of them took place. There was too much to tackle at home. St. Luke's was being built in readiness for Dr. Aubert's occupation. The fact that Dr. John Elliott, who had been her visiting physician from the first, had to ask what was being built down the drive, only goes to show the acute pressure of work under which Dorothy laboured. The house was blessed and ready for occupation in June, and Edward and Deidre Aubert and their family moved in. Dorothy had first met Edward in 1957 when he was the senior partner of a practice on the island of Guernsey.[2] She had immediately "seen" that Edward belonged to her work and at the time had told a friend that he would be her successor. One of his first duties at Burrswood was to warn Dorothy that she could not go on overtaxing her health with impunity. He told her he found it hard to believe it was God's will that she should drive herself to such an extent and begged her to take a day in bed at the first opportunity. But still life went on.

The golden jubilee of Dorothy's healing was celebrated on Sunday, 18th February, at a service of thanksgiving in St. Martin-in-the-Fields. The church was packed to capacity and chairs had to be placed in every possible place in the aisles. It was to be the last time that Dorothy would address the Fellowship whose love and support was given in such ample measure, as was evidenced on that February afternoon. Before the blessing by Bishop Cuthbert, the choir sang Handel's "Let the bright Seraphim", accompanied by the famous trumpeter of the time, David Mason. It was heady music for the 2,000 present and even more appropriate words, since it was Dorothy who had heard the angelic music at her healing just fifty years before:

> Let the bright Seraphim in burning row,
> their loud uplifted trumpets blow.
> Let the Cherubic host, in tuneful choirs,
> touch their immortal harps with golden wires.

In May, she went on a holiday to Italy, much against her own inclination and to please three friends. This was, to say the least, unusual for she never disobeyed a prompting. She did go, but suffered, for most days she had a painful heart attack. She managed to get home and at the insistence of the doctors spent three weeks in bed. She asked for the Anointing and Father Browning administered this Sacrament of healing in her private oratory in the presence of a few friends. As they prayed on after the short service, Dorothy stood and stretched out her arms to the crucifix while her face, which had previously looked drawn, became radiant with light. Her eyes seemed to be fixed on Someone visible to her and not to the others though they knew the room was charged with a "power from above". Dorothy then spoke in a voice that seemed strangely not her own, "He says, 'I will make unto thee a new heart'."[3] Dorothy and the

191

small group of colleagues at first took this to be a promise of complete recovery. Later they realised it was a promise to be fulfilled in the fuller life of the world to come. Her vision had been of the hereafter.

She did recover well enough to carry on life as normal and took a full part in the dedication of St. Luke's, this time by an American friend, Bishop Grey of Connecticut. She congratulated the Russell brothers once again, who "with their usual ability and skill have built a house of grace and beauty which we hope will be a very happy home for our beloved Physician". Once more her standards of nothing but the best for God had been maintained by the building brothers. It still is a very happy home for the "beloved Physician" of today.

There was no lessening of the pace. She actually increased the number of healing services in the week from two to three, adding Sunday afternoon to Thursday morning and Saturday afternoon, a programme which is still maintained. The mission to the USA was in fact postponed from their side, to Dorothy's regret, although it was probably providential. A new interest occupied the summer; she found a new "Ark" or retreat, in Gladys's cottage at Fairlight, which proved to be a God-given and restful haven. She planned to write another book there in the spring of 1963. The first chapter would relate the vision of the Acorn.[4]

In early December she gathered together the Bishops of Rochester (David Say), Coventry (Cuthbert Bardsley) and Tonbridge (Russell White) and invited them to be trustees of a Burrswood Trust when it was formed, and they agreed. She had been pressed before now to do this but her reply had always been, "I have received no guidance in the matter." There still seemed to be delays and questions and the answer was always the same. But surely this *was* the answer, the very positive answer. No guidance, no decision. It was as it had always been. Obviously she was not meant to tie up the estate in a neat and rational way. Her successors were to have the freedom to develop the work as they were led.

192

It would continue as it had begun, in total obedience to the Lord's bidding. "Where God guides, God provides" was her dictum, and she knew full well he would not provide for an unguided ship. It was a handing over of her obedience to the person on whom the mantle would fall in each generation.

She bought and wrapped her Christmas presents as usual, a mammoth undertaking in her case, though sadly only Francis, the eldest of her children, was to be at home that Christmas. The last present was laid by the Christmas tree and she went to her room to prepare for Midnight Mass. On the way down she paused at the bottom of the stairs and said with a sob, "I can't go on". She turned to go back to her room, fell half way up and could not move. Her two faithful doctors carried her to her room, where she insisted that all should go to the Midnight Mass apart from Kathleen, whom she asked to stay. She never left her room again.

As the snows descended for that record winter early in 1963, Dorothy had frequent heart attacks and endured prolonged pain. Never once did she complain and always longed to be able to say with a smile, "It's better now", in order to reassure her staff. Bishop Cuthbert came on 22nd January for the night and gave her and the whole staff Communion in her oratory the next morning, the last time they would be together around an earthly altar. Her staff maintained all-night vigils of prayer in the church. Everything that modern medicine could do was being done. The body was worn out, but the vision was still there. As she was talking to Edward Aubert "about the present and the future",[5] she fell forward and breathed her last. She had told him that she *saw* Burrswood continuing. In recent years she had told Gladys, "As long as time is, Burrswood will go on. I have lit a torch that will never go out." History has so far vindicated her vision, and whatever else is destroyed, the message of her life will inspire more visions in the centuries to come.

Notes

1. *Dorothy Kerin: Called by Christ to Heal* by Dorothy Musgrave Arnold (Hodder and Stoughton, 1965) p. 221.
2. It was here also that she found Frank Drake. At her instigation he built the miniature Church of Christ the Healer there.
3. Dorothy Musgrave Arnold, op. cit. p.224.
4. Ibid. Chapter 4.
5. Ibid. p. 229, from Dr Aubert's statement to the community the same afternoon.

Part IV

Her Legacy

A new vision for the Church and Medicine

18   THE NEED FOR VISION

Generally a vision is regarded as an ecstatic experience in which new knowledge or insight is revealed through something that is seen. Such visions were the particular experience of the Old Testament prophets, among whom Ezekiel would seem to have developed a heightened capacity for visionary experience. All refer to what was given them to proclaim in terms of vision at the beginning of their writings. It was the one factor that gave them credibility in the eyes of the people, something for which the people looked in their leaders, and without it they knew themselves to be distanced from God. As the writer of Proverbs put it, "Where there is no vision, the people perish" (29:18).

All the prophets also knew that they had to respond to such visions with obedience, and stories such as that of Balaam (Num. 22, cf. 23:12–26) were timely warnings of what disobedience would bring in its train. For the perfect response to a vision in terms of obedience, we have to wait for the revelation of the New Testament – in Mary's vision of Gabriel. The insight given to Mary of God's plan of salvation needed her *fiat* in terms of perfect obedience. Only when such a response is given to a vision can its fruit be productive.

Dorothy had been given such grace throughout her life that she was able to respond in whole-hearted obedience to the divine bidding. This was the secret of her life. In a letter dated 18th May, 1958, to James Davidson Ross, when he had asked about her years of preparation, she wrote:

197

In visions and dreams He revealed to me many things in His pattern for the future. As these plans unfolded and have continued to unfold through my life, I humbly and thankfully affirm that *I never* consciously disobeyed Him. All that He has asked me to do in faith for Him has been done through His power, thanks be to God. That which was once faith has now become knowledge and I know of a truth that where God guides, God provides; and never in any instance has work embarked upon through what I believed to be His command, failed to come to fruition . . . the cruse of oil has never failed and the barrel of wheat never wasted.[1]

This was the secret of the fruitfulness of her visions. She listened, she saw, she obeyed. This was how the Lord's will was fulfilled in her. And because her obedience to the visions and words she received from Him was so manifest, others took notice of the company she had kept, of the command she had obeyed and frequently of the cost of obeying that command. Like the people in the days of the early Church, who noted that the Apostles had been with Jesus because of the radiance that shone out from them, so those who met Dorothy knew her as one who had been in the Lord's company, as one who had seen. What was this quality of life that shone out from God's servants in the early days of the Church? If we can find an answer to that question we may well ascertain the secret of Dorothy's vision.

The main qualification of an Apostle was to have seen the risen Lord (1 Cor. 9:1). He was essentially a witness to the resurrection of Jesus. In the earliest tradition of the gospels, we learn that Jesus himself made preparations so that He was seen after His Resurrection by the disciples; furthermore, that He was seen by them in Galilee, in the environment where they could not possibly mistake Him and which would recall to them the days of their first beginnings in His service. It was essential that they saw *Him*, in the glory and power of His risen life, an experience given to the chosen three as a foretaste on the mount of the Transfiguration. Such an experience was not to be shared with others until after the Resurrection at His express orders. After that, it must be told to the world that they had seen him alive after his Passion.

. This emphasis on seeing with regard to the person of the risen Christ was very much part of the primitive tradition of the early Church. The tradition surrounding the Empty Tomb came later. The first tradition concerning the person of our Lord was the earlier one and even crept into the text of the later traditions, as in the Matthean account where the angels say to the women, "He has risen from the dead and is going ahead of you into Galilee. There you will see Him" (28:7). This is the message they are to give the disciples; the disciples must *see* Him risen. In fact the whole matter receives confirmation and emphasis when Jesus Himself meets them on their way and repeats the angelic injunction – "there they will see me" (28:10). It is the sight or vision of the risen Christ and all that follows that renders them such dynamic people who influence others. From the moment of the vision they have an inner compulsion to witness. They are to be witnesses of the Resurrection (Acts 1:8, 22): that is the essential content of the witness for it is the Resurrection that has changed their lives and will change the lives of others. They had seen the risen Christ and that was the experience that would turn the world upside down (Acts 17:6), just as it had radically changed their lives. It was St. Paul who above all counted the experience of seeing the risen Christ as life-changing. His claim to be an Apostle rested on his having seen the risen Christ in front of the Damascus gates. He had further visions also: the reminiscence at 2 Cor. 12:2 ff. is probably autobiographical. At the end of his life, and this was the supreme statement which made his visions so fruitful, he was able to claim in his defence before Agrippa that he had never been disobedient to the heavenly vision (Acts 26:19). It is the act of obedience to the vision that invests it with such power and influence over the lives of others. It is the fact that God has spoken and that

199

He has been obeyed that together makes the life-changing experience. It is all God-given and it is all God's power because it is the Holy Spirit, the author and giver of life – Resurrection life – who gives the grace to see, to obey, to proclaim and to be a son or daughter of the Resurrection. It is His gift alone which effects the change in us, as the disciples experienced on that feast of Pentecost. The gift is either accepted or refused. St. Paul was able to say he had always been able to accept it. It was the energy that came from this positive response to God's grace that empowered him tirelessly to proclaim the gospel, travel, suffer, write, counsel, heal, give of himself completely, and behind it all, to which his obedience was but the response, was the vision of Christ risen.

This was also the secret of Dorothy's life and ministry, and of her amazing influence on the lives of thousands. It seemed impossible to encounter her and remain the same person. An interview with her, often not more than ten minutes duration, was a life-changing event, marked frequently by physical or mental healing, and invariably by comfort, new faith and a new view of life. The burden brought to her was left behind. The vision and the response of obedience was of such power and energy in her own life that it affected the lives of all with whom she came in contact. It is this infectiousness that is one of the characteristics of the saints. Because they have seen holy things, they are able to open and widen the vision of others.

Frank Drake, who later became chaplain at Burrswood, wrote of his son's remarkable "healing" in death in *Thy Son Liveth*, to which reference has already been made. In his intimate dealings with Dorothy concerning his son's illness, he acutely observed her motivation and wrote an extended account of what he found, which is worth quoting for our present purpose:

Dorothy is Irish, middle-aged and essentially feminine in all her ways. She is not tall. She is not plump. She is round, and compact and adorable. She is full of laughter. She practically never smiles, because the moment she begins to smile joy overcomes her and the smile develops into a laugh; not a deep-throated laugh, as men and women laugh who are amused, but a little explosion of happiness. No word that I know will do for Dorothy's laughter. Our ordinary words . . . laugh, chuckle, giggle . . . express amusement, humour, embarrassment, sometimes even scorn. We want here a word which will express above all a rippling of joy; and not mere human joy either, but the unmixed delight of young angels whose home is in Heaven and can think of little else. For Dorothy has much of the angel about her, is eternally youthful, and half of her, the half you cannot see, has actually, as we believe, been to Heaven and met Our Lord there. Not an exuberant or noisy laugh, for that might contain something of self, but the joyful outward expression of a deep inward tenderness. Dorothy's laugh never stays with her. It romps gently across the room to where you are sitting and wraps you round. You cannot picture Dorothy without understanding this, for her laughter is a vividly personal thing, one of the great gifts which God has given her as a means to carry the Peace and Reassurance with which her own soul is filled.

Extremely pretty, I am sure, in girlhood and full of beauty in middle age, her face lights up into an intense loveliness when her heart is stirred by sympathy or joy or other deep emotion. Full of peace, it is yet the face of a woman vitally alive, capable, intelligent; smooth and unlined, for the years of deep suffering, both physical and mental, which she has endured, have never been allowed to express themselves in resentment or bitterness, even in the remote fastnesses of her mind. She has a lovely skin, very pale, of a colour and texture most rare. Her eyes, which to me are hazel, are deeply expressive of the love and tenderness which fill her soul. Her mode of dress is simple and charming, but never striking or distinctive, for

201

she does not dress to please herself, or indeed any human being. She seems to possess few clothes. She wears no jewelry. She has no mannerisms. Her hands are quiet and still. She never gesticulates as most women do.

Broadly speaking, Dorothy has three interests only: Her Master, the people whom He sends to her, and their needs. She is an intensely active person. Up early, to bed late; she cooks, gardens, tidies, plans and orders as an immensely efficient chatelaine should, whenever the need or the opportunity arises. These things she does because it is the will of her Master, or the need of her children, her patients or her staff. She does not read the newspapers, listen to the wireless, watch television, knit or even chat save on those occasions when by so doing she can serve a purpose for her Master. She is never idle. She eats little, sleeps a few hours only. She has strength for whatever comes, and remains throughout intensely human. Scores of people depend upon her. Her two chief occupations are prayer, and the ministration of her outstanding gift for bringing help to the sick, the suffering and the distressed.

Dorothy receives constant guidance from Our Lord. And I believe that frequently in the silent hours of the night, when at last she is alone, she visits Heavenly places. Complementary to the prayerful attitude of the mind is the permanent desire to obey. Adoration of Her Lord and obedience to His wishes make up the sum of her life. As with St. Paul, so with her, "To live is Christ."

Just as one who had recently climbed Everest would speak with calm assurance about the conditions he found on Everest, so Dorothy speaks with calm assurance and certainty about the ways of Heaven and earth, at least in so far as her experience goes. This experience, immensely limited no doubt in comparison with the saints who have passed through the Veil, is yet immeasurably greater than that of the average person. She speaks of what she has actually seen and heard. For the rest, all who have received her help will remember the distant look in her eyes, the rapt expression of her face, which so often show that she is turning, for immediate guidance, to Heaven.

Those who know her realise that this small saint, so perpetually joyful, so perpetually occupied with ministering to the sick, running a great house, and travelling to different parts of England, invariably manages to spend many hours out of the twenty-four in prayer. What few realise is that, side by side with all this, she has a vast and aweful capacity for suffering, far beyond the power of ordinary people even to imagine, and that this suffering, arising directly out of the sins and sufferings of those whom she would help, descends upon her not infrequently. Happily, to those who are called to share a little part of His suffering, Our Lord Himself grants, we believe, the strength to bear it.

Many people have been cured of sickness, often of "incurable" sickness, through the prayers and ministrations of Dorothy Kerin. But she never, never, I am sure, primarily brings them healing. She brings them Christ. This then is her priceless and immeasurable gift, that Christ Himself, no less, honours her presence, accompanies her into the life of the patient, and, when it is for the best, heals them physically. That is her secret. She brings them Christ.[2]

"She brings them Christ", and that is the secret indeed. Her first-hand vision of Him and her immediate response of obedience are the powerful combination of spiritual energy that united to forward the Kingdom of God on earth. There is need for the vision: that is paramount, and more and more channels able to receive such a vision are the insistent need of today. But there is also the need for that obedient response, for men and women able to say with St. Paul, "I was not disobedient to the vision from heaven" (Acts 26:29). Dorothy learned to accept the grace of obedience especially during the years of preparation under Dr. Langford-James. In that same letter to James Davidson Ross she wrote, "During those years of waiting and preparation the thing

I thank God most for is the fact that, by his Grace, I was helped to discover the great secret of obedience. This secret I believed to be the foundation of the supernatural life, without which we cannot abide in God's will." After those years of discipline it became second nature. The life-changing partnership of vision and obedience was the essence of Dorothy's spiritual life, so powerful in its effect on others that they also were led to a new vision for their lives.

Notes

1. Quoted in his book *Dorothy* (Hodder and Stoughton, 1958).
2. From *Thy Son Liveth* (Hodder and Stoughton, 1959) pp. 50–6.

19 "HEAL THE SICK"

O MOST MERCIFUL,
  hear my prayer for grace
  to be a good workman in thy kingdom;
and when thou hearest,
      forgive.

Work in me of thy good pleasure
  both to will and to do thy work,
  the work thou willest, when thou willest,
      as thou willest;
– thine own incessant work
  of truth, sympathy, healing, joy;
work that speaks, none knows how, nor I,
  the tongue of heaven;
      and reveals thyself.

Thou, O God, art in love with all thy work;
  it flows, it pours, out of thy heart.
In the bounty of thy grace
  make me, O Father, an instrument of it;
the thought be thine, the word thine, the deed
  thine,
      the glory all thine:
enough for me
  the obedience. Amen.

Eric Milner-White[1]

From her earliest years we have seen how Dorothy
was given a special empathy with the sick. Her own

suffering intensified it. It was a natural reaction to their suffering to intercede for them and this she did continuously, even throughout her own times of acute suffering. She saw it as the work of God and in that regard prayed to be "a good workman" in His kingdom; and this she duly became, for she continually resonated with her Lord's "own incessant work" of intercession. Her own call to "heal the sick" was well grounded and prepared for when it came.

Dorothy's great gift was to discern the divine in people, and therefore she was able to see their potential, indeed to see them as they could be if they allowed the divine part in them to come out of its prison and have full play. With her piercing eyes, used to seeing heavenly things, she would search with her total attention for the Christ within. When she said to Gladys Modin's relation after such a search for several minutes, "You need loving", she saw how the embers of the divine could be fanned into a living flame once again. She would have agreed with Jung who wrote,

Among all my patients in the second half of life, there has not been one whose problem in the last resort was not that of finding a religious outlook on life. It is safe to say that every one of them fell ill because he had lost that which the living religions of every age have given their followers, and none of them has been really healed who did not regain his religious outlook.[2]

For Dorothy "the living religion" was Christianity and she sought Christ in all her patients, so that their "outlook" would be with His eyes. As we learned from Frank Drake in the last chapter, "That is her secret: she brings them Christ". We could add, "She also brings Christ out of them".

Part of the therapy, therefore, was to surround her patients with beauty in order to encourage the divine spark in them to ignite. We have seen how she lived in the belief

206

that nothing but the best was good enough for God. She saw that the gardens of her homes were sheer beauty and a privilege to behold. Similarly, the furnishings of the rooms had to be tasteful, of good material and matching colours, warm in tone. If one of God's children was to come to stay in one of her rooms, it had to be prepared to perfection. One day she accepted a patient for immediate treatment. The room was being decorated after previous occupancy and her staff had to hurry the proceedings. In the end there was only time to do a rushed job on the curtain pelmet. Dorothy came in to inspect and her unerring eye fixed on the offending cobble in the pelmet. Slowly she said to the housekeeper, "I wonder if our Lady would have approved of that." It was taken down at once and hung properly. The glory must all be God's: enough for her, and her staff, was the obedience. Beauty was one of God's attributes and had to be reflected in the environment of her patients. That is why she adored flowers and saw that they were fresh and colourful in every room.

This healing environment is one of the great legacies she has bequeathed to her Burrswood, where the beauty of the place, both inside the house and church and outside in the gardens, still receives emphatic priority. It is good to be there. This was the therapeutic atmosphere Dorothy sought to create so that the embers, sometimes near to dying, of a person's soul could be awakened and brought back to life, fanned by the beauty of the place as well as by the caring, devotion and prayer of herself and her staff.

All these things Dorothy saw as essential factors in carrying out her commission to "Heal the sick". They needed tender loving care in abundance, but that care had to be offered in an environment of beauty that would evoke the life of the Creator of beauty within them. It was all conducive to the regaining of their "religious outlook on life" and so made them receptive to the spiritual treatment and life of prayer which were the essential therapeutic agents Dorothy was so well equipped to offer.

A study of her "A Little Way of Prayer" reveals her method

in this regard. It is frequently read out at the healing services in the Church of Christ the Healer.

A Little Way of Prayer
Let us by an act of the will place ourselves in the presence of our Divine Lord, and with an act of faith ask that He will empty us of self and of all desire save that His Most Blessed Will may be done, and that it may illumine our hearts and minds. We can then gather together ourselves and all those for whom our prayers have been asked, and hold all silently up to Him, making no special request – neither asking nor beseeching – but just resting, with them, in Him, desiring nothing but that Our Lord may be glorified in all.

In this most simple way of approach He does make known His Most Blessed Will for us. "For so He giveth Himself to His beloved in quietness."

The first step in intercession was to *realise* the divine presence, to be aware of the Lord's power present to heal. The second step was a *kenosis*, a self-emptying, both of the self that obtrudes and of desires that atrophy our concentration; and by this act of faith only one desire was to be allowed to remain – the doing of the Father's will, praying that in all things "Thy will be done". His will, and His will only is to be the light of our hearts and minds. Third, there is to be *a gathering together*, of ourselves (this is usually a corporate act) and of those for whom we have a particular burden of prayer; it is the time of concentration, when all distractions have been put aside and God is all-pervading. And then the fourth act is to *enter the silence and lift all those for whom we intercede up to Christ,* leaving them before the throne of grace, in His eternal silence; making no specific petition, "neither asking nor beseeching", but "resting". This is the climax of the prayer – "*resting, with them, in Him*". Here is the high point of intercession, resting in Him, with the people on our heart. And finally, the one desire in this transfiguring moment is "*that our Lord may be glorified in all*"; that His glory may shine in them and from them to others. Such is the essence of healing and wholeness, a manifestation of the glory of Christ the Healer. It is in this kind of silent offering of intercession that the Lord's will is made known and that He comes among us "in quietness", according to His promise "where two or three come together in my name, there am I with them" (Matt. 18:20).

David Flagg, the present chaplain of Burrswood, calls this idea and concept behind the prayer a "resting" theology and sees it as one of Dorothy's legacies to the healing work of the Church. Many churches today, including the Church of Christ the Healer, have an altar book in which the names of the sick are placed and regularly "prayed over", perhaps at a healing service. This is not an escape from the real work of prayer, but is rather a letting go, allowing God to be God, not trying to manipulate him into our pre-arranged movements but rather letting his perfect will be done. This is central to Dorothy's theology and to the present practice and philosophy of Burrswood. She knew Christ's work to be accomplished in the sense of His cry from the cross, "It is finished." He has completed His work: we only have to rest in it. And we have to be patient with Christ. We have to "wait for the Lord" (Psalm 27:14), or in Coverdale's fine translation, "O tarry thou the Lord's leisure" (v. 16). This beautiful phrase is incorporated into the final thanksgiving of the Burrswood healing service which Dorothy wrote and compiled.[3]

This contemplative approach to healing prayer, resting in the Lord and seeking only His will, was indeed one of Dorothy's legacies to the praying church. The perfect trust that shows itself in the assurance, "for so He giveth Himself to His beloved in quietness", is a welcome antidote to some of the frenetic praying that is sometimes heard in churches and house groups today. It speaks more of the majesty of God than our own desires, and the quiet searching for the will of God and the trusting of that will is very near to the heart of true prayer. It is this prayer of desire for God to "be glorified in all" that is central to all healing prayer. And it is by the offering of this true prayer that the Church can fulfil its *raison d'être* and so make its contribution to the healing of people and nations.

From this depth of prayer, which is the essential factor in a ministry of healing to the sick, sprang a great desire for the healing together in one ministry of the Church and Medicine. We have seen how Dorothy took the decision to register Chapel House, Ealing, as a nursing home and the sponsorship she had from senior men in the medical profession as well as in the Church. This act set a pattern and a method of working from then onwards. It laid the foundation for the Burrswood of today and the unique interworking in equal partnership which occurs there. Dorothy did not allow either side to be dominant to the detriment of the other. She trusted and relied on her nurses and listened to them. She expected them to listen to her. Constantly they were amazed at her correct diagnosis. It is only when there is a true partnership in this way that the patient can receive full therapy. The Church's contribution is to minister the gifts of the Spirit, without which no one is entirely whole. Medicine has its own role of ministry to mind and body which, it is hoped, will bring about *mens sana in corpore sano*. But that is not the ultimate equation. There must be an interlocking of the two so that the spiritual insights inform the treatment of the body, just as the treatment of the body and a caring and understanding medical team lift the spirit. The Christian ministers should have a medical sensitivity and the doctors a priestly consciousness so that there can be a perfect healing of the therapists to enable a better healing of the patient.

It was such a humility with authority that Dorothy exercised with her doctors and nurses and she expected them to have the same humility, commitment and dedication. Anyone who has worked in such a team will not want to go back to the old ways of departmentalism and standing on professional dignity. The mutual support in prayer during the combined and separate ministering to the patient brings blessings to

210

all the team, of which the patient is a member, as we shall see later on. This kind of cohesion and working together in partnership could be the source of a new vision for Church and Medicine. Little wonder William Temple, in founding the Churches' Council for Health and Healing to encourage this partnership, said that it was a tragedy the work of the two had ever been separated. Like Dorothy he would have agreed that just as it would be folly for a priest or lay Christian to fight disease without medical expertise or help, so it is like tying one arm behind one's back to fight disease without the armoury of faith and prayer. These facts have to be faced if there is to be serious discussion about partnership.

Dr. John Elliott was at the time the only doctor to volunteer his services to Burrswood and he served the work there devotedly for forty years. Speaking on the twenty-fifth anniversary of the start of Dorothy's work on the 25th October, 1955, he had this to say:

> I feel very proud, but diffident, in getting up to say a few words from the medical point of view on this wonderful day. It is a very great honour to be associated in even the must humble capacity with this work. I must frankly state that when Miss Kerin asked me to help her in this work seven years ago I knew nothing about it. That is an important point to remember. I talked to her for a short while, and immediately I had an overwhelming desire to help in any way I could. From that time onwards it has been a wholly thrilling and tremendous experience. If I have been able to help in even a small way in alleviating pain and suffering, I have learned from Miss Kerin and from what this place means to be more tolerant in my outlook, to believe more in medicine in the widest sense, and to realise the significance of Miss Kerin's great doctrine that medicine and religion go hand in hand.
>
> In a recent talk on divine healing one or two points were mentioned which should be considered from the medical viewpoint. One was, "Don't you think that the healing

211

which took place could have occurred in the natural course of the disease; that it would have happened anyway?" I have a medical and scientific mind; I also have a degree in psychology, and I have applied all that knowledge dispassionately. I have the strongest conviction that healing in some form or another does happen invariably. The benefits are not always immediately obvious; it may take some time before they do become apparent. In some cases which have come through here we have become a little disheartened that they have not made the apparent improvement that was hoped, but the happy thing is that months or years later we have received messages to say that the person was helped, and helped primarily through Miss Kerin's ministrations.

If I were speaking purely as a doctor, various events which have taken place here would compel me to say that some influence other than medicine has helped the patient. *We* know what the influence is; but the basic fact is that the patient improved – and what more could anybody desire?

Does hysteria and emotionalism play a big part in this sort of work? Emphatically, no. From the psychological point of view, we can state that mental illness is just as important as physical illness. Miss Kerin, by her unique gifts of sympathy, love and understanding, is able to reduce the nervous tension and get the patient to think of something other than self. In this way, the happy state is produced where the patient can receive, through Miss Kerin acting as a channel, the help which nobody on this earth can give. That is the furthest thing away from hysteria and emotionalism you can think of.

There have been one or two cases where, clinically, I have found that the patient has had a fracture. I have ordered the ambulance to take the patient to hospital; I have rung up specialists fifty miles away to come and see the patient. And then something – we know what – has happened. When the specialist has arrived at the hospital we have found his services are not required. Some people may say there was no X-ray evidence of a fracture. More often than not we have had no time for an X-ray. In the old days, the clinical acumen of the good old-fashioned G.P. was never doubted, so why should it be today?

Another very fascinating and exciting case was that of a young boy who came down by ambulance from a London hospital with a letter stating that he would die within a few days. He was being given massive doses of morphia to relieve his pain. Miss Kerin spent hours and hours with him; and a few days after he arrived, about four-thirty one morning, his mother, who was staying at a nearby hotel, woke up with a start and thought she heard her son calling. At the same time, in an entirely different place, Miss Kerin had the strongest conviction that the boy had been touched. In a third place I was awake, and I felt that something had happened to that boy. Next morning I went to the nursing home. I went up to the boy, and he said that he had woken up at four-thirty that morning and all his pain had gone. He was radiantly happy. On examination there was no doubt that his pain had gone, and although he was dreadfully ill, he was very, very markedly better than any medicine or any other form of treatment could have made him. That afternoon he sat out in his chair for the first time; four weeks later he was able to go home to his own people. I do not know what you would call that other than divine healing.

It is wonderful to be able to work with Miss Kerin in this atmosphere, knowing that any medical treatment which it may be possible to give will have its maximum effect because the patient is receiving that help through Miss Kerin.[4]

It was to this first part of her call Dorothy gave herself unremittingly and with real devotion. No adverse conditions of weather would prevent her travelling the length of the country for just one sick person. Peggy Simpson's brief account of this ministry is instructive:

To visit the sick and those in need, Dorothy travelled the length and breadth of the country. At first we made very early starts on long journeys, but eventually found that travelling through the night was more convenient, as Dorothy could sleep and rest in the car, and arrive, when possible, in time to go to early Mass in some church nearby and then have breakfast. Then she would make her visit and perhaps have a short rest and we would start our homeward journey, doing this in easy stages.

We have watched the dawn come up over Dartmoor in company with wild ponies. We have crept through thick fog, snow, over icy roads and through floods, but have been rewarded countless number of times with glorious scenery, and above all with the joy and happiness and peace which Dorothy took to each patient and which showed so visibly in their faces. On these journeys Dorothy always had her time of prayer before we reached our destination, and on over-night journeys she kept always to her early morning prayer hour, when we would drive in silence broken only by her when she had finished. To Dorothy it was unthinkable that anything or any journey should break in upon this sacred hour.

The longest journey we had was to Edinburgh some years ago where Dorothy was to visit a sick woman. This was in early December. The weather reports for the north of England were bad and the papers were full of stories of people buried in the snow, and ambulances working at full pressure rescuing people from cars. Miss Friend read them to Dorothy and did her best to prevent the journey, but Dorothy, knowing the dire need of her patient, was determined to go. Finally we left after evensong on a Sunday, taking Lady Ypres with us. It was an uneventful journey to Grantham, where we ran into freezing fog which was dense over the Yorkshire moors, but we followed the rear lights of a lorry until daylight. Even so, it was difficult right to the Scottish border where it turned to heavy rain all the way to Edinburgh, which we reached finally at

214

11.20 a.m., and pulled up at our destination on the dot some ten minutes later. The sick woman ministered to, greatly cheered and comforted by Dorothy's presence at her bedside, we had early lunch, a rest and then down to Princes Street for tea, and off home again at 5.30 p.m. We encountered the same kind of weather on the return journey, arriving at 8 a.m. at Baldock where even Dorothy enjoyed a breakfast of bacon and eggs! She then found the energy to shop on the way through London! It was a memorable journey, not because of the big mileage but because it made me realise how sustained I had been by Dorothy's prayers, and the giving to me of strength for what was necessary.[5]

Dorothy had great gifts which she used in her commission to "Heal the sick". There is no doubt that people felt better after being in her company, even for a short interview. Nor is there any doubt about the complete dedication she showed in her intercession for her patients and the long hours she spent with them. It was literally her life's work. Also, as we have seen, she worked in partnership with her medical team who at once sensed that her house was a special place because, as she used to say, "the Lord walks these corridors". In all this she offered a new vision for such a partnership to Church and Medicine. She would also be the first to say that there is only One who heals the sick and we act as His channels. The secret of all ministry to the sick was for her the bounty of Christ the Healer.

It seems fitting to close this chapter with two extracts from letters her patients wrote to her:

Last Saturday I had the pleasure of attending the Healing Service in your Church. I was most moved and impressed by the beauty of the Church as well as the wonderful atmosphere of peace and tranquillity. In no other Church have I ever felt that JESUS was so near to us, and I received not only a wonderful blessing but healing as well. When you

215

laid your hands upon me I felt a new strength come into me. For a year I have suffered from a heart condition and have been unable to walk very far. The Sunday after my visit to you I walked to the bus and went to church, and did not get any pain. When my Doctor visited me on Wednesday he said there was a vast improvement. I was overjoyed. I know now that I will in time get completely well.

I feel I must write to tell you about Audrey. Following her operation, she got a pulmonary embolus which gave her very great pain. She was whisked back into hospital again, and was told that she would have to have three weeks' complete bed rest. Last Thursday, I came over to Burrswood to receive the Laying-on-of-Hands especially for her. I wrote to tell her about this, giving her the time of the Service – "Hospital dinner" is usually at 11.45 – but by a series of different happenings, she was left undisturbed between 11.0 and 1.0. She had ten hours' normal sleep without drugs and woke up on Friday morning with no pain. The Doctor when he did his rounds examined her thoroughly and said she was perfectly fit and could go home.[6]

Notes

1. Eric Milner-White, *My God, My Glory* (SPCK, 1954), p. 111.
2. Carl Jung, *Modern Man in Search of a Soul*, p. 229.
3. It is helpful with regard to the subject of this chapter to study the balanced theology of her service, still used at Burrswood, which can be found in Appendix C.
4. *Dorothy: A Portrait*, James Davidson Ross (Hodder and Stoughton, 1958) pp. 113–16.
5. Dorothy Musgrave Arnold, *Dorothy Kerin: Called by Christ to Heal*, pp. 194–5.
6. Ibid. pp. 180 and 178.

20 "COMFORT THE SORROWING: GIVE FAITH TO THE FAITHLESS"

> By the bruising of my whole life,
>   strengthen me with sympathy for every
>   wounded soul,
> and let my prayers be a balm for
>   the wounds of thy children,
>   that they may be healed,
>   O Lord, my God. Amen.
>
> *Dorothy Kerin*

We live in a fallen world and the joys of life will always be mingled with sin, suffering and sorrow. Dorothy prayed that her own experience, having offered it all to Christ, would make her alert in sympathy "for every wounded soul", and that her very prayers would equally be the healing balm to bind up the wounds of God's children. It is a fine prayer and it came out of a life so dedicated.

The sorrowing as well as the sick sought her out in their thousands. Many, many tragic cases were brought to her. Some, like the boy in the last chapter, had a happy outcome. Others did not. She stayed with people in their grief and they stayed with her while the tragedies of their lives were healed or at least lessened. Like us all she had her own experiences of grief. She had deeply felt the death of her mother, with whom she was totally attuned. They were extremely close and had an intuitive relationship. They both had an irrepressible sense of fun and love of music.

Her mother shared her spiritual experiences with Dorothy, especially towards the end when she completely recovered from blindness and deafness after a heart attack, during which she underwent the life/death experience. Dorothy later told this to Marina Chavchavadze who related the story thus:

Mum told her that she had been to a most beautiful place, where there were trees, water, the scent of flowers, and where the whole of nature was filled with light and inexpressible beauty. The atmosphere was alive with a joy such as she had never experienced before. "And then," she said, "I saw Him coming towards me, and there were others with Him. He told me you were very dear to Him, and He would always take care of you. Our Blessed Lord also said you were not coming yet. He made that very clear, and He added that He was very pleased . . ."

Dorothy did not repeat the concluding words, but the context was obvious. She had wept as she had listened to this message from the Kingdom for which she yearned: her heart was divided between the joy of it, and the sorrow of all it implied about her mother. Thus it followed that a month later Mum became critically ill once more, and this time Dorothy went down with a temperature of 103°.

Jummie (Sister Friend) nursed them both, with only me to help her, dividing her time between the two invalids as best she could. Then, on December 13th, in the early hours of the morning, as Jummie and I were watching over Mum, Dorothy suddenly came into the room, hardly able to walk, and collapsed into a chair beside her. Hastily we wrapped a blanket around her and bolstered her up with pillows, and then we sat and waited, praying for the approaching end.

Mum lay very still, her hand in Dorothy's, and I could see the outline of both their faces in the shaded light, both so withdrawn and yet at one, in that moment of separation. I became conscious of the stillness that lay about us as a

218

cloak of peace, and the room was filled with an invisible Reality, impossible to describe. This peace and its activity deepened with our silence; only occasionally, Dorothy's gentle voice could be heard murmuring a prayer, and then the silence would flow through us on its progress towards eternity.

I wondered how Dorothy would know whether Mum was still with us or not, but shortly I heard her say: "Into Thy Hands, O Lord, I commend her spirit." As she spoke, Mum gave a little sigh, and bowed her head in a movement of assent. She had fallen asleep.[1]

With this kind of personal experience, especially having been so close to her mother, she was able to be in sympathy with, and impart her strength to, the many who were in the grip of sadness and sorrow. She herself had experienced her Saviour's love in the sadnesses of life. She knew Him to be especially near at such times.

One of her matrons was particularly impressed with Dorothy's ministry to such people. She spoke of how Dorothy only entered a sick room if asked to do so and called herself "only a little piece of pipeline". She was moved by this humble phrase which she called a dynamic statement, because in fact "her step across the threshold was a transforming moment". She went on to give two examples of her ministry to sorrowing people:

Dorothy sat by the bedside of a depressed woman. The sad face was covered with unsightly abrasions. Between them lay a jigsaw puzzle. The patient saw a broken piece of wood. Dorothy saw a broken life. One hand moved wood. One heart moved in prayer. The puzzle was completed. The face was healed.

"Behold, I make all things new"
"No one can take this sorrow from my heart," sobbed a heart-broken Mother. Here was a story of human error

ending in tragedy beyond recall. The Faith and mental discipline needed to surmount the memory was not known to this woman. She sobbed for ten days.

Bowed with grief she met Dorothy. Within a matter of minutes an upright, composed old lady left Dorothy's study. Dorothy had looked on her and loved her. In the Greater Love, the memory of the tragedy burnt up.[2]

Letters were received in growing numbers from grateful patients and it is obvious from a reading of them how people's spirits were lifted by a visit to Burrswood, an interview with Dorothy or their attendance at a healing service. A grateful wife wrote:

> My husband and I were deeply grateful to you for telling me to come to Burrswood; having been there for over a week, we want to thank you even more (a hundredfold more) for your goodness in arranging it. This is indeed a Home of Healing – an abode of peace and joy. My experience hitherto having been chiefly of mental homes, I had no idea there was anything remotely like Burrswood.[3]

Another wrote of the elimination of her personal sadness:

> I write to tell you what help and comfort you have brought to us. Everything seems to have come right in my mind, and I think all the fear, worry and sadness have quite gone.[4]

It seemed that so many were given a new vision for their lives and the strength to go on again. Yet another patient, expressing her gratitude for "the love and caring of all your Burrswood band" wrote of how her stay had been "so rich in a new vision of life".[5]

It is at this point that the undoubted comfort imparted through her ministry merges into the giving of a new faith, a new strength, indeed "a new vision of life". When the person is led to Christ and given an experience of His presence and power, the gift of faith is an inevitable consequence. When the Lord Jesus meets people "in the way" as He met His early disciples, particularly after the Resurrection, the bonus of such a meeting is that faith is given or restored. When the people experienced the power manifested in His healing miracles they believed. This is why the Christian healing ministry is such a vital, if still to be recognised, tool of evangelism. Without it, to evangelise is a formidable if not impossible task. It is like trying to raise money without first moving the heart of people. The media can teach us some lessons in this exercise. It is when men and women see Jesus at work in all His healing power that their hearts will be warmed and that faith will be kindled. This was why Dorothy's threefold call was in fact one. It was Christ's ministry to the sick at her hands that constantly led to the comforting of the sorrowing and the giving of faith to the faithless. The following letter is not untypical:

> Life can never be the same. It was my experience of Burrswood, the most wonderful thing that has ever happened to me. I am so very happy about your wonderful work. It was something I thought I would never live to see, although I have dreamt of it. Will you please give my sincerest thanks to everyone, including the doctor and the nurses, for all the wonderful help they gave me. And what of your dear self? All I can say is that you have brought me nearer to our Lord than I have ever been. The only way I can really thank you is to assure you I shall now hold you and your work up to God in very sympathetic prayer.[6]

One of the seemingly incessant afflictions which attack people is fear. It may well be responsible for much of the sickness around today. Fear indeed has torment (1 John 4:18) and it can knock the immune system for six. It is therefore interesting to note how many of the letters

221

Dorothy received were on the theme of replacing fear with faith. One man wrote:

> I am the man who, with my wife, attended your wonderful Service for the first time yesterday. I feel that you would like to know that the Power which was vouchsafed through you is already at work. The *fear* which has nagged at me for years has gone, and this morning, for the first time for years, I attended two Services without difficulty of breathing. I know where my thanks must be given, but I am deeply grateful to you for being the channel, and also for your kindness in giving me a twenty-five minute interview before the Service.[7]

Another expressed his gratitude in this way:

> It was such a joy to meet you and talk to you yesterday, and I loved every moment of the Healing Service. The feeling of fear and tension about which I talked to you left me very soon after the Service started. I shall always remember the feeling of heat that came through your hands on my head at the altar-rail.[8]

In addition to the personal ministry or a visit to Burrswood, people received blessings at Dorothy's hands in other ways. Prayer was, of course, the main weapon in her armoury and many wrote to testify of its effectiveness and its miraculous results:

> Will you please tell Dorothy that the little boy who was born without any gall bladder or bile ducts, and of whom it was said by doctors and surgeons at the Gt. Ormond Street Hospital, and by doctors and surgeons here (Portugal), he could not possibly live, and for whom we asked Dorothy's prayers for God's healing, has just come back from a visit to London with his mother for a check-up, and these brilliant doctors and surgeons are all absolutely mystified

over the child's condition! They say he can now be treated as any normal child and that there is no reason why he should not live to any age, and they add they simply do not understand what is happening inside him![9]

It was a fact that distance was no obstacle in this regard, as again the following letter shows:

I am so glad to be able to tell you that my Mother has made a wonderful – in fact what seems to us a miraculous – recovery. Even the specialist told me that her recovery did not tie up with her symptoms, so convinced was he that she had cancer of the liver. No words of mine can express to you the heartfelt thankfulness for your prayers for her because I am sure they turned the tide for her. She was a dying woman when I arrived in New Zealand and my sister had been told by the doctors that her days were numbered.[10]

There was also another way in which her ministry was exercised and that was through her writings. Dr. George Searle, F.R.S., a former university lecturer in experimental physics and Fellow of Peterhouse, Cambridge, gave his witness in *Fulfilling*, where he related how he had been suffering from nervous trouble on and off for thirteen years. Then he chanced upon *The Living Touch* in a Cambridge bookshop in November 1914. He read it several times and as a result the old weakness left him and he was able to continue his work as university lecturer until the age of eighty. He wrote of his experience in *Fulfilling* at the age of eighty-seven. He became a great friend of Dorothy's and referred to her book as "the dynamite" which had given him new life. When he stayed at Burrswood he marvelled at the stamina Dorothy was given to cope with the incessant round of interviews and ministrations.

From the Visitors' Book and in other ways I realised anew something of the range of her appeal. Of many nationalities and of many faiths, people have come from many countries at all times of day or night, seeking help for their bodies, or, more importantly, for their souls . . . Time has shown that as her need is, so is her strength . . . when I saw her, she let out a great secret by saying, "What a lovely thing it is to feel that you have come to the end of all your strength."[11]

This great friendship and Dr. Searle's health both flourished because he found her book. When he died, an old, battered and well-thumbed copy was found in his pocket. It was his constant companion as a kindler of new faith. And he was not the only one. Hundreds have received "ministry" through her writings, finding the story of her healing to be an experience that has inspired new visions.

Dr. Searle mentioned that people of other faiths were drawn to her for help and ministry. This was especially true of Jewish people. Gladys Modin gave an account of such a ministry to sorrowing parents:

Jews were strangely drawn to Dorothy's spirituality. There seemed to be some affinity between the practising Jew and his Old Testament spirituality and her deep Catholicity. They listened and respected her and her faith. At Chapel House, Speldhurst, Dorothy brought us one day a couple of Jews, a husband and wife, whose little boy was doomed to die quite young – some rare disease common to Jewish parents in certain circumstances about which I know no more. This couple had already lost one little girl about four or five years and they had been warned they must not try to have another child; but they did, and their little boy, at about the same age, was brought to us to see him through the inevitable end. He was the most beautiful and perfect boy one can possibly imagine, and Dorothy and I used to look at him and think how the little boy Jesus must have resembled him. It was tragic to watch the end drawing near. I never heard any conversation

between Dorothy and his father but I carried out my
instructions that he should be treated in every way as one
of our Christian patients, and this with the father's consent
but not with the mother's. One day the father came to me
in deep distress and said, "I want him baptised before it
is too late. Please arrange for this at once." Quietly and
quickly this was done and little Francis was baptised by
our Chaplain and in the presence of Dorothy and of the
boy's father but not his mother, and very soon after he
died and was buried in our churchyard as a Christian.
The sequel to this story is that not long after I heard from
the father that he had himself become a Christian and
been baptised into the Roman Catholic church but still
his wife remained obdurate. Once again they ignored the
warning and had another child, another little girl, but she
also died at a very young age. After that I lost touch with
them, except to learn that he had become a wholehearted
Christian.

One can only pray that the marriage was reconciled in some
way in due course, but it illustrates the breadth of Dorothy's
ministry.
For this ministry, one has to be a good listener and
certainly Dorothy was that. She always listened to the end
of the story and, in the words of James Davidson Ross, who
spoke from personal experience,

when we have finished speaking, then softly, gently, she
begins her work of comfort and healing. With economy
of words, that we might understand more clearly what she
means, she tells us that nothing is impossible to God; that
we must take this trouble to Him and ask that His will be
done in it and for it . . . under her guidance and prayers we
start looking in a different direction – away from ourselves
and towards God. She shows us that our religion is not a
special part of our lives, however sincere it may be, but
is a rich, living power which can take the sting out of the

most terrible situation. We go along to the Chapel with her and listen as she prays about us and our trouble, speaking, as only Dorothy seems able to speak, to the Master she knows is always there ever waiting to help those who come to Him. Almost without realising it our burden starts to lift. We begin to understand that nothing, no matter how dreadful, can harm us if we bring it squarely before God. In the presence of a love which knows no bounds we feel love rising within us, and a longing to say: "Thy will be done" – and to mean it. Quietly, with her whole mind and spirit a channel for the outporing of God's love, Dorothy leads us on, and our "tragedy", as we had once thought it, is one day resolved.[12]

There was one other part contained in her commission to heal the sick, comfort the sorrowing and give faith to the faithless; it was that she would encounter many rebuffs. These she knew in full measure, mostly at the hands of people, both those whom she knew well and also those who had never set eyes on her. It is never easy for anyone to encounter a saint of God. Anger wells up as the feeling of insufficiency to match such a life comes into awareness. So does the feeling of power over such a humble soul. The power of evil is seldom absent when sheer goodness is around. All these factors and more, sometimes of her own making – she could be difficult to live with and she did show she was human by making mistakes – combined to make life far from easy and she did as a result meet with many rebuffs. The secret of her life was how and where she took them: in prayer, straight to the throne of grace. She was then given grace to leave them there so that her Lord was able to effect the healing.

It may be appropriate to end these two chapters (19 and 20) with a prayer, as they both began. It was how Dorothy frequently used to end her interviews:

May the eyes of Jesus behold you,
May the lips of Jesus speak to you,
May the ears of Jesus be open to your prayers,
May the hands of Jesus bless and heal you,
May the feet of Jesus guide you,
And may the heart of Jesus pour forth His great
  love upon you,
and hide you, and keep you in peace and safety,
  now and evermore. Amen.[13]

Notes

1. Dorothy Musgrave Arnold, *Dorothy Kerin: Called by Christ to Heal* (Hodder and Stoughton, 1965) p. 115.
2. Ibid. p. 183.
3. Ibid. p. 175.
4. Ibid. p. 176.
5. Ibid. p. 175.
6. Ibid. pp. 174–5.
7. Ibid. pp. 175–6.
8. Ibid. p. 176.
9. Ibid. p. 181.
10. Ibid. p. 179.
11. Dorothy Kerin, *Fulfilling* (Hodder and Stoughton, 1952), see pp. 18–21.
12. J. Davidson Ross, *Dorothy: A Portrait* (Hodder and Stoughton, 1958) pp. 19–21.
13. Ibid. p. 62.

21   BURRSWOOD: CHURCH AND MEDICINE AT WORK TOGETHER

Doctor Edward Aubert, as her immediate successor, led the Burrswood community through a difficult time after Dorothy's death. There was the inevitable vacuum left after the departure of a charismatic founder. There was also the financial uncertainty until the estate was settled. It was hard to maintain the standards amidst the need for stringency. But the community under his leadership weathered the storm.

The medical side of the work was getting stronger. Doctor John Elliott continued to give his unstinted support as physician and Trustee, while Doctor Aubert himself was able to give both medical and spiritual help to all who came. He now had Maria Preston as the senior member of the nursing staff, Johanna Ernest transferring to bursar. Maria had been trained at the Middlesex and served as an Army nurse in the war. She had come five months before Dorothy's death and nursed her in her last illness, having been attracted to this ministry by Dorothy whom she had met on a previous visit. She was to continue with this responsibility throughout Dr. Aubert's time and has played many responsible roles ever since, quietly witnessing with her colleagues to this day, to the vision that grasped them all through Dorothy and her Burrswood, and interpreting it to each generation.

A community is always enriched by its senior members who enable and encourage growth. At Burrswood it is essentially a growth into Christ. As in the rose window in the Church, *He* remains at the centre. Doctor Aubert saw

228

in the senior members the community's greatest treasure. He was another St. Laurence who, when asked to produce his church's treasures, paraded the congregation before his inquisitors. He saw they had all been grasped by Dorothy's vision and that was the cohesive energy at the centre of their dedicated and tireless work. They had caught her spirit of obedience.

It was Doctor Aubert's intention that the acorn should be tended with that same obedience; he constantly held before the community and wider fellowship the call of Dorothy to heal the sick, to bring comfort to the sorrowing and to give faith to the faithless. He thus steered Burrswood on the same course charted by its founder. As a doctor of deep Christian commitment, his emphasis was naturally on the first two parts of the commission he inherited. As the years went on he was slightly concerned that the bringing of faith to the faithless was not receiving the priority it should have at Burrswood. He felt it should expand on the teaching side "to meet the needs of the young". The teaching was to receive emphasis under Primrose Cooper when joint seminars for theological and medical students were hosted by the community. The present director, Dr. Gareth Tuckwell, has now fleshed out the hope expressed by Dr. Aubert, in a concentration on forming a community in which young people may come and experience a Christian way of life, through serving the needs of others in the Christian healing ministry.[1]

The community and its facilities today are larger than they have been previously. The nursing home (St. Michael's and St. Faith's) has thirty-one beds. The guest house (Chapel House) can accommodate thirteen. There is a therapy swimming pool, an activity centre and a playgroup. The most recent addition, incorporating a lift to the church, a new staircase, a chaplain's room and more bedrooms, also houses a most comprehensive bookshop for the healing ministry and Christian spirituality. At the centre of the whole life of the community stands the Church of Christ the Healer. With the increasing number of visitors, especially to the healing services, the whole undertaking needs a large staff, efficient organisation and an annual budget of over a million pounds. There are in fact over one hundred staff on the payroll, nearly a third of whom live on the campus as the residential community. In addition there are a hundred volunteers. Two doctors, two chaplains, a matron, a sacristan, a housekeeper, an estates manager and head gardener all live on the campus, in addition to others of the house and nursing staffs. The registered nursing home is fully staffed day and night. The staff is integrated through daily staff prayers, a system of prayer partners which is varied regularly, and the Sunday Eucharist. There is also a Community Council and other gatherings of community members, including an annual quiet week, when the staff is given space to listen and to be. All who come to Burrswood are welcomed in a positive and loving way and yet are given space to be themselves. The same standards of beauty in the house and gardens which Dorothy set at the first are maintained. It is obvious that people are helped from a stay in the place: they love it and seldom want to leave. To be soaked in loveliness of all kinds is a therapy in itself and the morning and evening stillness gives a peace that enters the soul. It is not unknown for people to be healed in soul, sometimes in mind or body, purely by being there.

The wholistic care offered to patients is a testimony to the standard of integration achieved by the various disciplines. The care team consists of doctors, chaplains, matron and nursing staff, physiotherapist, counsellor and always, where possible, the patient. Prayerfully each morning and immediately after staff prayers, each patient's case is discussed, with reference back to the patient before decisions are taken. Special needs are met by special prayer groups in the community as well as by medical skill and ministry from the chaplain. There follows a meeting with the admissions secretary and very great care is taken in ensuring a balanced intake of patients. Usually not more than four of any particular category are admitted at any one time. Most categories are taken, including the dying, after prayerfully considering the doctor's referral letter and the patient's own letter of application. All are considered for admission, the less well off and those who are unable to pay are helped by a large bursary fund for which a major appeal is under way. Many come through referrals from the major hospitals. The average stay is for two weeks, longer if necessary, and the bed occupancy over 75 per cent.

Miracles continue to happen alongside great suffering and one of Dorothy's great legacies was to hold these two experiences in creative tension. Marina Chavchavadze recalls Dorothy emerging from a room in which a young patient was dying of a particularly painful disease and saying, "Why? Why?" That she was so stunned by this, the person whose hands were used by God to heal, helped her senior nursing sister. The same contrasts exist today. In recent times there have been occasions when the cases of acute suffering were so severe that the whole community had to be called to prayer, partly to sustain the medical and nursing staff. On the other hand, a male patient was admitted after surgery for recurrent cancer, who had no faith. After a few days he said to the doctor, "This place is different". After his questions were answered, he was given one of the gospels. A few days later he asked for another. He then talked with one of the staff and said he had only been baptised and that he would now like to make a commitment for himself. He was confirmed in his room and so came to a living faith. He went home and nothing more was heard. Six months later he returned under his own steam, nearly wrung the director's hand off and told him he had been pronounced fit and well by his doctor.

These are occasions for great thanksgiving, but so are the beautiful and positive deaths people die, and the remarkable healings received on the way, with the family and within themselves. One of the blessings for them is that they are cared for by a Christian staff who can help them on the journey and are available to talk to them, and especially listen to them, at any time of day or night. The maintaining of this balanced care and the holding of the miraculous with the ongoing suffering in a creative tension is handed down from the founder through each generation. The present chaplain sees it as a contribution to the whole theology of the healing movement today.

Theology and medical practice are always developing and evolving. Each has given and proven premises, but each needs to move on and interpret present situations. It is exciting when they move together, and the contemporary world with its uncertainties and sufferings is a veritable crucible within which to forge a combined stance on many pressing issues. In this spirit, it is the present policy of Burrswood to meet the challenge of the new decade; it is of particular importance that the healing movement should play its vital role in the decade of evangelism. The director has given much prayer and study to future policy and strategy, and the present author is grateful to him for sharing what he has already prayed through and planned with his team. It is a bold and adventurous way of renewing the vision for the twenty-first century.

The importance of community is underlined from the first. The realisation that for a community to grow there should be a greater dependence on God for corporate and individual needs carries with it the implications of deeper worship and fellowship with each other in the Lord. It also demands a constant caring for the spiritual welfare of its members and an extension of their theological education. The demand for a greater stillness and more space for contemplative prayer will also have to be met if the community is to maintain its loving and faithful ministry to all who come, for it is even now a good experience to be there, as it was in Dorothy's day. The quality of love is paramount; for a community to be strong and effective in its mission, that quality of love offered to those outside has to be at full stretch in the internal relationships, for living in a community is to

232

live in "a place of pain, growth and struggle". Christians living in community most especially must have the mind of Christ. They have to demonstrate by their lives that they are "a letter from Christ . . . written not with ink but with the Spirit of the living God, not on tablets of stone but on tablets of human hearts" (2 Cor. 3:3).

All this and more is necessary to be alongside the one who is sick in order to "pray the person into new being". The person has to be aware of an integrated community of loving care surrounding them in their sickness, just as the community has to realise that each member is making a vital contribution to that caring and should have "an awareness that all work done to the glory of God is of equal importance". This ensures that the home is a safe place where there is space both physically and in people's lives for the Holy Spirit to be heard and to move "setting the captives free", offering the weak the opportunity to soar or to run, but above all to walk (Isa. 40:31). Again there is need for space, both for patient and members of the community, since both need to listen to each other and especially to the Lord. This is greatly assisted by the beauty of the surroundings. The gardening and maintenance teams know full well that these are integral to the wholistic care and healing offered to all who come. Burrswood and places like it are oases in the desert of modern life where people can come to be refreshed and restored. Again Dorothy saw her foundation as "a city of refuge" in the context of the end time. Many in church and political leadership, as well as those working "against the odds", need to find such a refuge, such an oasis, as Burrswood can and does provide. More and more "lights in the darkness", "cities set on a hill", will be needed.

Dr. Gareth Tuckwell has a vision for Burrswood as "a glorious bonfire – if you will – an eternal fire glowing on earth with the love of God, to bring His love, His power and His truth to a disbelieving world". He has sat down to count the cost – in financial but also in spiritual terms. There is a realisation in the community that "a house divided against itself cannot stand". They are careful about feeding dissension and know the importance of forgiveness and reconciliation that goes deep and is tackled sooner rather than later. His hope is that "every day should become a celebration of the Spirit of love", though he is also realistic about Burrswood always being "a place of pain as well as of joy and healing".

This will not be achieved without personal cost if spiritual progress is to be made. Dorothy was very direct with her staff and so kept good relationships. There is a need, too frequently bypassed in favour of sloppiness, "to care enough to comfort" (David Augsburger), to speak the truth in love and so lay firm foundations for a relationship. In terms of policy also, if the weakest have the greatest say, a weakened policy will result. A community has to have a good vision of the hindrances in its way towards progress in order to see through them to the distant scene. It is the intention of the present leadership to follow Dorothy in never losing sight of the ultimate vision – to promote the Kingdom of God by bringing healing to the sick, comfort to the sorrowing and faith to the faithless. In doing this, they are determined to ensure that the less well-off will also be enabled to come and be cared for, that Jesus may still stretch out his healing hands to the poor and needy. And such is their determination that this should happen that they are prayerfully seeking guidance about the abandonment of pay structures related to those of the world, moving instead towards a new dependence on one another.

One of the specialist ministries of Burrswood is the care of the dying. There are close connections with the hospice movement enabling the maintenance of updated skills, medically, in nursing and pastorally. There is a real desire to help people "to die well and to be released to go on their journey as they enter the gate and goal of life". The community is the first to realise that the benefits and blessings are not all one way. "The community is enlarged and given the courage

234

to go on through the ministry it receives from the dying."
This is of supreme importance and something that should
be heard by all professionals in Medicine and the churches.
It is essential for the corporate health of humankind that
eternal issues should not be lost in the rush and tumble of
the daily routine. Where they have been lost, humankind has
not only been impoverished but has also become unhealthy
and diminished. The dying are a very precious part of the
life of any community.

What of Burrswood's contribution to the life of the Church
and Medicine today? Dorothy said she had kindled a light
that would never go out. Burrswood will remain true to its
vision while it seeks to be that light in every changing and
evolving situation. It is supremely a place to which people
may come for Christian wholistic care and healing, an oasis
in the desert of life. It may well be increasingly important
that members of the caring professions – from Medicine and
the Church and the other healing professions – should come
to "tarry the Lord's leisure" in that place. They will make
their contribution: they will certainly receive. It could give
those who make the pilgrimage a new vision for their own
particular part of God's vineyard, indeed for their own life.
Burrswood is a resource that will be needed increasingly.
There are also other "acorns" that have been planted and
are offering like resources to those out in the regions, and
to one of these we must now turn.

Note

1. I am grateful to Dr. Gareth Tuckwell for sharing his vision for
   Burrswood and for his consequent contribution to this chapter.
   The quotations on pp. 233 ff. are from the notes he made available
   to me. Enquiries about the work and ministry offered at Burrswood
   may be addressed to him, The Director, Burrswood, Groombridge,
   Nr Tunbridge Wells, Kent, TN3 9PY.

22   THE ACORN CHRISTIAN HEALING TRUST: RESOURCE FOR THE CHURCH AND MEDICINE

One of the lasting influences on Dorothy's life was her childhood vision of the acorn. It will be recalled how the Lord came to her with an acorn in His hand, saying, "Tend this with obedience, and I will water it with the dew of my love, and one day you shall behold a mighty oak".[1] We have seen how the obedience theme has been woven at every point into the tapestry of her life. When she recounted this experience she prayed that as the Church of Christ the Healer "extends its branches and drops it acorns", there would be others who would gather up the acorns and tend them with like obedience. So would her Lord water them and have them as plantings in his Kingdom.

The Acorn Christian Healing Trust (A.C.H.T.) has gathered up one of these acorns. All who are now committed to its vision know that same strong call to obedience, not without cost, and yet are continually refreshed with the dew of the Master's love. My wife, Anne, and I were given the vision of a Church and nation renewed in the service of Christ the Healer. The vision was fanned into flame during a sabbatical partly spent at Burrswood, fed by listening walks in the beauty of Ashdown Forest, with its extensive views of the Sussex Downs, and regular visits for contemplative prayer to the Church of Christ the Healer. The former gave the vision immensity and long-sightedness; the latter gave it focus, as the circular east window, with the head of Christ

236

in the centre, became the icon. The response could only be obedience.

Anne and I returned from Burrswood to our home in York, knowing what we had to do: the step of obedience and faith was to resign my episcopal see. It would be a wrench to leave York and its people after twenty-five years in the diocese. Mercifully we had a sympathetic chief in Archbishop Stuart Blanch of York who also "knew", because he too had been listening. The work was to be adviser on healing to the Archbishops of Canterbury and York.

Once the commitment had been made, there seemed to be a vast company of people whose hearts God had touched, which is testimony alone to the prayerfulness of the healing movement in the churches. The Archbishops had with true discernment taken the tide on the full. Four Trustees of deep Christian commitment offered their services: Frank Baker, a trustee of Burrswood, who was to be chairman for the first five years; Charles Longbottom, one-time M.P. for York, now a businessman, who is the present chairman; Raymond Hylton, a Roman Catholic peer with a national healing ministry of prayer; and Peta Baker, a Christian writer-to-be.

A.C.H.T. was formed in order to give the necessary financial, as well as the prayerful and practical, support to our ministry and to build up the infrastructure for the Archbishops' Adviser's office. From the first it was committed to investing its funds in people and not in buildings. Additional finance meant additional staff, who have incarnated the generosity of God's bounty. The home diocese of York showed itself to be a truly loving family, not least in its Archbishop, who master-minded the whole operation; gifts of prayer and money and love flowed and still continue to flow. The new diocese of Bath and Wells, especially its bishop, John Bickersteth, gathered us into our new home while the gift of encouragement came from all parts of the British Isles as the constant round of travelling, which was to last for five years, got under way. It was a time of overwork

237

and tremendous blessing. Gradually contacts were made and the vision shared throughout the home country and Ireland. For the time being we were led to offer an obedience to work only among our island race and invitations to go abroad were declined. There was this clear call to concentrate and focus the work here so that the acorn would be strongly planted and its growth nurtured and not dissipated. Others would develop the immensity and long-sightedness of the vision once they had been schooled in its demand of obedience. As for Dorothy, the acorn was first a symbol of obedience, before the growth which would follow.

One of the major objectives for the fulfilment of the vision was the healing of the healing professions, particularly a reconciliation between the work of the Church and Medicine. This had been part of Dorothy's vision; it had also been part of William Temple's for the rebuilding of the nation's spiritual life after the Second World War. Two avenues of advance had been borne in upon us as part of our vision. The first was that there had to be in our society a living experience of the professions working together as at Burrswood. The other, that there was a great dearth of listening, not only in us, but in the life of the Church and Medicine: we did not make sufficient time for God and for each other.

The Acorn Apostolate

With regard to the first avenue, it seemed that the example of Jesus in sending out the disciples in pairs – which led to him naming them Apostles, the Greek equivalent to the Latin word missionary – was given to his Church with good reason, especially as the disciples were so unlike each other that they were bound to complement each other's gifts! If there could be pairs of Christians today with a commitment to prayer and Christian healing, and one of them had had a medical training, then they could act as a sign of the healing Christ in their locality and of the partnership of the Church and Medicine. This would involve the taking of initiatives – in the interface between Church and Medicine, in seeing that teaching on the Church's healing ministry was being given in the local churches, in encouraging the formation of clergy/doctor and other caring professional groups, in forming groups of Christians who would undertake a commitment of prayer for the sick and undergird the healing ministry of their local churches. There would be the minimum of rules, but one commitment would be to say regularly the Acorn prayer, which was adapted from Acts 4:29 f:

> Lord, look upon this work;
> Grant to your servants to speak your
>   word with all boldness,
> While you stretch out your hand to heal,
> and signs and wonders are performed
> through the name of your holy servant Jesus.
> Amen.

It would also be a priority to attend the annual conference which was the essential way of keeping together and cross-fertilising the visions, ideas and initiatives of the members. In fact, as the numbers grew each year, more organisation was needed. Regionalisation took place into eight groupings throughout the country. The conferences which had been south of the Thames were moved to a permanent venue at the All Saints Pastoral Centre, London Colney, for ecumenical as well as geographical and practical reasons. A Trustee organised a regular prayer leaflet. The conference has now become the annual gathering of the whole Acorn family.

For the first five years the "apostolates", as they came to be called, were chosen by the founders, who are the members of staff in charge of this project, on their regular preaching and teaching tours. Now there are a minimum of two days in the year when prospective members meet representatives of the staff, Trustees and apostolates to learn together where God is leading them, and then recommendations are made for our final consideration and decision.

Out of this project, many initiatives have been taken to advance the work of the Christian healing ministry. After a challenge on this matter at the 1986 conference, one pair, a doctor and a Surrey landowner, decided to open a Christian Cancer Help Centre at Loseley Park, near Guildford. Once a fortnight, a meal of organic food, a pilgrimage of prayer, an open sharing of "where I am", counselling by a doctor, priest and layman, and Christian fellowship are available to all cancer sufferers and their families. Many are the blessings that have come from this initiative, including total remissions.

Another pair, a hospital chaplain and his assistant (a laywoman) in Leicester, brought together doctors and clergy of the diocese and began to plan the building of a day centre for the healing ministry. The laywoman, on whose land it will be sited, has already built three Christian homes for the elderly, where all is light and joy, and life is lived with a purpose. How good it is to see a brightness in the eyes of all the residents there. Yet another pair, Anglican and Roman Catholic, has opened a house of prayer in the Southwark (Arch) diocese for all who need quiet and help, to be listened to and loved. And a doctor and a priest, near Bristol, have made a study of integrating the work of the local church and general practice. Other apostolates have been appointed advisers on healing by their bishops or founded other methods of outreach like "the other ministry of health" in Essex. "Boldness", "Kingdom initiatives", "overcommunicate" have been some of the words that have given a theme and inspiration to the annual conferences.

Another fruit of the conferences was a request which the apostolates made to the staff, also in 1986, for resources – a training manual which they could have in their hands when they asked their churches and fellow health professionals to take the healing ministry into their system. The staff produced a draft manual for the following conference: the apostolates gave it a trial run during their ensuing winter programmes, and brought back their criticisms and suggestions.

240

The final product in printed form was available during 1988/9 and is now available on a national scale. The apostolates and their conference have given enthusiasm, structure and life to the whole Acorn enterprise, ably resourced and led by the whole staff.

Christian Listeners

The second avenue of advance that had been borne in upon us both lay in the realm of listening. Too many people seemed to be doing too many things leaving too little time to listen to too few of those in need. We were also convicted of the fact that we ourselves had spent too little time listening to God and that perhaps in the churches we were not alone in this. Would it be possible to train some of the vast number of prayerful Christians, many of whom were actively seeking for something to do in this field of healing ministry, to a certain standard of attentive listening in order to assist the hard-worked professionals in the caring professions? This was a question addressed to a working party which speedily came up with a positive answer. The result was the first appointment of a new member of staff, the Reverend Anne Long, a pastoral tutor at an Anglican theological college. She set to work with pioneer studies in training, which have resulted in a proven method and the production of training manuals of a high standard.

"Christian Listeners" – the title of the project – are committed Christians who have been selected in consultation with their local doctors and clergy. They are trained according to the A.C.H.T. method to work in teams of about twelve and to listen to referred patients and parishioners in an unhurried and uncritical manner. Each team is led and supervised by its own tutors. A good number of doctors, nurses and social workers are themselves now attending the courses. Christian Listeners also learn to listen to God in various ways in order to draw on His help and resources as they listen to the pain in others. Their own views are

241

THE VISION OF DOROTHY KERIN

not forced on others: their work is done in obedience to Christ and in His strength. Among those referred to them are people with anxieties and worries, with decisions to make, with a recent bereavement or other trauma, or those under stress at home or at work. They include all age-groups and all sorts and conditions of men and women, including health professionals themselves. There are currently nearly forty groups working up and down the country, in parishes, hospitals, hospices and in a prison. As the work has developed and grown, more staff have been taken on and now include a doctor (Moy Gill), an ex-vice-principal of a college (the Reverend Margaret Jones), and an ex-teacher (Sharon Stinson). The Reverend Russ Parker, a full member of the Acorn staff, also gives half of his time to this project. In the years to come there will be more demand for Christian Listeners to play their part in Christ's healing ministry.

Whitehill Chase

The greatest fruit of an appeal for funds in 1984 was a letter from the Whitehill Chase Foundation Trustees who generously offered the use of their house and grounds in Bordon, Hampshire, for the work and a substantial financial input to run it. The agreed purpose was

> to establish a resource centre for teaching and training in the Christian healing ministry and a meeting ground for the coming together of religion and medicine, to extend the ministry locally in co-operation with those already committed to Christian healing and nationally in support of the wider activities of the Acorn Christian Healing Trust.

The first director of the centre was a consultant haematologist, the Reverend Dr. Roy Walford, with his wife, Norma, a nurse and health visitor. These were pioneering days as the methods of training were being hammered out.

When they went into hospice work three years later, the Trust appointed as director and domestic bursar respectively the Reverend David Smethurst and his wife, Dorothy. David Smethurst was an experienced parish priest, Dorothy a head teacher, and they had just returned from a Deanery overseas. The Whitehill Chase Trustees responded by putting in motion a complete redevelopment programme to meet the extra demand for the facilities as the work grew locally and continued to grow nationally. As a result, the A.C.H.T. Resource Centre, as it has now become, has a fine chapel dedicated to St. Luke and All Saints, a conference room for sixty delegates, residential facilities for twenty-four and a comprehensive reference library and bookshop, offering audio and video tapes and journals concerning the healing ministry, in addition to a comprehensive list of books. The Acorn office, under Nigel Beazley, the executive officer, who is a Roman Catholic, is also housed in the building. This is surrounded by beautiful grounds well kept by Terry Wright, the estate manager, and is adjacent to a small hospital and a Shaftesbury home for the elderly.

The two Trusts work together in partnership and the centre is now attracting conferences, training weeks, staff meetings, long-term training and sabbatical placements as well as being a resource for the dioceses and congregations in the vicinity. An open day each Tuesday is attracting growing numbers. The turnover of the bookshop shows a very great hunger for literature, tapes and training packs on this ministry, which the Acorn staff continue to produce to meet known needs. Two new members of staff, who are both Welsh Presbyterians – Peter Ashton, a retired doctor, and Sheila Wyatt, a nurse – have recently been trained there to work from their homes in Montgomery. It is hoped that this will be used as a major training centre for the Christian healing ministry and as a resource to enable Christians to follow the vision of bringing "healing to the sick, comfort to the sorrowing and faith to the faithless".

243

Trustees

A.C.H.T. has been richly blessed in its trustees because of their commitment as Christians to the Acorn vision. All have worked hard for the cause. Charles Longbottom, the present chairman, stewards half of his time to the work. He has seen the budget grow to nearly twenty times its original size. He and one of his colleagues, Alan Lewis, also a Christian businessman, have brought drive, commitment and vision to the work, enabling its advance and growth. Frank Baker, the first chairman, and Raymond Hylton, who has nurtured the ecumenical dimension of the work, have already been mentioned.

Other trustees who have joined since the Trust's foundation number among them a housewife, Anne Eggar, whose special concern is Whitehill Chase; Martin Cruttenden, a banker, whose organisational skills are proving their worth in a time of expansion; John Russell, a priest in south London with an ecumenical parish, who is the chairman of the Whitehill Chase Foundation Trust; and John Richardson, the Provost of Bradford, who had worked closely with us from the first and had acted as one of the chairman's advisers. Mr. James Thomson, a Harley Street surgeon, was also a trustee for a time until pressure of work made it impossible for him to continue.

Return to Burrswood

The initiatives taken during and after the 1986 Apostolate conference led to the demand for more training and resourcing. It seemed right that Anne and I should move to a place of resource to which members of the apostolate could come for short courses of teaching and visioning. We received an invitation to come to Burrswood from the director, Dr. Gareth Tuckwell, and the trustees and we readily accepted. Burrswood has proved to be an ideal place for such training and an average of forty each year have come on the courses which we conduct and to which the Director or Chaplain of Burrswood contribute. The doctors have particularly appreciated a chance to see at first hand an integration of Medicine's ministry with that of the Church.[2]

Bishops' Advisers

Another major project has been to encourage bishops of the Anglican and Roman Catholic churches to appoint advisers in the healing ministry for their dioceses. Conferences were held in three successive years in the Midlands, the South and North to which bishops of both churches were invited to send representatives or advisers if appointed. There was a very positive response and as a result most bishops have now made appointments. This has formed a useful line of communication through the Archbishops' Adviser's office and is a creative means for developing this ministry in the churches, as well as enabling the healing ministry to play its part in the healing of the churches. A major advance was made towards both these ends by the Lambeth Conference of Anglican bishops in 1988. In the course of a statement concerning the healing ministry they said: "We urge all Bishops to encourage, to oversee and to be themselves involved in the ministry of healing in their dioceses".[3] They then made twelve points as to how this might be followed through. This has been the most formative statement made by a mainline church about this ministry in the twentieth century.

A.C.H.T. has taken two recent initiatives to support the bishops and their advisers. Archdeacon Trevor Nash has been appointed as executive co-ordinator of this work and a full-time member of staff, to work with us in training and servicing the advisers. Together we are also seeking to involve the equivalent advisers in the Free Churches.

The first course for bishops' advisers was held at Burrswood and Whitehill Chase for the south of England in 1990; the second at Ampleforth for the north in 1991. It is of interest that three of the bishops' advisers were already part-time members of A.C.H.T.'s staff: Canon Roy Lawrence (Chester), and the Reverend Peter Hancock (Bath and Wells), and Canon Dr. Russell Hunt (Leicester).

Prayer and resource for the churches

A.C.H.T. seeks to be a servant of the Church of Christ. Its trustees, staff and all its members are deeply committed to a life of prayer for the promotion of this ministry in all the churches, so that it becomes the true resource for the Church of God as Jesus intended it to be. The Acorn Prayer Fellowship (A.P.F.) was initiated by the director of Whitehill Chase for this purpose and to bring together prayer groups and individuals praying on their own. The foundation of all the work is a continual linking together in prayer – the Acorn focus of prayer is at 12 noon each day – as it was in the life of Dorothy. Out of this concerted prayer come new visions and initiatives to provide resources for the churches and individual congregations. More and more are seeking advice, practical help and literature to forward the ministry in parishes and congregations up and down the country. The Christian healing ministry seems to be the growth industry in today's Church; the need for it is so pressing and increases all the time. Did not Jesus intend His mystical Body to be a healing Church? All this, however, cannot be accomplished without an enormous body of prayer.

A.C.H.T. is deeply committed to offering a resource to the churches of prayer and encouragement, teaching and training, listening skills and business expertise to assist Christians individually and congregations corporately to live out the truths of Christ's healing gospel: in a word, to become a healing Church.

Notes

1. See Chapter 4.
2. These courses will now be continued at Whitehill Chase, High Street, Bordon, Hampshire, GU35 0AP.
3. *The Truth Shall Make You Free*, Report of the 1988 Lambeth Conference (A.C.C., 1988), p. 48. See Appendix D.

23 "GO AND TELL": A NEW VISION FOR THE CHURCH AND THE WORLD

Almighty and everliving God,
whose Son Jesus Christ healed the sick
and restored them to wholeness of life:
look with compassion on the anguish of the world,
and by your healing power
make whole both men and nations;
through our Lord and Saviour Jesus Christ,
who is alive and reigns with you and the Holy Spirit,
one God, now and for ever. Amen.

> *ASB*, Collect for 8th Sunday before Easter

In the thirty years or so since the death of Dorothy, the world has become very different. The advent of telex, fax and calculator, and above all the computer, has stretched the capacity of the human mind, which has been confronted with an unceasing input of facts and the consequent need to make instant decisions. Possibly because of this, everyone seems to be on the go, mostly by land, where the motor car has taken over vast areas of countryside, or by air. News and people travel fast: there is little time to stand and stare and with silence virtually outlawed, even holidays can be counter-productive with the hassle of airports and busy hotels. The word "stress" looms large, in daily conversation and among therapists of all kinds.

This pace of life is undoubtedly stressful and has led to great changes in society. There is no longer the opportunity for a leisured life in which there is time to recharge the batteries. Less time is spent in the company of family and friends with consequent breakdowns in relationships. All this has contributed to a more materialistic way of life and for many, money is their god. This in its turn has led to a loss of values and discipline and a neglect of spiritual belief. These are sadly now glimpses into the obvious. There is, however, another side to the equation. God has been at work on a massive scale.

The year 1963, the year Dorothy died, also saw the deaths of Pope John XXIII and President Kennedy, the latter by violence, another tragic factor of modern life. Pope John ushered a new springtime into the Church and changed the whole ecclesiastical scene, challenging hitherto unchallenged presumptions. His papacy was a watershed not least because it changed the attitude of non-Christians to the Church. A Christian leader could be a saint, had power to effect great changes, and was able to embrace all humankind in love. All churches have certainly been warmed by his papacy and their healing together advanced.

President Kennedy appealed to the young and was the kind of politician for which they had hoped: someone who would stand up to bullies and pit his country's and his own honour against them. His violent death sent out tremors of shock to every corner of the world. Most people can recall what they were doing on that November day in 1963.

In a similar way, Dorothy made her contribution to this new springtime and on a world scale. A senior member of the Swedish church on one of her visits to that country commented that she brought to them "a vision of the United Church of Christ". After her talk in Geneva a United Nations official said, "her luminous presence has made a lasting impression". Mother Joanna Mary, one-time Superior of the Community of the Resurrection of our Lord in Grahamstown, wrote at the end of the 1960s of how Dorothy's

THE VISION OF DOROTHY KERIN

work and influence live on, not least in South Africa. Though few ever met her, many have been brought to a closer knowledge of Christ through her books and through reading *Called by Christ to Heal*. It seems that her spirit is still very close to us and that she is still being used to heal, though her physical presence has been withdrawn from us.

Like Pope John, her charisma lifted all whom she met to heights previously unperceived. "During the address," wrote Dr. Laurence Blackburn of the occasion at the Marble Church in New York, "there was an ethereal stillness as we were all lifted to a higher plane of consciousness". Such "giants" did show another side to normal news of gloom and doom. God had not left himself without witness; even in such a traumatic period of human history, God had been working "on his usual magnificent scale" (David Edwards).

It is in the context of such violent times that the tokens of God's presence and the signs of new visions are given to those with eyes to see and ears to hear. St. John, in exile on the isle of Patmos, himself the victim of violence, was given prophetic visions of what God was about, not least in the final vision of the Holy City. The first vivid impression was that God was doing a *new* thing. There was to be a new Heaven and a new earth (Rev. 21:1). The Holy City was the *new* Jerusalem and the whole atmosphere spoke of new life, likened to a bride adorned on her wedding day (21:2). God would from now on dwell among His people and the old order of sorrow, pain and death would be replaced by a new order of healing and life (21:4). The voice from the throne proclaimed the newness of creation – "I am making everything new" (21:5), for He was none other than the Alpha and the Omega (21:6). There was no need for the temple in the city: God and the Lamb are its temple because of their eternal presence (21:22). There would no longer be any need for the sun or moon: the glory of God is its light and the Lamb its lamp (21:23), and the nations and rulers of the earth will walk by its light, the light of God who alone reigns (21:24).

Right at the centre of the city, flowing down the middle of its great street, are the waters of healing (Rev. 22:1). Their source is the throne of God and the Lamb: their function is to irrigate the tree of life on each side; their purpose, to produce the leaves which are for the healing of the nations (22:2). And then, when all is made new, that is the end time, and Jesus will come again: "'Yes, I am coming soon!' Amen. Come, Lord Jesus!" (22:20).

The work of healing and the Second Coming have always been held together, not least by the pioneers of the Christian healing ministry including, of course, Dorothy herself. In the healing dimension of the ministry, a foretaste of the power of God is manifested, the power that will be fully demonstrated at the end time when the Kingdom, the power and the glory are fully revealed. That is why the healing experience is so vital for all Christians, who, to engage effectively in their prime function of evangelism, must themselves be open to the power of God, so that they may speak from experience. They have, therefore, to be found watching and ready for the Lord's second coming. Experiences of His comings in manifestations of His healing power help them to be ready and prepared, while they also enable Christians to be better communicators of the essential gospel. Having experienced the power of God in healing, they will be ready to be channels of His healing power to others, who will all the more easily be grasped by a living faith, and this is the central purpose of evangelism.

The year in which this book sees the light of day, 1991, marks the beginning of what the major churches have assigned as a decade of evangelism or evangelisation, a time when all Christians are called upon to take new initiatives to spread the Good News of Jesus Christ. In the same way that the purpose of Medicine has in recent years been thwarted by an over-concentration on scientific advance to the detriment of preventive medicine and community health education, so the *raison d'être* of the Church – the furtherance of the Gospel – has been seriously atrophied by an over-concentration on a cerebral faith and an over-emphasis on organisation and non-essential priorities. In both cases the root cause has been the neglect of the healing dimension of the ministry, medical or spiritual, and the consequent loss of vision as to the overall purpose of the life of each institution. In the churches some basic thinking and praying, with consequent re-visioning, has to take place before such an ecclesial enterprise as is planned can be embarked upon. To the pioneers of the healing movement in the churches the healing dimension of ministry was not only essential to the faith of Jesus Christ, but also to its propagation. It was in fact the core of the evangel because it met people where they were, but even more important than that, God could be experienced in power. They knew that nothing less would change people. It is this experience that is the chief need of men and women in any age, and it is paramount for this decade.

It might provide the right objectives to the whole scheme of things in these last years of the second millennium if the churches assigned to them the priority of healing, for it is this dimension that will communicate most powerfully with world needs in the years to come. It was for this that Jesus so prophetically prepared His Church. Preach/heal was and is Jesus's method of evangelism and by His own experience He showed us that never did He engage in the preaching without the healing. It has been not only the height of folly but also of disobedience when His Church has attempted to separate the two or neglect the one in its evangelistic task. If nothing else, the life of Dorothy Kerin has recalled the Church to a new vision of the healing Christ whose word is to be obeyed if people's lives are to be changed. Her own example in the field of obedience to His every prompting is a powerful legacy to today's Church, not least in the field of evangelism.

As the years draw on towards the third millennium, Christianity's relationship with the other religions of the book,

Judaism and Islam, is bound to come under fiercer scrutiny. With its implication of the end time, Christianity's healing dimension will the more easily communicate with them. To those of other faiths, the outward face of western Christianity is not attractive at the present time. Its apparent insincerity and inconsistency for them remains an enigma. To the majority of westerners, who view the churches as introspective and engaged solely on priorities of their own choosing, it is an irrelevance. This need not be so. There could be other priorities, not only of greater relevance to those of other faiths and of no faith, but also nearer to the Divine Will. Here again the prophetic life of Dorothy, with her attentive and disciplined listening to the Lord's voice and her attuning in total obedience to His will, might well be the message which corporate Christianity, as well as individual Christians, needs to hear today. What she heard and the method of her obedience could well be the legacy of her life most relevant to the evangelistic and communicative needs of Christianity in regard to other faiths. For the common desire of all the great religions is that God shall be obeyed and His will respected. When other faiths see such an obedience among followers of the one who obeyed His Father's will even to death, there will be a greater healing in their relationship; and the more devoted the obedience, the deeper will be the healing. For the healing comes from the heart of God and He alone can put in motion so great a salvation until He is all in all.

What, then, would be some of the new vistas that might open up for the Church and for the world if we were able to take a contemporary view through the eyes of Dorothy Kerin? What would be her vision for them? And has she left them a legacy relevant to their needs?

First, the will of God has to be obeyed. This always involves a costly and prolonged listening to His Word by His Church and by individual Christians, with a refusal to take major decisions until that word has been heard. This may well mean a period of waiting, but as every spiritual director knows, the blessing is in the waiting. The Psalmist certainly

253

knew about waiting on God to ascertain His will (Psalm 62:1 especially in Coverdale's translation) and so did the eighth-century prophets. Nothing would make them speak out unless they had listened to and heard the word from the Lord. In the same way, Dorothy knew that her undertakings would only receive the divine blessing if she had listened to and heard the word from the Lord correctly and then, and then only, would they be in accordance with the Divine Will. This was the essence of her obedience which was always such a major factor in her life: its end was to be perfectly attuned to the Divine Will. Two obvious examples we have already found were the making of a will, which she declined to do because she had not received "instructions" in that regard, and the building of the Church of Christ the Healer, which she was only permitted to do towards the close of her life on earth.[1]

Listening is therefore a prime necessity in today's church. It is the only way that the Lord's will and the needs of others will be heard. But those who should be particularly good at it because they are called to be people of prayer, waiting upon God, have not always excelled in this regard. In fact, the message of a sabbatical was to impress upon myself and my wife that our listening was far from adequate. That is why one of the major projects of the Acorn Christian Healing Trust, in which half its staff is employed, is a training system in listening (Christian Listeners).[2] The training seeks to ensure that we shall listen totally and attentively to God and to the needs of others.

It is this kind of project which seems to be an essential need in the Church's contemporary life and should be given a massive priority in any future planning. How *on earth* can we know when to jump if we have failed to attune our ears – and wills – to *Heaven*? Our chief hope lies in the revival of spiritual growth, for instance in Ignatian spirituality, prayer schools and studies in the Christian mystics, which seems to be burgeoning in our time, and also in the real desire one senses among ordinary Christians to be more and more extended in the spiritual life. In these listening ways, the will of God may be better heard and, we pray, the better obeyed. It will be an uphill struggle in a world which has outlawed silence. It is a harsher world in which to dream dreams and see visions, but the medical profession may soon have to be prescribing space and silence in which this may be done if the human race is to remain human. It is essential to human survival that *homo sapiens*, if he is to remain *sapiens*, has the opportunity to listen to his Creator. A priority in the churches should be to create such spaces in which people may listen, that they may hear again the "Word made flesh" and, hearing, may obey.[3] Obedience has to be a priority of the Body of Christ who both learned and taught His followers that obedience by the things that He suffered (Heb. 5:8). Towards the end of her life, Dorothy Kerin was able to look back and say,

> Through the long years of my life, through the Grace of God, I have come to know that obedience is the golden key which unlocks the door to every true spiritual experience, and I humbly believe it is the most important thing in the life of all Christians.[4]

Second, and flowing out from the first priority of obedience, *the whole healing dimension is a fundamental part of the Christian life.* Dorothy was called through her own healing to heal the sick. It was for her a way of life, a natural outflowing of her life in Christ, who had given healing a very special place in His own life and ministry. There has been sufficient evidence to see how mightily Dorothy was used by Christ to manifest His healing power. But, of course, it was costly. Graham Ikin wrote in 1969, "Dr. Searle was sure the secret of Dorothy Kerin's being used by Christ to heal, lay in the utter surrender to Him, and the great need for repentance and the awakening to the dimension of holiness".[5] Healing is becoming a keyword in the proclamation of the Christian gospel today. It is also being matched by that greater "surrender to Christ". It is not easy to be a Christian in today's world: surrender to Him is the only means of survival. This leads on to the "need for repentance". There is a longing in the heart of people today which can only be realised by a total *metanoia* or turn-round in their present life-style and their intuitive sense tells them this is true. Lastly comes that "awakening to the dimension of holiness", which we have noted to be one of the encouraging signs of new life in the Church, shown in a desire for a deepening spirituality among those turning to Christ today.

If healing is one of the significantly Christian words for today, what new vistas could it, does it, open up for the gospel? Obviously a very great opportunity is being offered by the mainline churches deciding to give the major emphasis to evangelism during the last decade of this millennium. It has already been inferred that the Church's lack of success in this field in the past has been consequent upon its neglect of the healing dimension. Since Jesus obviously meant this to be at the centre of His Good News and since the early Church gave it a central place in its proclamation, this subsequent neglect seems foolhardy to say the least. It would be tragic in the extreme if the healing dimension were ever to be neglected again in the Church's evangelistic task. There is, however, great hope that this will not be so.

An objective observer of the whole scene might fall to wondering why there has been such a revival of the Church's healing ministry in modern times. He or she would note the dedicated lives of the pioneers such as Dorothy Kerin, James Moore Hickson, George Bennett, Leslie Weatherhead, not to mention William Temple himself, and conclude that this was no hole-in-the-corner affair. She or he would note the upsurge of the ministry in parishes and congregations and conclude from the increasing number of ministrations – both in the sacraments and at healing services – and the desire for teaching and experience, that this was a movement among the people of God which would only grow. He or she would then observe how the hierarchy of the churches has gradually been giving encouragement to the movement and conclude from their pronouncements and directives, for example the Lambeth Conference Reports of 1978, and 1988, the workbook of the Methodist Division for Social Responsibility, and the appointment of diocesan advisers, that here was a dimension of the Church's witness which had returned to stay and which was being welcomed at all levels. Our objective observer could be forgiven one more conclusion, namely that here was an instrument for the proclamation of the gospel, for it opened new vistas for suffering humanity and could be the most likely facet of the Good News to meet them in their particular need or situation. It had, therefore, to be a vital and indispensable part of any essay in evangelism.

If any further substantiation or affirmation were needed, the New Testament itself would provide a superabundance. Possibly, then, in the usual and perfect timing He gives these things, God has raised up this dimension of mission and ministry in His church for this present opportunity. The integration of healing and evangelism was an ever-present part of Dorothy's vision.[6] The decade of evangelism will assuredly be blessed if that same integration can be part of the vision of the contemporary Church.

Third, this integration has implications for many other parts of the Church's life and witness. The healing dimension, because it speaks of the presence and power of the risen Lord, is a necessary part of all Christian endeavour. Not the least of these is the area of ecumenism, for the healing balm of Christ has certainly been poured out upon all ecclesiastical relationships in our time. The healing of the *churches* with each other is in fact the context within which the healing ministry to individuals takes place. And where there is an active healing ministry in the churches of an area or within a city it is remarkable that the walk towards unity is engaged in with greater zeal and that there is a more advanced integration of work, worship and witness by the Christians of differing denominations. Where healing services take place in such communities, there is a sense that they are preparing the ground in a powerful way for organic unity. The differences of history and organisation pale into insignificance as the vision of a oneness in the Christ who heals becomes a living experience. The healing and ecumenical movements need each other to demonstrate to the world the credibility of a unity in the will of Christ, even if present differences seem to dominate for the time being.

The healing balm of its Lord is undoubtedly being poured upon the Church today in its long and tireless struggle for unity. The new initiative taken in September 1990 by the churches in Britain and Ireland gives renewed hope to the ecumenical movement. For the first time the Roman Catholic Church is fully involved in the coming together of the churches, in the C.T.E. (Churches Together in England), in A.C.T.S. (Action of Churches Together in Scotland), in the C.Y.T.U.N. (Churches Together in Wales) and in the C.C.B.I. (Council of Churches for Britain and Ireland). All who took part in or heard on radio the inaugural services cannot doubt the new depth of commitment and enthusiasm among Christians in being together. This brings new hope for the healing of the Church, for only the healing power of its Head can effect the unity that accords with His Will, in His way and in His time.

An obvious corollary to this must surely be the healing of the *healing organisations* themselves. The Churches' Council for Health and Healing (C.C.H.H.) is the "parent" body, forming the house base centre of communication. There needs to be a greater reciprocity and working together of the "children". The annual conference for the heads of healing homes is a step in the right direction; the pooling of resources at the Christian Resources Exhibition is another. Joint initiatives are pioneering new ways and there is more communication between the leaders of the various organisations. The healing organisations must never lag behind

in the healing process. It is their task to present to the
Church and to the world a united message concerning the
healing Christ, so that all who come to them for resource
and teaching may be inspired to go out and infect others
with their new-found faith in the healing power of Christ.
It was this gift that characterised Dorothy and which caused
most frequent comment: time spent with her Lord led to
a sharing with other people in the presence of Christ, a
consequent turn-around and life-changing experience and
a going forth as the bearer of Good News. All involved
in the healing organisations, when acting corporately or
individually, could have no better objective for their ministry
today.

We have also seen how Dorothy had a total commitment
to the *working together* of Church and Medicine. This commitment was lived out in all her foundations and continues
to be so lived and practised at Burrswood today. In the same
way, the majority of healing organisations have a similar
objective. It is essential that more initiatives should be taken
to bring about a closer integration. The hospice movement
has greatly assisted with this and ideas and initiatives from
both Church and Medicine have combined to give a deeper
all-round care to the patient. At the present time we await
the result of a working party under Dr. Robert Twycross on
the relationship of the hospice movement and the healing
ministry. Mrs. Prue Clench also continues to keep the Chris-
tian/Medical dialogue in hospice care at full stretch through
her conferences for the St. Columba's fellowship which she
founded. She also runs an advisory service on terminal care
in the community in association with the Dorothy House
Foundation of Bath.

These are welcome initiatives in the hospice movement
whose lessons are now spilling over into the medical world.
Initiatives such as the Acorn Apostolate, joint resource centres of Christian healing and the constant round of courses
for doctors, priests and lay folk at Burrswood, Crowhurst,
Whitehill Chase and at many other places throughout the

country, all move forward a further step the integral work of the Church and Medicine. It is essential that more efforts are made to heal the professions together into an integrated whole. The starting point is the patient who, for total health, needs wholistic care. This seems a statement of the obvious, but is still far from gaining credence in much of the contemporary medical thinking and training, as it is in the fundamentalist theology that is gaining ground in the major faiths today. Prayer and medicine are of equal necessity in patient care because a human being is an integration, not only of the physical and mental but also of the spiritual. If there is to be true healing, it is essential that the whole person receives treatment and care. Should it not be high on the agenda, therefore, that opportunities are sought for the Church and Medicine to work closely together? As we have seen, not only Dorothy but William Temple saw this as a priority in the healing of society.

Anyone who still doubts the power of God to change society has only to examine the events that have happened in eastern Europe since 1989. Of course, the changes have been traumatic and not without suffering, but the paradigm shift has been cataclysmic. Official communism has been dismantled. The life of fear has given way to the life of freedom. The Christian religion, almost persecuted out of existence, kept its lamp burning through seventy years and like its Lord has risen again. The first Liturgy since the revolution, in the Cathedral of St. Basil within the Kremlin, on 14th October, 1990, must have seemed like the miracle of the Resurrection to the thousands of worshippers who thronged the cathedral and Red Square. In the estimation of many, it is the prayer of Christians that has brought about such healing from oppression, not only in Russia, but in all the countries who were once her satellites.

If God is able to work "on His usual magnificent scale" in these countries, is He not more than capable of bringing about a greater healing in our own? The structures of our society are extremely complex and it is hard for many corporate bodies, let alone individuals, to survive in these pressurised times. But if we look with healing eyes and can glean something from the vision of Dorothy, then we shall see God at work in the lives of many individuals and also in the structures of society. It is not that we have to take God into society, as the over-enthusiastic industrial chaplain vowed to do: God is already there at work, waiting for us sleepyheads to join Him. But let us first watch and wait, so that we shall see clearly, as Dorothy always sought to do, where we are needed and what action or word can best convey the wonders of His healing power.

That healing power was unleashed through the Cross and Resurrection recorded in the Gospels. Jesus gave the healing gifts to His Church to carry on His redemptive work (1 Cor. 12:9; Eph. 4:8–13). This work, and the power with which to effect it, is for the healing of society. As Jürgen Moltmann wrote: "The text is the gospel of Jesus Christ but the Church's context is society". It is here that God's mighty work of healing and reconciliation has to be played out. The end product of the redemptive process is the healing of creation. So shall the Kingdom of God come on earth.

Fourth, it is therefore essential that the Church should provide its members with a *freedom-under-obedience to take initiatives for the Kingdom*. Dorothy could never have accomplished what she did without a freedom to move and act when she felt constrained to do so. She rejoiced in this freedom, but we have seen it was a disciplined freedom. Never would she take any action without praying it through and without "a word from the Lord". If at all possible she would consult her spiritual adviser, who, throughout her ministry, was someone in episcopal orders. It was in fact a "freedom-under-obedience".

This way of life has always been the natural way of doing things in the Church. Hierarchy is a word that has gathered pejorative overtones in our time, but it has a noble meaning – ruling in a holy or sacred way, that is, giving people freedom to act and take initiatives under a non-restrictive obedience. A Christian is under the rule of God and owes Him the first obedience. The Church in its hierarchy is there to pray through, test and bring wise counsel to the aspirations of the faithful. The faithful are discouraged from taking initiatives when a paternal relationship is substituted by a committee rule with its many and various voices. To whom is the obedience due? A long and hard look is needed at the unsacred way of ruling – the reversal of hierarchy – which tends to creep into ecclesial government under the best of motives and inhibits the taking of initiatives for the Kingdom. Something of Dorothy's vision, for whom order and discipline were a priority and yet who fought for the freedom to act under obedience to her Lord, whatever He demanded, could be helpful to hierarchy and faithful alike in today's Church. We have tended to pursue an upside-down or "through the looking glass" way of life. The faithful have tended not to do things of their own initiative – among Anglicans it was always thought to be the vicar's task – but to leave it to the hierarchy. In reality, those who have the sacred rule over us, whether as pastors, group leaders, spiritual directors, priests or bishops, are in the business of keeping the Lord's company and seeking His will in collegiality so that they may the better guide into concerted action what the Lord is telling His people, both individually and as a Church. In the history of the Church, all major movements have come "from the pews". The initiatives have been taken by the people. The hierarchy has guided and enabled such initiatives to come into fruition and eventual fruitfulness.

For this to happen, a firm discipline of time is necessary at all levels. Here again, Dorothy's own discipline was an inspiration to all who worked with her. Her time with God, very early in the morning, sometimes for most of the night – "the night belongs to the Lord", she used

to say – gave substance to her work, which began with
an hour at the letters before breakfast. For most of the
remainder of the day she was with people, those in need
of any sort, then family, friends, staff, but always listening
to the "still small voice". It is obvious that many Christians,
especially those in leadership, have similar disciplines. Perhaps they should not be reticent in disclosing the secret of
their spiritual life because it would certainly be an inspiration to others. If they are to lead, they so clearly need
a disciplined life, not only to accomplish the work they
have before them, but also to provide the kind of "sacred
ruling" that can affirm, guide and enable the initiatives of
the faithful which manifestly are of God. This is a priority for which many of the peripheral concerns should
be jettisoned. In business terms, Christians today need
a "hands-on" leadership if we are to see increasing initiatives for the Kingdom of God's sake. But only those
with a hand firmly in that of God, which Dorothy's life
so luminously demonstrated, will provide such an enabling
leadership.

*Last, the provision of resources to enable God's work
of healing and redemption to proceed without human let
or hindrance* was an object near to the heart of Dorothy
throughout her ministry. It could well be a vision for the
churches today, a vista opening up to each of the churches,
locally and centrally. For Dorothy it meant the provision
of a "city of refuge" staffed by a dedicated team – with a
"hands-on" leader. The place itself had to be one that would
lift the spirits of all who came, kept entire in the beauty of
holiness. It had to speak of the divine, it had to be a little
bit of Heaven. We could well afford to initiate in our day
such standards of excellence. The "shoddy leftovers" have
sometimes adorned our ecclesial plant; what is needed is
something that will not only lift the spirit but speak of God.
A resource centre actually means a place of Resurrection.
It was such a light that Dorothy kindled at Burrswood, a
place where people invariably are lifted by their visit and

leave better equipped to face life again, many with new life in themselves.

Every Christian and every place set apart for the worship of God is also a resource. They offer the person who comes to them the possibility of meeting God. A Christian is the *alter Christus*, the other face of Christ in the world, while a church, be it barn or cathedral, is where Christians meet together and where that happens, Christ has promised to be among them. The Church, the Body of Christ, is in fact the extension of the Incarnation. Those whose responsibility it is to be the Church, need to be themselves resourced. It is for this reason that the healing movement is attempting to provide resources for those in the churches who are in the front line of resourcing others, to enable them also to be signs of healing and reconciliation in the world.

In some instances these will be healing resource centres. We have seen how the Whitehill Chase Foundation Trust has combined with the Acorn Christian Healing Trust to create a major new centre at Whitehill Chase in Bordon, Hampshire. Like Burrswood, it is now a place that lifts the spirit. The standards of excellence, of which Dorothy would have approved, are present in all the unified design and in every fitting and small detail. The chapel, dedicated to St. Luke and All Saints, lifts the eyes to the constantly changing pattern of reflected light, while the surrounding garden on all sides inspires worship of the Creator. With the Sacrament chapel of St. William of York it forms the centre of the resource, out of which prayerfully flows the life of the community in its conference facilities, opportunities for study in its library of books, video and audio tapes, its comfortable bedrooms and excellent catering facilities. It is hoped that this will only be the first centre of its particular kind in the country. What is encouraging is that there are always Christians available for training to run such centres.

The purpose of these centres is to resource Christians

in the churches and congregations in inner city, town and country, hospital and school, as well as those who work in prisons or serve in the armed forces. All need the message and touch of the Christ who heals. These are centres of resource to enable the churches to fulfil their function of incarnating Christ in the world today. The world, in the political scene, in the sphere of relationships between the major faiths, amidst cultural differences, in industrial relationships, in domestic and family matters and in all that it means to live in a community and society, is searching for and in need of the healing power of God.

Dorothy Kerin, "called by Christ to heal", was enabled to see a vision of healing for the Church and for the world. This vision she was ordered to "go and tell". She obeyed. In the contemporary world this is a time of great events. The whole scene is changing, the world map is being redrawn. Empires, not only political, decline and fall. Others rise in their place. To many, world events speak of the end time. This may or may not be so. One thing is essential: that the Church of God, filled with Christ's followers who have offered their obedience to His healing and reconciling purposes, and whose only desire is to be attuned to His will, shall be found watching. "Amen. Come, Lord Jesus."[7]

Notes

1. Between the building of the church and her death two-and-a-half years later, she told three people on different occasions, while she was with them near the sanctuary, that she would one day rest there. "There" was a place to which she pointed in front of her stall which was then outside the altar rails. It is now within them. Since she said this on three separate occasions, it was obviously something she felt was right and true. In the event she was buried in the churchyard of St. John's in Groombridge on the east side of the church. It will be for a future generation to decide what is right in this matter.
2. See Chapter 22.
3. There is a "listening room" designated for this purpose in the

Anglican cathedral in Bradford, where the Provost is a trained "Christian Listener" and an Acorn Trustee.

4. Johanna Ernest, *The Teaching of Dorothy Kerin* (Dorothy Kerin Trust) p. 23.
5. Ibid. p. 26.
6. It was remarked how her presence in a congregation inspired the preacher to greater heights which gave a significant challenge to others in the congregation.
7. Revelation 22:20.

APPENDIX A

Further Accounts of Dorothy's Healing

1. This second account was written for her second book, *Fulfilling*, and appears on pp. 12–17.

My beautiful day

On Sunday morning, February 4th, I received the Blessed Sacrament, and as the priest came towards my bed with the chalice, I saw a golden light radiating from it which enveloped the priest. I had never seen this before, though all through my illness I had made my communion once a month, sometimes more often. It was a beautiful experience. The Divine Presence was indeed a reality. When the service was over, everything around me seemed to grow dim and misty and I could not see anything clearly. In the evening I asked my little sister to sing "Abide with me": it was all so dark. She did not know it well enough to sing, but, as she sat by my bed, her hand in mine, we heard it sung from beginning to end so beautifully. My sister heard it as distinctly as I did, and said: "O how wonderful!" We were certain it must have been the Holy Angels singing for there was no one singing in the house or outside. After this I seemed to drift into space, no longer conscious of my body but my spirit overflowing with joy and love, and a transcendent feeling of supreme happiness impossible to describe in human language. I passed on and on. As I went the way grew brighter and brighter until I saw in front of me a wonderful Altar, formed, as it were, by Angels. There were six at the back and one in the front, more beautiful than the rest. He was holding a chalice from which he gave me to drink. They all disappeared; as they went they chanted words which I could not understand. I passed on again, and soon I heard a great flocking sound, and saw, coming from every direction, white-robed figures. Some of them were carrying lilies, some had haloes. Their movements made lovely music; they all looked as though they were coming and going with some definite purpose. No words of mine can express or exaggerate the exquisite beauty of the scene. As I looked I saw One coming towards me. I thought He was coming for me and held out my hand towards Him, but He smiled and said, "No, Dorothy, you are not coming yet." Again I passed on; this time I seemed to go a much greater distance, until I could go no further, when I heard a voice say "Dorothy" three times. I answered, "Yes, I am listening. Who is it?" Then a great light came all around me and an Angel took my hand in His and said, "Dorothy, your sufferings are over. Get up and walk." He passed His hands over my eyes and touched my ears, and then I opened my eyes and found myself sitting up in bed. My mother and a number of friends were standing around my bed, all looking very frightened, and some clutching at each other. It all seemed so strange to me and I could not understand why they were all there. I asked for my dressing-gown, telling them that I was quite well, and that I must get up and walk. They were all too astonished to speak or move.

The Angel again said to me, "Get up and walk." They brought the dressing-gown. When I had put it on I got out of bed unassisted. Part of the light which emanated from the Angel came to the right side of my bed. I put my hand on it, and it led me out of the room, along a passage and back into my bedroom. Though I had not walked for nearly five years, I now walked quite steadily, not the least bit shaky; indeed I felt well and strong and might never have been ill at all. Soon I realised I was hungry and asked for food. They brought me milk in a feeding cup, which I refused, finally going in search of food myself down two flights of stairs, returning with a real meal. How I enjoyed it, too! It was the first solid food I had been able to digest for a long time and I had not the slightest pain or discomfort after eating it. There were sixteen people in my room all very mystified and amazed at what they saw. I was perfectly well. ALL pain had left me, my sight was restored, and I felt better and stronger than I can ever remember feeling before. It was half-past nine in the evening when I got up, and at twelve o'clock midnight, I went back to bed, and slept until eight o'clock the following morning. When I got up, my mother and friends, who knew that I had been like a skeleton the day before, were amazed to see my body quite normal and in a perfect condition. I was quite plump, all my bones being covered with firm, healthy flesh. This in the space of twelve hours! Blessed be God.

At nine o'clock Dr. Norman was sent for. When he heard that I was up and well, he thought it must be a mistake, and came to the house post-haste, expecting to find that I had passed away. On entering my room, he asked my mother what it all meant? I ran to meet him, and he turned to my mother and said, "Is it possible that this is the girl I left dying yesterday?" As soon as he had recovered from the shock he examined me and pronounced me perfectly healthy and well. He then asked me to go up a steep flight of stairs to test the strength of my muscles. When he saw me run up, he said, "Great God, what is the meaning of it all?"

When approached as to the cause of my present condition, he could give no explanation, but said it was certainly the most marvellous recovery he had known during the course of his experience. Next day he made

269

the following statement, published in the *Daily Chronicle* of February 22nd:

"When I heard the girl had got up and was about the house I would not believe it until I had been to see for I left her on Saturday night apparently dying." Asked "Did she really suffer from consumption and diabetes?" he replied, "Oh certainly, there is no question whatsoever about that." "Then what is your theory?" asked the representative, "as to the cause of her present condition?"

"I have no theory," he replied. "Had I read of it, I certainly should not have believed it. She is well, but how she got better I don't know."

In an interview with an *Evening News* representative, Dr. Norman stated that "he had always hoped that the girl might recover, but that on Saturday he gave up hope. She had suffered enough to kill half-a-dozen people," he said. "In attending her he had found all the gravest symptoms of advanced tuberculosis, of diabetes, and other complications. She had been attended, under him, by twelve nurses up to the present, and a chart was kept of her temperature. This chart shows that her temperature rose and fell in the most alarming way . . . sometimes reaching as high as 105."

This statement was published in the *Evening News*, 20th February 1912.

At the request of Dr. Norman, a number of medical men examined me and were amazed when they heard the past history of my case, and admitted that my healing was something beyond their ken. A fortnight later I was examined by two X-ray specialists and found by them to be perfectly well.

Tests for the presence of tubercle both by Von Pirquet's and Calmetté's methods made by Dr. Murray Leslie were negative, no reaction being produced in either case.

Three days after my healing, I was invited by Dr. Edwin Ash to his home in Seymour Street, that I might receive rest and quiet, away from the crowds of people who

constantly came to see me, many from mere curiosity.
I remained with Dr. Ash for several weeks. It was here
that God revealed the purpose of my healing to me. I
had prayed much that God would guide me into the way
of His Will, and show me what He had brought me back
to do, and was waiting in Faith for His guidance, when
it was made quite clear in a vision.

On Sunday, March 11th, I was roused from sleep by a
voice saying "Dorothy". I sat up, and saw at the foot of
my bed, a wonderful light, out of which came the most
beautiful face of a woman. She was holding a lily in her
hand, and came quite close to my side saying, "Dorothy,
you are quite well now. God has brought you back to use
you for a great and privileged work. In your prayers and
faith, many sick shall you heal; comfort the sorrowing;
give faith to the faithless. Many rebuffs will you have, but
remember you are thrice blessed. His Grace is sufficient
for you. He will never leave you."

After making the sign of the Cross over me with her
lily she disappeared. When I awoke in the morning, the
scent of her lily still remained.

The answer to my prayer had come. All unworthy as I
am, God has a work for me to do. I pray that He will
empty of self, and make more worthy, the very imperfect
channel He has chosen.

After this vision there came a period of waiting, when
one had to possess one's soul in patience. It was not easy
to be still and wait when there were so many in spiritual
darkness and sickness waiting for the light of God's Love
to illuminate their hearts and minds, and heal their bodies.
The longing to share the joy of my new-found health grew
day by day, and in His own way and time God made this
possible. The way of ministration was being made clear,
and one learnt that the Gifts of God can only be received
through prayer and faith in accordance with His Will. True
spiritual joy comes to us through communion with God,
and bodily health and peace of mind follow, as growth

follows rain and sunshine. In Him is no darkness. If we put
our hands in His, and by His grace, follow in His footsteps,
we shall know the truth and realise the wonderful power of
the Love that is infinite. We can live in the very presence of
God, in the midst of the promised land. We are no longer
pilgrims and strangers, but can, here and now, enter into
our inheritance as heirs of the Kingdom of God.

2.   This third account is a recording made by Dorothy Kerin
during the early part of the nineteen-sixties, in her own room
in Chapel House, Burrswood.

Many years ago I had a personal encounter with our Living
Lord. By this I mean that I met Him face to face. He
laid His hand upon my life and restored me to perfect
wholeness in the twinkling of an eye. My healing was
instantaneous and complete. There was no moment of
weakness or convalescence, and this after five years of
so-called hopeless illness. During this time I had been
bed-ridden, suffering from general tuberculosis and other
complications. The last of twenty-eight doctors had said
that nothing more could be done to help me, and we
must expect death which was inevitable. Everything that
love and skill could do had been done, and now the end
was expected at any moment. There had been weeks of
semi-consciousness during which time all efforts to prolong
life had been abandoned.

   A little company of friends and relatives were gathered
around my bed waiting for the last flicker of life to depart,
when some of them saw a great light over the bed. They
first thought it was Jesus taking this little spirit to Himself,
but as they watched they saw this little emaciated form
raised to a sitting position by unseen hands. She opened
her eyes and began to speak, and this is what she said, "Do
you hear, I am well." "I must get up and walk." No, they
did not hear, but as they watched they saw her who was
dying, get out of bed and stand before them, every whit

whole – every whit whole, and this in the twinkling of an eye. Jesus had touched her, she was healed. There are two significant things concerning this miraculous healing. The first is had it been any other voice than the voice of the living Lord, nothing would nor could have happened. Secondly, the servant to whom the Lord spoke knew it was the Lord, and obeyed without hesitation or question, and so this miracle happened.

It is noteworthy that during the period of unconsciousness I was oblivious to the suffering that was endured by those who watched and tended me. For me it was a time of indescribable joy and bliss in a place and environment of exquisite harmony. I seemed to be going somewhere with a definite purpose, when suddenly I was aware of a lovely form clad in dazzling white. He was coming towards me, and I knew it was Jesus.

He said, *"Dorothy, will you go back and do something for Me?"*

To which I answered,

"Yes, Lord."

Then it was I was commanded to get up and walk.[1]

Note

1. I am grateful to Miss Filmer for allowing me to use a transcript of her recording.

APPENDIX B

Centenary Sermon by Bishop Morris Maddocks
St. Martin-in-the-Fields, 8th October, 1989

When Dorothy ministered and spoke in this lovely church thirty-one years ago, she gave this testimony.

> Today I stand here all unworthy and sinful as I am and dare to say to you in the presence of God and all the company of heaven that I have seen Jesus. I have heard his voice, I have felt his touch and I know that Jesus Christ is the same yesterday and today and forever.
> And that is the text I offer you tonight, Hebrews 13:8, "Jesus Christ is the same, yesterday, today and forever."

Dorothy did at least know her Lord intimately. In her childhood she had a Julian-of-Norwich-type vision when the Lord came to her holding in His hand an acorn and said, "Tend this with obedience and I will water it with the dew of my love. One day you shall behold a mighty oak". Many acorns have grown from her ministry especially, of course, at Burrswood. Among others, we might mention its first cousin, the Acorn Christian Healing Trust, and so many more. Perhaps the mighty oak may be the amazing growth of the healing ministry today, to which her foundation at Burrswood bears such living testimony. Be that as it may, the time of her intimate knowledge of her Lord of yesterday, today and for eternity was her miraculous healing on 18th February, 1912. The comatose period of the last fortnight

275

of her mortal illness she called her "beautiful day" in which she was told of her healing and sent back, as she learnt later, *to heal the sick, comfort the sorrowing and give faith to the faithless.*

And the healing was so akin to that of Jairus's daughter, which is why Dr. John Elliott read that lesson tonight, and why the picture of Jairus's daughter is in her memorial window in the Church of Christ the Healer at Burrswood. How appropriate for Dr. Elliott to read that lesson. He was the first doctor to come and help her and remain with her throughout her life, and he has only just retired.

In Dorothy's case there was this same immediate response of obedience to the Lord's command to get up, and from her healing – her spiritual birth – onwards, there was always the same obedience to the Christ of yesterday, today and forever.

The remaining fifty-one years of her life conveniently divide into three periods of seventeen. The first seventeen years we might call *the obedience of preparation*. She prepared for her ministry under the discipline of a spiritual director, Dr. Langford-James, and it was during this period that she received the stigmata or the wounds that Christ was given on the Cross. In his testimony of this phenomenon Father Fynes-Clinton wrote, "She appeared to be endowed with a great humility and told me that she shrank very much from the showing of the marks to others, but that she obeyed in the matter. She was evidently still suffering and spoke of having prayed that she might suffer if it were God's will on behalf of others." And that was in 1915 and suffer she did, especially through indifferent health, because it was during this time that her out-of-body experiences transported her to the battlefields of the First World War. Sometimes, she told her confidants, she would find herself kneeling by dying men on the battlefields, undiscovered in the no-man's-land between opposing armies; a symbol truly of healing and peace in a world of conflict.

Dorothy in this first period was surely at one with the Jesus of yesterday, the suffering servant. Like Him, her master, she learnt obedience in the things that she suffered, like a beautiful Stradivarius violin, finely tuned to the will of God. Such was her obedience of preparation and always marked by long vigils of prayer, sometimes throughout the night. Probably each of us here will have known something of this discipline of preparation, as the Christ of yesterday gradually moulded our frail earthen vessel into the shape He wanted and made us ready for what He would have us be and do. Obviously it is a process that goes on, until the life of the world to come. But certainly the Christ of yesterday is always preparing His Church and its members for the reality of today, and so he did with Dorothy, preparing her for the next portion of her life.

That second period we might call *the obedience of ministry* – the today period. She began her ministry in Ealing, in this diocese of London, in 1929, and here the Christ of today inspired a mighty work for the Kingdom as people began to come in their hundreds to touch the hem of His garment. There was never enough accommodation, never enough staff, never enough hours in the day but no one was ever turned away, and gradually the whole of Mattock Lane in Ealing was given to this work of ministry in Chapel House and the surrounding houses. Here was a direct act of obedience to the contemporary Christ worked out in a remarkable healing ministry. May the Christ of today continue to inspire this generation never to cease from taking initiatives to promote the Kingdom of God; initiatives that will demonstrate to contemporary human kind the love and the power and the glory of Christ who heals today; initiatives that will cut through the bindweed of bureaucracy, the confusion of committees and the plethora of paper, so that the hungry and thirsting people of today may look up and find their Saviour and Healer in the Lord Jesus Christ of today, whose touch does still have its ancient power.

But there is also an obedience to the Christ of tomorrow, the Christ who is constantly calling His people to move on.

"Tell my people that they go forward" – the summons to the Israelites at the Red Sea – as much a word for the people of today from the Christ of tomorrow. Here is *the obedience of looking forward*. Dorothy's obedience to this call was expressed in her move out of London, first to Speldhurst and then, in 1948, to Burrswood. It was a move that gave her space to widen her ministry and to build in more senses than one so that there could be a full integration of the work of the Church and Medicine. The final building was the Church of Christ the Healer shortly before she died, the focal point of all the Christian wholistic care that goes on at Burrswood today by a dedicated team. It was the place God had chosen where she could answer more fully the call within her call – "In your prayers and faith many sick shall you heal, comfort the sorrowing, give faith to the faithless". And as we know so well, the Christ of tomorrow never allows us to stay still for long, never allows our tent pegs to be hammered home. "Move forward, move on, my gospel must be proclaimed in all the world" is His relentless call.

The obedience of looking forward. What is it demanding of you tonight? Jesus started with twelve. What couldn't we do if we offered ourselves in total obedience tonight?

So Dorothy began a few years before her death moving on – her missions abroad to the United States; to Sweden (where Dr. Gareth Tuckwell has been following in her footsteps on a fortnight's lecture tour); her speaking and ministering in all parts of these islands, either to large congregations or to individuals in their beds of pain; travelling sometimes the whole length of the country, sometimes by night, for one of God's children. Here in this church when she ministered at this altar rail where we shall be tonight, she noticed her shoes were soaking wet with the tears of the men who came up for a healing blessing. And the secret? Her acute listening to the voice she knew so well, her Lord and Healer, the Christ of tomorrow and always answered by that immediate obedience.

Possibly the greatest problem facing the Church of God is

encapsulated in the words of the Venite, "*Today* if you will hear His voice". Our listening powers have been atrophied by our busyness in the day-to-day rush and tumble of ecclesiastical life. We are a very active church and in many ways as we look at some of our yesterdays, that is no bad thing. But not if our very activity today leads to deafness to the insistent summons of the Lord of tomorrow who calls us to the obedience of looking forward. We need to major on listening rather than talking. We shall not be heard for our much speaking, but worse, we shall fail to hear the call of Christ. Dorothy was always expectant of, and listening to, the Christ of tomorrow, calling forward His Church, calling His Church always to be His instrument in the healing of Creation.

And I believe that the Christ of tomorrow is indeed urgently and insistently beseeching His Church to hear His word today in a new way, so that we may be able the more boldly to proclaim His Good News to others in the last decade of this millennium, designated by the major churches as a decade of evangelism, of proclaiming the Good News. Listen, yes, we must listen in a new way. How dare we, for instance, proclaim the Good News by preaching alone when the healing dimension of the proclamation is absent? Jesus taught us that both had to go together. Where is our obedience?

Now it is for this act of obedience that so many of us have gathered here tonight. Like Dorothy Kerin, one of the unsung saints of our time, we long for the healing ministry of Christ to be restored to its central place in the Church of God. Wonderful developments to this end have taken place in this decade which would rejoice, does rejoice, Dorothy's heart. Resource centres for Christian healing are being founded up and down the country and money is being raised by devoted men and women for these projects. An ever increasing number of congregations hold regular healing services. Medicine is taking this to heart and in many cases working in partnership. The Lambeth Conference has urged all bishops, "to encourage, oversee and be themselves involved in" (I quote directly) this ministry. Roman Catholic bishops have sent their healing advisers to our Advisers' Conferences. But we cannot rest there. Our obedience to the Christ who heals, who is indeed the same yesterday, today and forever, demands that all of us here, and so many brothers and sisters in Christ who are praying with us and are one with us tonight, will not cease our labours until the healing dimension of the Church's ministry takes its full place in the ministry of every church and congregation; until every Christian heart beats with the Sacred Heart of the healing Christ. You know, or you would not be here tonight, how vital is this healing dimension to everything we are and do for Christ. It transforms our caring, it gives our evangelism conviction, it gives our practice of the faith credibility, it gives all our work for Christ a depth and sincerity redolent with His love.

Jesus Christ is the same yesterday, today and forever. He has blessed our yesterdays and given us a burning and shining light in people like Dorothy Kerin, for whose vision and healing ministry we praise God this evening. He is blessing our today as we see the healing ministry transforming the witness of the Church in our time, meeting people at the point of their need. As we come forward for ministry tonight let us make our pilgrimage a rededication, knowing that He will bless our tomorrow if we can offer like obedience with Dorothy. For His call is to trust His promise that our little acorns will become His mighty oak.

And so to Him be the glory, now and for ever, Amen.

Centenary Sermon by the
Rt. Reverend Michael Turnbull, Bishop of Rochester
Church of Christ the Healer,
Burrswood, 28th November, 1989

As the abounding grace of God is shared by more and more, the greater may be the chorus of thanksgiving that ascends to the glory of God. 2 Cor. 4:15

"Don't speak of me, speak of Christ", I can almost hear Dorothy Kerin saying. Of course, I can't hear her voice because I never heard her speak. I had been ordained barely two years when she died. And yet in another sense, I can hear her. Her voice lives on. Such is the miracle (I use the word advisedly) which is Dorothy Kerin, that generations which never knew her sense the light shadow of her presence across their lives. For me, the pictures and the messages have come through close friendship with Bishop Cuthbert and his experience that healing is an indispensable part of evangelism; through my admiration of the work of Bishop Morris which has brought the ministry of healing into the mainstream thinking of the Church; through the writings of Johanna Ernest which have put me in touch with Dorothy's life and wounds; and not least through my unforgettable first encounter with the community which is Burrswood and which vibrates with Resurrection spirituality.

The transmission of a tradition by oral communication, by writings and by community, has a New Testament ring about it – so that those of us in subsequent generations can feel the pulses of earlier times – and yes, hear the voices of the saints who have passed on their light to us.

So there is some authenticity about Dorothy Kerin's plea, "Don't speak of me, speak of Christ".

What then is this "abounding grace of God which is shared by more and more"? It is, firstly, the grace which comes through knowledge of the incarnation. Verse 11 of our chapter speaks of the life of Jesus being revealed in this mortal body of ours. Jesus becomes human through our bodies. That is an astonishing thought. And yet it is given to some to reveal this truth to us. They are able, through their closeness to Him, to see others through His eyes. They are able, through the depths of their compassion, to see the suffering and risen Lord in the lives of others. This kind of sensitivity is at the heart of all healing, and the Church down the ages has been given gifts of saints whose lives have displayed it for us.

281

Secondly, the "abounding grace" is that which comes through knowledge of the Cross. Without the Cross we should have no knowledge of grace at all. Verse 12: "Death is at work in us." Our true knowledge of the Cross is not just as a historical event or a theory of the atonement, important though they may be. Knowledge of the Cross comes from an experience of death. Death in those interiors which war against the soul. We can glimpse this for ourselves – but it is gloriously affirmed by those whose lives are a working out of costly obedience and long hours of prayer. The saints are those who are surrendered into the hands of death.

Thirdly, "abounding grace" is that which is experienced through knowledge of Resurrection. Verse 14: "We know that He who raised the Lord Jesus to life will, with Jesus, raise us too." The saints are those who exhibit this grace through their simple trust that Resurrection – the piecing together of several parts to make a whole – is God's will for all and that He brings it about today. The risen Lord promises wholeness and healing. There are beacons in His Church who take Him at His word and believe miracles to be no less evidence of the grace of God simply because they become commonplace.

Fourthly, "abounding grace" is evident through knowledge of the kingship of Christ. Verse 17: "the outcome of our troubles is an eternal glory which far outweighs them." Christ in glory is perceived by the saints, even in the midst of pain and sorrow and trouble. It is this which could be said to be the *vision* of the saints. Thanks be to God there are those with this spiritual vision in the twentieth-century Church. It is not our plans and strategies which we then attribute to God. Vision is the perceived will of the glory of God which is then ascribed to man. The writer to the Corinthians goes on in Verse 18 to speak of "eyes fixed, not on the things that are seen, but on the things that are unseen". Men and women of vision have the ability to so fix their attention that the will of God is revealed to them. A saint has the tenacity and the obedience and the courage to follow it. I have been speaking of Christ and the saints of the Church who bring reality to the grace which is there in Incarnation, in the Cross, in Resurrection and in glory. I haven't mentioned Dorothy Kerin. Perhaps you have. It would not be surprising, for her life, beginning 100 years ago today, spoke of incarnation and death, and new life and vision and glory.

All these elements are necessary if the Church is to recognise God's healing grace today. The ever extending panoply of modern medicine is part of that. It is part of what God gives to us to both prevent and to heal sickness. But Resurrection life and the glory of God is bigger than overcoming disease. It is the making whole of dismembered mankind – the bringing together again of body, mind and soul. And not just to individuals but to communities, which is why the Burrswood story cannot be separated from the Dorothy Kerin story. Not only communities but nations. Not only nations but the whole of mankind. "For the Sun of Righteousness shall rise with healing in His wings" (Mal. 4:2).

It is not without significance that we celebrate Dorothy Kerin's one hundredth Anniversary as we are on the brink of a decade of evangelism, now embraced by most of the mainstream churches. What a travesty it would be if that evangelism became narrow proselytism. For the call to evangelism is not to ask the world to believe what we believe, nor act or worship or decide as we do. It is an invitation to the world to see what we see, to be healed as we are being healed, to become part of a new wholeness of mankind of which each of us is a member. Evangelism without healing is neither a New Testament pattern nor credible in our modern world. Healing without evangelism has a hollow and sensational ring about it. It could be that some of Dorothy Kerin's most compelling visions will find a Church ready for them in these coming, crucial years.

For we give thanks today that she knew the abounding grace of God; that that grace is being shared by more and more; that the chorus of thanksgiving is building up to a crescendo; that new visions are being caught and fresh discipleship discovered. But most of all we give thanks that Dorothy Kerin's life and all that we are called to do in this generation "ascends to the glory of God".

APPENDIX C
The Burrswood Healing Service

An order of service for the laying-on-of-hands, 1989

A little way of prayer
LET us by an act of the will place ourselves in the presence of our Divine Lord and with an act of faith ask that He will empty us of self and of *all* desire save that it may illumine our hearts and minds. We can then gather together ourselves and all those for whom our prayers have been asked, and hold all silently up to Him, making no special request – neither asking nor beseeching – but just resting, with them, *in* Him, desiring nothing but that Our Lord may be glorified in all.

In this most simple way of approach He does make known His Most Blessed Will for us. "For so He giveth Himself to His beloved in quietness."

Dorothy Kerin

Order of Service

Hymn   *Stand as the Ministers enter*
   God is our hope and strength; a very present help in trouble.
Versicle:
   Lift up your hearts;
Response:
   We lift them up unto the Lord.

285

V   Let us give thanks unto our Lord God;
R   **It is meet and right so to do.**

Thanksgivings
Let us thank God:
First let us thank Him for who He is
(here the Minister may use his own words)

V   Let us bless the Lord;
R   **Thanks be to God:**
     For the movement of His Spirit in our time, and for the renewal of the Church's Ministry of Healing.

V   Let us bless the Lord;
R   **Thanks be to God:**
     For His abundant blessings in this and other places, for the growth of fellowships of prayer and healing, and for the prayers of many, especially at this time . . .

V   Let us bless the Lord;
R   **Thanks be to God:**
     For those many who have known His Healing Touch upon them . . .

V   Let us bless the Lord;
R   **Thanks be to God:**
     And for the new hope of those who have been released from fear, saved from despair, and delivered from the grip of moments past . . .

V   Let us bless the Lord;
R   **Thanks be to God:**
     Finally, let us give thanks for the life and prayers of all the Saints (*especially . . . and for Dorothy Kerin, founder of Burrswood*) . . .

V   Let us bless the Lord;
R   **Thanks be to God.**

Intercessions
(*Second Minister:*)   Let us pray: *Kneel or sit*
  For boldness, wisdom and humility amongst those called to Christ's Ministry of Healing . . .

V Lord, hear our prayer;
R **And let our cry come unto Thee.**

For Doctors and Nurses, for Ministers and Counsellors, and for all in training for these and other caring professions and for the increase of understanding of health and salvation . . .

V Lord, hear our prayer;
R **And let our cry come unto Thee.**

For the life and work of fellowships of prayer *particularly the Burrswood Fellowship*, that God may continue to bless, inspire, and use them for His glory . . .

V Lord, hear our prayer;
R **And let our cry come unto Thee.**

For all who have gone forth from this place, that God's blessing may rest upon them . . .

V Lord, hear our prayer;
R **And let our cry come unto Thee.**

And for the complete healing of those who have passed through death to the fullness of life with Christ . . .

V Lord, hear our prayer;
R **And let our cry come unto Thee.**

For all who are in hospices and in hospitals and homes of healing, *especially for those here* . . .

V Lord, hear our prayer;
R **And let our cry come unto Thee.**

For the disabled and those who care for them *and especially for those who use St. Peter's Pool at Burrswood* . . .

V Lord, hear our prayer;
R **And let our cry come unto Thee.**

And for all who have asked for our prayers: together with those whose names now lie upon the Altar here; and especially for the children. All these we now lift to God in the silence of our hearts . . .

V Lord, hear our prayer;
R **And let our cry come unto Thee.**

Finally, let us pray for the blessing of Almighty God upon all who are here now, about to seek the Touch of our Living Lord Jesus Christ . . .

V Lord, hear our prayer;

R **And let our cry come unto Thee.**

Pause for silent prayer

O God,
Who hast prepared for them that love Thee
Such good things as pass man's understanding,
Pour into our hearts such love towards Thee
That we, loving Thee in all things and above all things,
May obtain Thy promises, which exceed all that we
   can desire,
Through Jesus Christ our Lord. Amen.

The Lesson
An Address may be given

Recorded music or anthem

Kneel or sit

V O Saviour of the world, who by Thy Cross and precious Blood hast redeemed us:

R **Save us, and help us, we humbly beseech Thee, O Lord.**

Psalm 91 (Selections) or another psalm or hymn
WHOSO dwelleth under the defence of the most High: shall abide under the shadow of the Almighty.

I will say unto the Lord, Thou art my hope, and my stronghold: my God, in Him will I trust.

For He shall deliver thee from the snare of the hunter: and from the noisome pestilence.

He shall defend thee under His wings, and thou shalt be

safe under His feathers: His faithfulness and truth shall be thy shield and buckler.

(2nd Part) Thou shalt not be afraid for any terror by night: nor for the arrow that flieth by day.

There shall no evil happen unto thee: neither shall any plague come nigh thy dwelling.

For He shall give His angels charge over thee: to keep thee in all thy ways.

They shall bear thee in their hands: that thou hurt not thy foot against a stone.

Thou shalt go upon the lion and adder: the young lion and the dragon shalt thou tread under thy feet.

Glory be to the Father, and to the Son: and to the Holy Ghost;

As it was in the beginning, is now, and ever shall be: world without end. Amen.

Confession
Anything falling short of the glory of God is sin. In particular, resentments, anger, unresolved frustration, and lack of forgiveness to any who have wronged us, can be powerful blocks to healing. Repentance is the willingness to change one's whole attitude, relationships, and way of life, seeking the new direction of Jesus Christ and His Holy Spirit.

If we say that we have no sin, we deceive ourselves and the truth is not in us, but if we confess our sins, God is faithful and just to forgive us our sins, and to cleanse us from all unrighteousness.

Pause for self-examination

Let us humbly confess our sins to Almighty God.

> **Almighty God, our heavenly Father,**
> **we have sinned against thee,**
> **through our own fault,**
> **in thought, and word, and deed,**
> **and in what we have left undone.**
> **For thy Son our Lord Jesus Christ's sake**
> **forgive us all that is past;**
> **and grant that we may serve thee**
> **in newness of life,**
> **to the glory of thy Name.   Amen.**

The Absolution

ALMIGHTY GOD, our heavenly Father, who of His great mercy hath promised forgiveness of sins to all them that with hearty repentance and true faith turn unto Him: Have mercy upon you, pardon and deliver you from all your sins; confirm and strengthen you in all goodness; and keep you in life eternal, through Jesus Christ our Lord.   Amen.

(Third Minister:)
V   Lord, have mercy upon us.
R   **Christ, have mercy upon us.**
V   Lord, have mercy upon us.

Our Father, who art in heaven, Hallowed be Thy name; Thy kingdom come; Thy will be done, on earth as it is in heaven. Give us this day our daily bread. And forgive us our trespasses, As we forgive those who trespass against us. And lead us not into temptation; But deliver us from evil. Amen.

V   O Lord, save Thy servants;
R   **Who put their trust in Thee.**
V   Send them help from Thy holy place;
R   **And evermore mightily defend them.**

V Help us, O God of our salvation;
R **And for the glory of Thy Name deliver us, and be merciful to us sinners, for Thy Name's sake.**
V Lord hear our prayer;
R **And let our cry come unto Thee.**

ALMIGHTY GOD, who art the giver of all health, and the aid of them that look to Thee for succour, we call upon Thee for Thy help and goodness mercifully to be showed upon us Thy servants, that being healed of our infirmities, we may give thanks unto Thee in Thy holy Church, and give ourselves into Thy service; through Jesus Christ our Lord. **Amen**.

A member of the congregation says this prayer:
GOD bless us, and grant that we upon whom Thou dost lay Thine hands may find healing and wholeness, through Jesus Christ our Lord. **Amen.**

These prayers may be used and the Ministers pray for one another and for those named in the Altar Book.

O Blessed Lord, Who hast promised that when two or three are gathered together in Thy name, there Thou art in the midst of them to grant their requests; we come to Thee now, just as we are, and we pray Thee, behold Thy servants, who, kneeling now before Thee, seek Thine aid. We pray Thee pour upon them the fullness of Thy blessing; abide with them, and never leave them; and according to Thy will, stretch forth Thine hand and touch them, and make them to be witnesses of Thy power, and use them for Thy glory.

(Ministers together:)
> *And now, O God, I give myself to Thee.*
> *Empty me of all that is not of Thee,*
> *Cleanse me from all unrighteousness,*
> *And according to Thy Will*
> *Take my hands and use them for Thy glory.*
> > *Amen.*

"Lord, I am not worthy that Thou shouldst come under my roof, but speak the word only, and Thy servants shall be healed."

> *(Remain kneeling or sitting)*

HYMN – Come Holy Ghost
> Come Holy Ghost, our souls inspire,
> And lighten with celestial fire;
> Thou the anointing Spirit art,
> Who dost Thy sevenfold gifts impart;
>
> Thy blessed unction from above
> Is comfort, life and fire of love;
> Enable with perpetual light
> The dullness of our blinded sight;
>
> Anoint and cheer our soilèd face
> With the abundance of Thy grace;
> Keep far our foes, give peace at home;
> Where Thou art guide no ill can come.
>
> Teach us to know the Father, Son,
> And Thee of Both, to be but One;
> That through the ages all along
> This may be our endless song;
>
> Praise to Thy eternal merit,
> Father, Son, and Holy Spirit. Amen.

The Laying-On-Of-Hands
"A little way of prayer" may be used.

The Ministers lay on hands and pray first with those unable to come to the rail. Then those wishing to receive the laying-on-of-hands at the rail come forward as directed.

Words such as these are used at the laying-on-of-hands:
In the Name of God Most High and through His infinite love and power, may release from all sickness and infirmity be given you. In the Name of Jesus Christ, may the healing power of the Holy Spirit make you whole, and keep you entire, to the glory of God the Father.   Amen.

Thanksgiving
And now O Lord we pray Thee give us grace to tarry Thy leisure, and to await with hope the fulfilling of Thy promises: "For they that wait upon the Lord shall renew their strength."

Response: **Thanks be to God.**
(Second Minister:)
Remember, O Lord, what Thou has wrought in us this day, and not what we deserve, and as Thou hast called us to Thy service, make us worthy of our calling, through Jesus Christ our Lord.   **Amen.**

The Blessing

Final anthem

Cantor:	Lead me Lord, lead me in Thy righteous-ness,
	Make Thy way plain before my face.
Congregation:	**Lead me Lord, lead me in Thy righteous-ness,**
	Make Thy way plain before my face.
Cantor:	For it is Thou Lord, Thou Lord only,
	That makest me dwell in safety.

293

Congregation: **For it is Thou Lord, Thou Lord only,**
That makest me dwell in safety.

Stand as the Ministers leave

On suitable occasions, the priest or minister may at his discretion add or omit such material as before God he may deem appropriate.

APPENDIX D

The Ministry of Healing –
Extract from the Lambeth Conference Report, 1988

79.   In the widest sense of the words, healing and salvation are two ways of describing the work of Jesus Christ. Within the work of Christ's salvation the healing of the sick holds a significant place because by it he both demonstrated the love of God and proclaimed that the Kingdom had come in his person (Luke 7:21–22). Jesus did not intend the good news to be proclaimed by word alone, but also by the mighty works of God. (See, for example, the use of words *seen* and *heard* in Luke 7:22 and in Acts 8:6; also the prayer in Acts 4:29–30.)

80.   Jesus commanded his disciples to heal the sick and cast out demons as well as to preach the Kingdom of God (Luke 9:1–2,6; 10:9,17; Mark 6:12–13; Matt. 10:7–8). This they continued to do after his Ascension, as Acts and various references in the Epistles evidence. This ministry did not cease with the Apostles but throughout the history of the Church, God has not left himself without witness in any generation to his power to heal. In most parts of the Anglican Communion today the healing ministry is pursued, along with the preaching of the Gospel, in obedience to Christ's command, and is seen as a normal part of the ministry of the Church to its members, and as a sign of the power and truth of the Gospel in evangelism.

81. The Lambeth Conference of 1920 called for a report on the subject, which urged the whole Communion to be involved in the ministry of healing by teaching about it, co-operating with the medical profession, and developing intercessory prayer groups in every parish. These same three words – teaching, co-operation and prayer – were taken up in 1944 by Archbishop William Temple when he set up in England the Churches' Council for Health and Healing.

82. "The Church is called to exercise a ministry of healing to the sick whatever their condition of mind and body. Such a ministry of love aims:

(1) to restore the sense of relationship with God and the community;
(2) to affirm the body's natural powers of healing
(3) to use all medical knowledge and skills to assist restoration or relieve pain;
(4) to establish peace as we acknowledge that we are mortal and yet are born for eternity."

83. This ministry is part of a total ministry which includes:

(a) medical research, the prevention of disease and the promotion of healthy life-styles;
(b) the work of the medical and caring professions;
(c) ministries of prayer and sacrament;
(d) the counselling and support of the troubled, the sick and the dying.

84. All the baptised and not only the clergy can be involved in the Church's ministry of healing (James 5:13 ff.), but there are those to whom the Holy Spirit gives special gifts of healings (1 Cor. 12:9; both words are plural in Greek).

85. Both in his earthly life and now through his Body the Church, Jesus' healing work is concerned with the wholeness of the person in body, mind and spirit. In obedience to

his command and with the guidance of and strength of the Spirit, we offer the prayer of faith for the sick (James 5:15) with humility and love, but we leave to his wisdom the way in which he acts. There remains a mystery why one person recovers and one does not when there has been equally faithful prayers for both, but acknowledging God's sovereignty in all things we continue to offer this ministry. Even physical impairment can be used to God's glory and, for the Christian, death itself is swallowed up in victory.

86. We urge all Bishops to encourage, to oversee and to be themselves involved in the ministry of healing in their dioceses. The following are some ways of being obedient to our Lord's commission:

(1) to declare that the ministry of healing should be a regular part of the ministry in every congregation;
(2) to encourage intercessory prayer by members of every congregation, remembering our Lord's promise about agreeing together in prayer (Matt. 18:19);
(3) to foster the use of the laying-on-of-hands with prayer by the clergy and members of the congregation;
(4) to bless and provide oil for the anointing of the sick and to encourage priests to make this anointing a regular part of their ministry;
(5) to develop counselling ministries, concerned with inner healing and the healing of relationships, and to provide for the ministry of absolution and the assurance of forgiveness;
(6) to provide and oversee ministries of deliverance from demonic oppression where this is needed, and, where appropriate, with medical consultation;
(7) to establish in each Province and/or diocese centres for the ministry of healing, both for ministry to the sick and for the teaching and support of those engaged in this ministry at the local level;
(8) to work in partnership with doctors, nurses and all

involved in the care of the sick, and to encourage medical research and the study of related ethical issues;

(9)   to ask for a fair distribution of resources and personnel so that all nations and all sections of the community may receive adequate health care;

(10) to embrace the sick and impaired, for example, drug addicts and sufferers from AIDS, as part of the fellowship of the whole Church;

(11) to support the Church's medical mission work throughout the world as a vital arm of its ministry and outreach,

(12) to work for the establishment of hospices for the terminally ill and to provide appropriate ministry for the dying and their families; this will need to include counselling regarding the continuance or otherwise of life-support systems.

BIBLIOGRAPHY

Arnold, Dorothy Musgrove, *Dorothy Kerin: Called by Christ to Heal*, Hodder and Stoughton, 1965

Ashton, Joan, *Mother of Nations: Visions of Mary*, Lamp Press, Marshall Pickering, 1988

Ashton Joan, *The Living Touch*, Dorothy Kerin Trust, 1914

Auerbach, David, *Surviving Trauma: Loss, Literature and Pschoanalysis*, Yale University Press, 1990

Augustine, *Confessions*, Hodder and Stoughton, 1983

Basil the Great, *The Long Rules*, OSS in his *Ascetical Works*, 1950

Coggan, Donald, *Cuthbert Bardsley, Bishop, Evangelist, Pastor*, Collins, 1969

Davidson Ross, J., *Dorothy: A Portrait*, Hodder and Stoughton, 1958

Drake, Frank, *Thy Son Liveth*, Hodder and Stoughton, 1959

Dumeige, G. (ed.), *Of the Four Degrees of Passionate Charity*, Vrin, Paris, 1955

Ernest, Johanna, *This House Named Burrswood*, CUP, 1989

Ernest, Johanna, *The Life of Dorothy Kerin*, Dorothy Kerin Trust, 1983

Ernest, Johanna, *The Teaching of Dorothy Kerin*, Dorothy Kerin Trust

Faricy, Robert, S.J., *Praying*, S.C.M. Press, 1983

Farr, Ruth, *Will You Go Back?*, Dorothy Kerin Trust, 1970

Julian of Norwich, *Revelations of Divine Love*, Hodder and Stoughton, 1987

Jung, Carl, *Modern Man in Search of a Soul*, Art Publications, 1984

Kelsey, Morton T., *Healing and Christianity*, S.C.M. Press, 1973

Kerin, Dorothy, *Fulfilling*, Hodder and Stoughton, 1952

Kerin, Dorothy, *The Living Touch*, 1914

Lambeth Conference Report, *The Truth Shall Make You Free*, ACC, 1988

Maddocks, Morris, *A Healing House of Prayer*, Hodder and Stoughton, 1987

Milner-White, Eric, *My God, My Glory*, SPCK, 1954

Nouwen, Henri, *Out of Solitude: Three Meditations on the Christian Life*, Ave Maria Press, 1974

Parker, Russ, *Healing Dreams*, SPCK, 1988

Teresa of Avila, *The Interior Castle*

Thérèse of Lisieux, *The Story of A Soul*, translated by Michael Day, A Clarke Books, 1973

Stacy Waddy, P., *Philip Loyd: Missionary and Bishop*, Mowbry, 1954

Underhill, Evelyn, *The Spiritual Life*, Mowbray, 1984

Underhill, Evelyn, *Mystics of the Church*, James Clarke & Co. Ltd., 1925

Waterfield, Evelyn, *My Sister Dorothy Kerin*, Mowbray, 1964

INDEX

Twycross, Robert, 259

Underhill, Evelyn, 1–2, 58, 66, 300

Virgin Mary, 18, 20, 21, 26, 29, 30, 33, 57, 59, 72, 75, 78, 83, 86, 88, 114, 124, 173, 197, 207
'vision', 1–2, ch. 18. *See also* Kerin, Dorothy

Wade-Brown, Winifred, 156–7
Walford, Roy and Norma, 242–3
Walpole Park, 114
Walworth, 2, 43

Waterfield, Evelyn (sister), 45, 48, 101, 104, 109, 110, 158, 170, 174, 300
Weatherhead, Leslie, 190, 256
White, Russell, 192
Whitehill Chase Foundation, 242–4, 246, 259, 264
Widdows, Mr. and Mrs., 70–1
Williams, Gwen, 113–14, 145
Winnington-Ingram, Arthur Foley, 112–13, 118, 120
Wood, Lawson, 156
Wright, Terry, 243
Wyatt, Sheila, 243

Ypres, Lady Violet, 173, 176, 214